W9-CAP-947

A TREASURY OF RESPONSA

A TREASURY OF

Responsa

By SOLOMON B. FREEHOF

The Jewish Publication Society of America

PHILADELPHIA

5723 – 1963

Library of Congress Catalog Card Number: 62–12951

Designed by Sidney Feinberg

Manufactured in the United States of America
by American Book–Stratford Press

To the memory of my beloved father

ISAAC FREEHOF,

who by his example and instruction
guided me in the paths of Torah,
this book is reverently dedicated

ACKNOWLEDGMENTS

The world of responsa, which extends over many lands and has endured through many centuries, is varied enough to maintain the interest of any student of this great literature. Yet for my continuing concern with responsa, I owe a debt to the many rabbis and laymen who have asked me questions in Jewish Law and tradition, and thus kept me turning, again and again, to this extensive literature.

My special thanks to Rabbi Wolf Leiter of Pittsburgh, whose phenomenal knowledge of the literature was constantly at my disposal.

My dear wife, Lillian Freehof, has given me encouragement and help, without which I could not have continued my studies.

My thanks are always due to Esther Tyrnauer, whose skill and judgment were constantly of help to me.

The Jewish Publication Society was more than an ordinary publisher. Deeply concerned with the dissemination of Jewish literature and literary history, it relates itself to an author in a manner very different from other publishers of the present day. I am deeply grateful for its helpfulness and its continuing interest.

Solomon B. Freehof

TABLE OF CONTENTS

INTRODUCTION

NATURE AND USES OF
THE RESPONSA LITERATURE

The Responsa Literature, published by The Jewish Publication
Society in 1955, is in effect an introduction to this volume. An
attempt was made there to give a general description of the responsa; the present volume, on the other hand, offers what may
be considered a fair sampling of this vast branch of Jewish legal
writing. The author would nevertheless like to explain why, because of the difficulties involved, his task cannot really be adequately accomplished.

The main difficulty is due to the fact that, while the responsa
literature has hitherto interested only specialists in the field of
Jewish Law, this volume attempts to enlist the interest also of the
general reader. Our book, therefore, faces the problem of addressing two separate audiences simultaneously on a subject that
would be difficult enough in relation to either audience alone.

Each of these audiences, moreover, presents problems of its
own. The scope of Jewish Law ranges over so wide a variety of
themes that each scholar of the technically-trained audience tends
to have his own specific interests. There are many learned rabbis
in America today to whom the laws of the ritual bath (*mikvah*),
which comprise a whole tractate in the Talmud and large sections
in the codes and hundreds of responsa, are of perennial and practical interest. Other rabbis, concerned with the problems of

kosher food, are interested chiefly in the innumerable responsa on slaughtering, on the mixture of meat and milk, and the like. There are, furthermore, scholars whose concern is not primarily that of making legal decisions, but rather of considering the responsa as a monument of Jewish legal literature which reveals, although usually without intending to do so, Jewish social, economic and political history. For each of these groups of the technically trained, a different sampling of the literally millions of responsa would seem important.

When turning to the general reader, not trained in Jewish Law, the problem is entirely different. The responsa were written by experts. Almost every responsum involves subtle analysis of the relevant talmudic text and of the earlier responsa which dealt with the subject under discussion. It is impossible for the general reader to understand even the general import of a responsum cited without constant explanations of the fundamentals of the law involved and the methodologies of talmudic and post-talmudic argumentation, which the trained scholar would find largely superfluous.

Since, therefore, neither potential readership can be fully satisfied, the sampling ultimately must be based upon the compiler's taste, his judgment as to what is significant, and his estimate as to what will prove to be interesting to the general reader. Undoubtedly, many experts will point out fields of law here not represented. Yet our collection may prove to have at least this merit: that beginning with a responsum of the gaonim and going through the entire history of the literature, down to the responsa of contemporary scholars, a general picture emerges of the extent and the growth of Jewish attitudes to the environment, and the relation of the environment to the ideals of Jewish Law. This book, therefore, could be subtitled: glimpses of Jewish social history as revealed in a selection from the responsa literature. One can but hope that the selection is representative and gives a fairly adequate total picture.

Each responsum is preceded by brief biographical information of the author, the background of the situation that called it forth, and some explanation of the law involved in the case. Excerpts from the responsum itself follow. Generally, the more subtle argumentation is omitted from these excerpts. Such omission is necessary, first, it must be confessed, because it is too difficult to transmit the translation without long and rather ponderous explanatory notes; and, secondly, because many of these argumentative passages were actually meant to be theoretical, even by the author. At least, these subtle arguments represent proof carefully marshaled that certain points of view in the Talmud, which were *thought* to be relevant, are really not relevant at all to the issue at hand. In other words, much of the detailed argumentation represents a mere clearing of the ground, which was necessary for the writer to undertake, but not important to the reader for his understanding of the problem.

It might, perhaps, be useful to add that the responsa themselves are not directly concerned with whatever history they may happen to reveal. Most of the thousands of responsa of the gaonim of Babylonia omit the name and the city of the inquirer. From the point of view of modern historical research, it would have been the most valuable if the gaonim had preserved such elementary data. A mere tabulation of the names and the cities of the questioners would have given us a statistical picture of where the Jews lived in those centuries and what the extent was of their Jewish culture. But the gaonim were not concerned with the fact that some day our interests would be social and historical.

Nevertheless, almost by chance or inadvertence, the responsa contain plenty of historical material. If the decision of a case depended upon the specific circumstances involved in the question, or whenever a specific historical event could serve as a precedent to a decision, the respondent might mention them. So there actually are thousands of unintended glimpses into the life of the Jews in the past.

One illustration may sufficiently exemplify this gratifying fact. Jair Hayyim Bachrach, of Worms, who lived toward the end of the 17th century, was asked by the son of a very pious person whether the fact that his father had imposed upon himself many observances of extra piety (fasts, special charity, etc.) obligated the son to follow the same pious practices. Bachrach answered that the son *was* so obligated. Then, to illustrate his decision, he described how, in the year 1699, the entire city of Worms was destroyed by the French armies, and, how of course, the Jewish community also was destroyed. Jewish refugees from the old community met Bachrach on his wanderings and asked him whether the old customs of special piety observed in the former community of Worms were still incumbent upon them now that the community no longer existed. He answered that they must never give up hope that the community would be restored; and that no matter where they might now live, they were still in duty bound to observe the old community pieties. Thus, Bachrach, wishing merely to illustrate a point of law, gives us an historical fact in fairly full detail and also explains how it was possible for the Rhineland communities, so often broken up by fire, persecution and expulsion, to find enough stability to develop local customs of such tenacity that many of them remained a permanent religious custom for all Ashkenazi Jewry. (See responsum 32, p. 173.)

Since, therefore, this selection, like all anthologies, depends upon the tastes and interests of the anthologist, it is to be hoped that other students of the literature, perhaps discontented with this collection, will gather other samples of the responsa literature and that thus, from book to book, this great monument of Jewish piety and intelligence will become known to an ever-widening circle of appreciative readers.

September 14, 1962

S. B. F.

A TREASURY OF RESPONSA

1

✡

THE HISTORY OF TRADITION: LETTER OF SHERIRA GAON

Rabbi Sherira ben Hanina was gaon of the Pumpeditha academy during the second half of the 10th century; he died at a great age about the year 1000. Famous throughout the Diaspora, he attracted many questions, none more important than that which elicited his letter to the Jews of Kairawan.

The responsa literature actually began with the letters from the gaonim (the "Eminences") of Babylonia to the Jews of the Diaspora. These "Eminences," the heads of the two great Babylonian talmudic academies, were the chief source of Jewish religious authority for five centuries. The talmudic literature, primarily the Babylonian Talmud, which was produced and grew out of the analysis and discussions of the predecessors of the gaonim, was now in their keeping, and they continued its study, explanation, and development, by the same processes by which it had been created. As Jewish communities matured in various lands, they sent questions to the gaonim of Babylonia, often across vast distances.

In reply, the gaonim gave direct guidance in religious worship and in matters of civil and ceremonial law. They thus became the guides of the growing culture and literary activity of world Jewry. As the study of the Talmud gradually took root in the various lands, the gaonim received questions concerning the meaning of certain difficult passages, and the legal conclusions which were to be drawn from them. These responsa were preserved in various manuscript collections and served as guides to the independent study which grew up in the newer communities, such as those of North Africa, Spain, France, and the Rhineland. Nearly all the scholars, in their own independent work in these lands, refer to what they had read in the collections of gaonic responsa in their possession.

The Gaonic Period lasted for about five centuries, from approximately the year 500 to the year 1000, and questions were constantly addressed to the gaonim during these five hundred years from all over the Jewish world. The total bulk of the gaonic responsa literature must therefore have been enormous. Manifestly the largest part of it has been lost. But gaonic material is still being collected. When the vast horde of manuscripts (the Geniza) was discovered in Cairo in our time, a great deal of the material in it was gaonic responsa. Evidently Cairo was the halfway point for messengers between North Africa and Spain to the west and Babylonia to the east. The responsa, on their way from Babylonia, were copied in Cairo and a copy kept. Hence in our own time, as more and more of the Geniza material is being edited and published, a fair amount of the great mass of gaonic responsa is being slowly recovered.

It is becoming increasingly clear from the gaonic literature that during the last two gaonic centuries, world Jewry was fighting for its existence with the new and powerful Jewish sect of the Karaites. These Karaites (text-followers) believed in the authenticity of the written Scriptures only and denied the validity of the rabbinic tradition: the Mishna, Tosefta, and Talmud. The Karaites continued strong, powerful, and influential for many centuries after the gaonim; but after gaonic times they became definitely isolated from the Jewish community. Therefore the questions that come up in the later responsa literature concerning them are whether it was permissible to teach them or to intermarry with them, and the like. But in gaonic times the questions had to do with the validity of Karaite claims and with the defense of the literature of Rabbinic Judaism against their attacks.

It was against this background, of the defense of Rabbinic Judaism against the Karaites, that we must understand a famous responsum of Sherira Gaon to the community of Kairawan, in what is now Tunis. In such communities, where the study of the talmudic literature under the guidance of the gaonim was still in its comparatively early stages, the polemics of Karaism, denying the validity of the entire literature, could have had a particularly devastating effect, for Talmud study in the west was not yet a well-rooted tree that could defy the storms, but a young sapling still reaching downward for a firm hold in the earth.

The chief charge of the Karaites was that the rabbinic literature (Mishna and Talmud) was merely the work of various rabbis who passed it off as Divine. The community of Kairawan, which for a generation had been already quite a center for talmudic studies, was now ready to go into the questions about the authorship of the Mishna and the time when it was written down. They therefore turned to Sherira Gaon and asked whether their impressions were correct, that it had been written in part by the men of the Great Synagogue (i.e., about the 4th pre-Christian century) and that Rabbi Judah the Prince (3rd century of the present era) had completed the work. If the Mishna was based on old tradition, going back to the men of the Great Synagogue, why then were the anonymous (i.e., the basic) parts of the Mishna said to be by Rabbi Meir, who lived in the 2nd century? And, they further asked, how did the Talmud develop, and how did it come to be written down.

The Gaon Sherira declares in his responsum that the *entire* talmudic material in its complete bulk was an ancient tradition (i.e., not a gradual accumulation, which would make it of doubtful authenticity) and that all Rabbi Judah the Prince did was to rearrange the material and clarify it. The essence of his answer is that the total material constituted an unbroken tradition going back to antiquity, and that all the various men whom we might think of as authors were not that at all, but merely interpreters and transmitters of this ancient tradition. While explaining this basic principle, namely, that the Oral Law as found in the Mishna, Talmud, and their accompanying books, is virtually of equal antiquity with the Written Law, and therefore of equal authenticity, he also lists the rabbis of the various generations who worked, expounded and transmitted this ancient oral material. Thus his responsum is the chief source for all later study of the history of talmudic literature, and is itself a great monument of Jewish literary creativity. In fact, it is one of the two, among the thousands of gaonic responsa which we now possess, which are basic to Jewish studies down to our day: one being the responsum of the Gaon Amram which gives the history of the development of the synagogue liturgy (*Siddur Rav Amram*), and the other this justly famous responsum of Sherira Gaon on the history and nature of rabbinic texts.

The responsum exists in many editions. One of the best, which is the basis for the following excerpt is found in *Medieval Jewish Chronicles,* by Adolf Neubauer (Oxford, 1887). A more recent and richly annotated text of the responsum is by Dr. Benjamin Levine (Haifa, 1921). In his edition, Dr. Levine publishes, in parallel columns, what may be called the French version and the Spanish version of the responsum.

TEXT

(Heading from the Oxford Manuscript:)
Isaac, son of Nissim, son of Josiah, turned with a question to our lord Sherira, head of the Yeshiva; (he asked it) in the name of the sacred congregation of Kairawan; and he (i.e., Sherira) ordered that the response be written here, in the year one thousand two hundred and ninety-eight of the documentary (i.e., the Seleucidan) dating, and the documentary dating is before four thousand five hundred and fifty-two (i.e., 986 of the Christian era).

Question:

As for your question, namely: How was the Mishna written? Did the men of the Great Synagogue begin to write it and the sages of succeeding generations write part of it until Rabbi Judah the Prince came and completed it? But if this is so, and since most of its text is anonymous, why are we taught that the anonymous parts of the Mishna were written by Rabbi Meir (Sanh. 86a)? Besides, most of the rabbis who are mentioned in the Mishna—Rabbi Meir, Rabbi Judah, Rabbi Yosé and Rabbi Simeon—all of them were pupils of Rabbi Akiba, and the rules (of decision) that the rabbis of the Talmud taught us (mention the same generation) saying that the law is according to Rabbi Akiba when he disagrees with his colleagues, and according to Rabbi Yosé when he disagrees with his colleagues, and according to Rabbi Judah the Prince in preference to his colleagues. All of these lived at the end of the time of the Second Commonwealth. If so (if all the authors mentioned lived so late), why did the more ancient rabbis leave so much to the later rabbis; and all the more (is it significant) if nothing of the Mishna was written until the end of the days of Rabbi Judah the Prince.

(The question implies that since the rabbis mentioned in the Mishna are all late and since the Mishna was not written down until the days of Rabbi Judah the Prince, it would be difficult indeed to answer the charge of the Karaites that the Mishna is not ancient tradition at all.)

Furthermore (the question continues), although the arrangement of the six main Orders of the Mishna are logical, what reason is there for the (seemingly illogical) arrangement of the tractates within these six Orders? Why, for example, was the tractate Yoma (dealing with the Day of Atonement) placed before the tractate Shekalim (which should precede discussion of the Passover)? And why does Sukkah come before the tractate Yom Tov? And why do both of them precede Rosh Hashanah? Thus (our question covers) all the tractates which are not in sequential relationship with the other tractates according to content. Furthermore, as to the Tosefta, which we have heard was written by Rabbi Hiyyah, was it written after the sealing of the

Mishna or was it written at the same time as the Mishna? And why did Rabbi Hiyyah write it (since it contains, though generally in a fuller form, the same material as the Mishna)? If he merely added material which expounds the material in the Mishna, why did Rabbi Judah himself omit it and fail to include it in the Mishna? Is not all of this material (in the Tosefta) quoted in the names of the same rabbis who are mentioned in the Mishna? And similarly, how were the *baraitot* (material similar to Mishna and Tosefta, but quoted only in the Talmud) written? And also, how did the Talmud come to be written? And so the saboraim? What was their order after Rabina? (Saboraim were the first post-talmudic rabbis, and Rabina was among the last talmudic rabbis.) And who bore authority after them? And how many years was each of them in authority from that time up to today?

> (In other words, the community of Kairawan asked for a complete history of the development of the talmudic litera-ture from its beginning and also, by implication, for the proper defense of its antiquity and its authenticity.)

Answer:

Our view is as follows: The saintly Rabbi Judah certainly ar-ranged the six Orders of the Mishna so that we might study the laws one after the other, without intending to add or to diminish. For thus it is said in the Talmud (Yeb. 64b): "When was the Mishna fixed? In the days of Rabbi (Judah the saintly Prince)." As for your question: Why did the earlier rabbis leave so much to the later rabbis? (As is evidenced by the fact that the rabbis mentioned in the Mishna were all contemporaries or pupils of Rabbi Akiba, which might imply that the Mishna is not ancient at all.) The earlier rabbis did not leave much for the later rabbis to do (i.e., to innovate), but all of the later rabbis studied and interpreted the words of the earlier rabbis (i.e., they merely ex-pounded; they did not create the tradition). For when Hillel the Elder was appointed by the B'nai Bathera as prince over them, he said to them (Pes. 66a): "What led to my being chosen prince over you? It was your own laziness, in that you did not serve sufficiently under the two great men of your generation, Shemaya and Abtalyon" (i.e., the knowledge had already been available in an earlier generation, but they did not take advantage of it).

The reason that the older rabbis are not mentioned by name, except for their prince and the head of the court, was that there never was any controversy among them. They knew thoroughly all the reasons for the teachings of the Torah and they knew the whole Talmud completely, and all the arguments, and they were careful in their study of every subject; for we see (B. B. 134a) that there were eighty disciples of Hillel the Elder, thirty of them were worthy that the Divine Presence should rest upon them as it did upon Moses our teacher; and thirty of them were worthy that the sun should stand still for them as it did for Joshua; and twenty were average. The greatest of them was Jonathan the son of Uziel and the least of them was Yohanan ben Zakkai. And they said about Yohanan ben Zakkai (the least of them all) that there was not a single text of Scripture that he did not know, nor Mishna, nor Talmud, nor laws, nor narratives, nor text details of the Torah or of the scribes, of all the arguments *a fortiori* and analogies and proverbs, etc., all matters great and small, and even the arguments of Abbaye and Rava (who lived four hundred years after his time). This tells us that even the arguments of Abbaye and Rava were not original with them, but were all well known to the ancients.

(Thus Sherira indicates that the total tradition recorded now in the rabbinic books was all known to the ancients; and the tradition, therefore, is authentic. If their names are not mentioned, it was because there was no need to record their names. In later times the names of various rabbis were recorded in order to explain who took one side of a controversy and who took the other. But among the ancients there was no controversy; they all possessed full knowledge. Now Sherira goes on to explain why it was necessary for Rabbi Judah the Prince to reorganize this vast material which presumably was perfect from the very beginning. He proceeds as follows:)

When the Temple was in existence, each one of the great teachers would explain to his disciples the reasons for the laws of the Torah, Mishna, and Talmud. Each teacher would put it in the words that appealed to him at the time, and thus taught it to his disciples so that they could understand. Abundant wisdom was then available and they needed no other effort (than just to explain the Law, each in his own words). The dispute as to the laying on of hands was the only dispute among them (i.e., hands laid upon the sacrifice on the holidays, whether such action was permitted on the holidays or not, that is, whether or not it was a violation of the requirements of rest on the festivals). When Shammai and Hillel arose there were only three matters that they disagreed on (Shab. 14b). Then came the time of Bethar (i.e., the Bar Kokhba revolt) and Bethar was destroyed and the rabbis were scattered in every direction. Because of these disturbances and persecutions and confusions, there were many disciples who never studied long enough with their teachers. Hence controversies arose among them.

(Sherira then proceeds to mention other controversies due to other persecutions and confusions, resulting in lack of time for sufficient study, and hence the increase of disputes. He continues down to the destruction of the thousands of pupils of Rabbi Akiba and continues from there, as follows:)

Rabbi Meir was more learned and more keen than all of them and Rabbi Akiba ordained him even though he was still young . . .

(He continues with the generation of Rabbi Meir and the following one, coming down to Rabbi Judah the Prince; and he writes:)

After the great calamity of the destruction of the Temple and the doubts that arose due to all the confusions of the time and all the divisions that arose in those three generations when the Law was not settled among the rabbis, there became known among the rabbis the words of individuals and the words of the majority. The rabbis went to great trouble to gather the exact wording of the Mishna; but they did not add anything to the words of the men of the Great Synagogue. They toiled and searched to bring to light what those ancients had said and what they had done, until all those doubts (which had arisen in the

three generations of confusion) were finally cleared up for them.
Not one of the ancients had written down his own original opinion, until the end of the days of Rabbi Judah (when it was
recorded). Nor had they all taught in the same phraseology, but
they all gave the reasons for the laws which were well known to
them and all were unanimous as to the meaning. They knew what
was the word of the majority and what were the opinions of the
individuals, but the wording was not fixed so that all might study
in the same language. It was the meanings and the explanations
that were known to them.

> (He proceeds to show how each rabbi taught in his own
> words and how much greater was the mentality of the
> ancients than that of their successors. Since they all knew all
> of the material, there was no real controversy among them.
> And then he continues:)

The rabbis found peace in the days of Rabbi (Judah the
Prince) because of the friendship between Antoninus (Pius, the
Roman emperor) and Rabbi (Judah); and he decided to arrange
the laws so that (thereafter) all the rabbis would use the same
phraseology and no longer teach each in his own phrasing. The
ancient (rabbis) did not need this (uniformity of phrasing) since
it was all Oral Law, and its explanations were not given to them
in fixed language, as was the Written Law. They knew the reasons
(of the Oral Law) by heart, and each taught them to his disciples
in any language he wished to use, as a man converses with his
neighbor. In the days of Rabbi, help came (i.e., from Heaven)
and they arranged and wrote down these words of the Mishna
just as Moses had done at the dictation of God as a sign and a
miracle. Not of his own invention did he (Rabbi) compose it; for
the words that had been taught by the ancients were all before him.

> (The rest of the responsum goes on to discuss the develop-
> ment of the other rabbinic books, leading to the development
> of the Talmud and to the post-talmudic era of the gaonim.
> And he concludes with a benediction extended to the con-
> gregation of Kairawan for its deliverance and blessing.)

The process and the justification and the grounds for authority of the Oral Law were thus made by Sherira Gaon in his answer to the community of Kairawan substantially as follows:

The entire talmudic tradition as we have it was already in its totality known to the ancients. Their names are not mentioned because they had no substantial disagreements. However, each one taught his disciples orally in his own language. In the centuries of confusion due to persecutions and national misfortunes, the various disciples would cite the words of their respective rabbis as they remembered them; but they had not studied sufficiently to recognize that, in spite of the difference of language, all the ancients agreed with one another. Therefore special work was needed to rediscover the true tradition; and when this was finally achieved, Rabbi Judah arranged the material in the fixed text which is the Mishna.

2

A RABBI'S LIVELIHOOD

Rabbenu Gershom ben Judah, "the Light of the Exile" (born in Metz, 960; died in Mainz, 1040), was the founder of talmudic studies in the Rhineland and in France. He was the teacher of Jacob ben Yakar, who in turn was the teacher of Rashi. He is best known for the far-reaching decisions which were made at the synod which he convoked about the year 1000. One decision was the prohibition of polygamy, and another was the requirement to secure the consent of both parties to a divorce. Although he lived well within the time of the gaonim of Babylonia, he was not overshadowed by them and he, too, received legal inquiries from many lands. His responsa, however, are scattered as citations in the works of later scholars and were not known as a separate book. Recently they were collected from all the various legal compendia and gathered into one book by Solomon Eidelberg (Yeshiva University, New York, 1955).

The responsum which we have selected is of special interest: first, because it gives a picture of the rabbinical career in those days; and, secondly, because it throws light on business arrangements within the Jewish community and between Jews and non-Jews. The rabbinate as a profession supported by community funds was unknown in the early days. The rabbi was a scholar who volunteered to teach and to decide legal questions. He supported himself through business. Since, however, the rabbi devoted most of his time to study and teaching, Rabbenu Gershom indicates that it is the responsibility of the community to aid the rabbi in his business in such a way that he should not have to devote too much time to it and thus enable him to do the more important intellectual and spiritual work. At the very beginning of the responsum, reference is made to the fact that "Reuben," the scholar involved, had a *maarufia* (a customer who was his alone). No one else was allowed to do business with this private customer. The responsum is no. 68 in Eidelberg's collection.

TEXT

Question:

As for your question which is as follows: "Reuben" had a *maarufia* with certain priests for many years.

> (In all responsa dealing with civil disputes the real names of the disputants were not given, but the names of the sons of Jacob were used as a substitute. Usually it is "Reuben" and "Simeon" who dispute with each other. If a third party is involved, it is usually "Levi," and occasionally some other son.)

This Reuben was a scholar. He taught Torah to the public without pay. His students, becoming aware of the profit that he made through his *maarufia,* trespassed into it, to his loss. (They sought to take these private customers away from him.) Complaint was made against the students and the community forced them, by ban and decree, to break off all contact with the *maarufia.* But the question that was in doubt was whether they (the community) had the right to exclude the rest of the people who were not his disciples (from trespassing into this business).

Answer:

From your question it is possible to infer that in your locality you do not have the general custom of *maarufia.* (In those localities where the custom prevailed, there would have been no question of anyone trespassing on anybody else's *maarufia.*)

Since you do not have that custom in your community, no one can compel the community to allow him (Reuben) to keep this business to himself. Rab Huna said in the Talmud (B. B. 21b): "If one who lives in a gateway sets up a mill and another one comes into that gateway and sets one up by his side, the law is that he can be prevented from doing so, for the first one can say to him, 'You are cutting off my livelihood.' " Yet (though Huna said that) the law is not according to him, because they (the other scholars) raised the following objection to him (in the same talmudic passage): "If a man establishes a store beside the store of his fellow, etc.," and in that discussion they traced the dispute to earlier scholars and concluded that it was Simon ben Gamaliel who said originally that one can prevent even one's neighbor (from opening a competitive store next door); nevertheless the law in that earlier dispute is not according to Simon ben Gamaliel, but according to the preceding scholar who said that one cannot prevent the competitor from opening the store. (Thus the law is in general that you cannot prevent a competing neighbor from opening a store next to yours.) Nevertheless (although that is the law), it applies only in localities where they do not have the custom of allowing a man to have a monopoly; but in places where they do have the custom (he may prevent a competitor from opening the store, since) everything depends upon the customs of the province.

Furthermore, the right of free competition applies to men in general, but not to a scholar who engages in the Torah and in the affairs of Heaven. It is proper to give such a person special status in order that he may not be distracted from his study. For Rabbi Nahman said (*ibid.*, 22a) that you may not prevent peddlers from opening a stall. Even the citizens of a city where the peddlers are strangers may not prevent them, since Ezra the Scribe arranged for peddlers to travel from city to city (the Talmud says Ezra arranged it so that the daughters of Israel might be able to buy ornaments). The peddlers may not be prevented from traveling about, but they can be prevented from establishing a settled business (next to a store that already exists. This applies to ordinary peddlers), but if the traveling merchant is a scholar, then he is permitted to establish even a fixed (com-

peting) business. Also we are told (*ibid.*) that Rab Dimi of
Nahardea brought a shipment of dried grapes to Mahusa by ship
and the exilarch said to Rava, "If Rab Dimi is a scholar, give
him a monopoly." Further it is said (Yoma 72b) Rabbi Yohanan
compared two verses: *Make for thyself an ark of wood* (Ex.
25.10 [i.e., that Moses should make the Ark of the Covenant
himself]). But another verse (Deut. 10.1) says: *Let them make
an ark of acacia wood* (here, using the plural, the verse indicates
that the people should make it for Moses). This proves (said
Rabbi Yohanan) that the people of a city are commanded to do
a scholar's work for him. Therefore Rabbi Yohanan concludes
as follows: How do we describe a scholar? One whose townsmen
are commanded to do his (secular) work for him; which means
that the scholar is one who neglects his own secular affairs and
engages in the affairs of Heaven.

For all these reasons we can conclude that the community is
in duty bound to make a special arrangement for this scholar
whose work is the work of Heaven and who teaches the Torah
in public without pay. (They must make arrangements) so that
he should not be disturbed from his studies. They should decree
against the *entire* community (not only against his own pupils,
who owe him a special debt) that they must abstain from interfer-
ing with his *maarufia*. They will receive a reward for this and
enjoy a long life. As it is written (Prov. 3.18): *It is a tree of life
for those who take hold of it and those who support it are happy.*

4

☆

CONTRACT WITH A TEACHER

Isaac Alfasi was the greatest Spanish authority before Maimonides, whom he antedated by a century. Alfasi, has in fact, remained one of the basic legal authors whose works are still regularly studied. He was born near the Tunisian town of Fez and studied in the great Tunisian rabbinical center of Kairawan. There he became recognized as an outstanding talmudic authority and there he lived until his old age when, due to some false accusations by informers, he was forced to flee. He settled in Spain, where he died in his nineties in the city of Lucena.

The work upon which his lasting fame rests was his abridgement of the Talmud, which he called *Halakhot* (Laws), but which is generally known as the RIF (after his initials, Rabbi Isaac Fasi) or *The Alfas*. It is a condensation of the Talmud, and therefore follows the talmudic tractates. He omits the non-legal parts of the Talmud and also those legal parts that apply only to Palestine. The work quickly accumulated a vast number of commentators and was studied all over the Jewish world. It was the first Spanish-Jewish legal work to become a subject for constant study in northern Europe and elsewhere. It can hardly be called a code, because it does not rearrange the talmudic material. It is rather a compendium of the Talmud, a practical abbreviation of it, and, further, offers decisions where the Talmud itself leaves the debate undecided.

Alfasi was also the author of many responsa which were known and used by scholars, as we can see from the fact of their frequent citation in the classical scholarly works. His responsa were long known as separate, individual documents; their first edition in book form appeared no earlier than 1781 in Leghorn. Since then many editions have appeared; the latest, richly annotated, was edited by Wolf Leiter (Maimonides Institute, Pittsburgh, 1954), from which text the responsum cited is taken.

Almost all of Alfasi's responsa are on matters of business law —mostly contracts, dowry disputes, inheritance and estates. We have selected one contract responsum because the subject of the dispute is of rather general interest. It is actually a dispute over the curriculum for an adult educational enterprise. Incidentally it reveals how scholars from other lands traveled to Spain and were welcomed there, as is well known from the fact that Asher ben Yehiel moved there from the Rhineland in the 13th century, and almost immediately upon his arrival became the head of an academy in Toledo. This responsum is no. 223 in the Leiter edition.

TEXT

Question:

Reuben and his wife and sons originally dwelt in eastern France, many days journey from Spain.

He (Reuben) left his wife and his sons in their native place and was content to wander through the communities in the land of Spain. He came to a certain province (in Spain) and preached in public. When five of the leaders of the community met him, they urged him to bring his wife and his sons to that province and dwell among them (i.e., to become their teacher). But Reuben hesitated because his wife was far away (and the expense of bringing his family would be great). But they continued to try to persuade him, and he ultimately agreed. They contracted with him, by formal contract (literally, "by complete acquisition").

(This refers to the fact that an agreement was made binding in a symbolic way, by handing over an object from one to the other. The acquisition of the symbolic object, a hand-kerchief or something of that kind, was the sign of the mutual agreement to the contract. The simplest translation of the phrase, "by complete acquisition" would be "with full formality.")

They agreed to give him 24 gold pieces, *maravedis*, every year for a term of three years; and he agreed to read before them Halakhah (i.e., some legal compendium or the Talmud), the Mishna and Scriptures, to expound the weekly portion, and to do whatever else they agreed upon by formal "acquisition," in writing, and in the presence of witnesses. Reuben further agreed, formally (i.e., by "acquisition"), that he and his wife and his sons would come to the community by the festival of Sukkot. When the time fixed upon came, he arrived and they welcomed him joyously. Some of them said: Let us begin by studying the Mishna; others said: let us begin by studying the Talmud. Finally they all agreed (on the course of study): they began with the tractate Berakhot ("Blessings," the first tractate of the Talmud) which they would study for four days out of the seven; on the fifth day, Scriptures; on the sixth day, interpretation of the weekly portion.

(It was customary to study the weekly portion on Friday, to be prepared for the public reading of it the next day in the synagogue.)

But after that, one of them, Issakhar, quarreled with his neighbor and said to him, "I cannot understand the profound Halakhah and I do not want it." And instead (of four full days of Talmud), he suggested, let there be read out to them (to the class) three lines of Talmud and then three lines of Mishna. But his companions said, "We do not want that" (scaling down our course of study). Thereupon Issakhar arose and said, "I do not desire to read (i.e., to study) and I will not pay my share." Thereupon Reuben (the teacher) answered and said, "I have a written contract in my hands, formalized by symbolic acquisition and witnesses. I may do no other than fulfill what is in my contract and what I had agreed upon with you."

Answer:

We studied this question and investigated all the conditions set forth in it. We see that they are strong and valid and that it is obligatory upon you to fulfill all the conditions that you made between you. As for Issakhar, who changed his mind and does not wish to fulfill the conditions which he agreed to together with his fellows, he has not done right. He is obligated to give Reuben all that he has taken upon himself as his part of the pay. If (when he has paid his share) he wishes to sit and study on the conditions that he had made, then all is well. If not, he has no complaint against Reuben, for note that he, Reuben, did not present an obstacle (to the fulfilment of the contract).

Now, although we learn in the Mishna (B. M. VI.1): "He who hires workmen and they deceive one another (as to wages, etc.) they have against each other nothing but murmurings."

> (I.e., they have no legal recourse, except that they can grumble about it. Of course, each of them, the workmen or the employer, is free to abandon the contract. See *Tur,* "Hoshen Mishpat" 333, and *Shulhan Arukh, ibid.* In other words, under these circumstances, the contract can be voided. But there can be no suit. All they have against each other are complaints.)

But where does this apply (i.e., that they can void the agreement if they feel they have been misled)? It applies only when the workmen have not yet begun their work, but if they have already begun to work, the employer cannot withdraw from the arrangement. As we learn (B. M. 76b): "Where does this apply (that they can do no more than complain and withdraw), only where the workmen have not gone down to work? If, for example, the donkey-drivers have started out, but did not find the grain (which they were to transport), or the farm-laborers went out and found the field wet (so that they could not work), then he must pay them their wages." So here (continues Alfasi), in the case of this Reuben (the teacher), if they had changed their mind before he had transplanted his family, they would be able to do so. Since, however, he has brought them from their native place and spent his money to bring them and, furthermore, has actually begun his new employment, now they can no longer retract and are in duty bound to pay him according to all the conditions. And, in fact, even if he had not yet gone (to fetch his family), since he has "acquired from their hand" (i.e., since the symbolic objects binding the contract formally have been passed between them), they are no longer permitted to change their minds, as it is said (Zeph. 3.13): *The remnant of Israel will not do wrong nor speak falsehood, nor will deception be found in their mouth.* (This verse is frequently quoted in the legal literature when an appeal is made to conscience and decency, beyond the strict requirements of the Law.) Of course, the court cannot rely merely upon their words; but if it is explained (to a court) that he has already gone (to his native town) and sold his chattels and spent money because of them, they are not permitted to deceive him, but are in duty bound to fulfill all the conditions that they had made with him.

As for Issakhar, if they wish, they can do him a kindness, provided Reuben agrees with them (they might make a special arrangement for Issakhar). This *would* be doing a great kindness, since they are not in duty bound to go beyond the law by setting aside a special time for him alone. Also, Reuben is not in duty bound to teach him individually, for he had only contracted to teach all of them together, but not to teach each one separately. Therefore, if Issakhar wishes to sit and learn, let him sit and learn. If not, let him give his share of the pay for the teaching.

(In other words, if they want to make a private arrangement for individual instruction for Issakhar, they may do so out of sheer kindness. The contract does not require it. But whether or not they do so, Issakhar must pay his share of the sum agreed upon.)

5

✡

MAIMONIDES TO OBADIAH
THE PROSELYTE

Moses Maimonides (Ramban: born in Cordova, Spain, 1135; died in Cairo, 1204) was the greatest all-around scholar produced by medieval Jewry. He was an outstanding philosopher, a famous physician, a great talmudist, and an unparalleled codifier of the Law. His famous philosophic work, *The Guide to the Perplexed,* is equaled in fame by his lucid codification of the entire Written and Oral Law, his *Mishneh Torah* (popularly known as the *Yad*). Though perhaps not generally reckoned among the great authors of responsa, he deserves high regard in this field also.

One reason why he is not generally counted among the great authors of responsa lies in the fact that he never seemed to consider responsa a special branch of literature, with each responsum following a certain pattern of talmudic reference, development and presentation. This treatment of responsa as essays, unique and important in themselves as works of literature, was not yet known in the time of Maimonides. Rather, the responsa of this period were simple practical answers to practical questions. Of course, when Maimonides wrote an answer to an inquiry of a learned scholar, he would, indeed, respond in elaborate fashion, giving references to the Talmud and analyses of them. But when he wrote to an average inquirer, he would simply dash off a direct answer, some of these answers being not more than a line or two in length. Furthermore, a great many of his responsa were in Arabic, the vernacular of the Mediterranean lands, and therefore were not easily accessible to the Jews of northern non-Mediterranean Europe.

Nevertheless, since his fame was world-wide and since he was the head of the important Jewish community of Cairo, innumerable inquiries were addressed to him, and many collections of his answers have been preserved. Upon these private collections were based the larger manuscript collections which are found in the great libraries. Some of these larger collections were entirely in Hebrew and many more were translated from the Arabic. The Geniza in Cairo has revealed very few Maimonides responsa; nevertheless, in modern times more complete editions are being published. The most complete is by Abraham Hayyim Freimann (published in Jerusalem, 1934).

The Freimann collection, of 386 responsa, contains three addressed to a certain Obadiah, a proselyte to Judaism who lived in Jerusalem. These responsa are of great interest because, written in the famous, lucid Hebrew style of Maimonides, they clarify the status of a convert in Judaism. His status needed clarification because, in the long history of Judaism, the mood of the Jewish community towards proselytes frequently changed. The Talmud records a warm hospitality towards them when it says (Pes. 87b): "God scattered Israel among the nations for the sole purpose of acquiring proselytes." On the other hand, the Talmud likewise records an opposite attitude (due certainly to some disillusioning experiences): "Proselytes are worse for Israel than leprosy" (Kid. 70b). With regard to this latter statement, it is worth recording the reaction of a proselyte in the 12th century in northern France. His defense of his fellow-proselytes is cited among the tosafists' notes to that passage (Kid. 71a). It reads as follows: "Says Abraham the Proselyte, 'Yes, we proselytes are a source of pain to the people of Israel because we are much more careful in the observance of all the laws than are the born Israelites, and therefore God rebukes them because of us.'"

Maimonides, in his three letters to Obadiah the Proselyte in Jerusalem, writes with respect and warm affection and asserts in
various ways the complete equality of the convert to Judaism
with the born Jew. As an example of Maimonides' responsa, we
offer the first responsum to Obadiah the Proselyte in Freimann's
edition, responsum no. 42.

The specific question which Obadiah the Proselyte asks Maimonides is the crucial one: Is a proselyte a child of Israel in the
full sense? He refers to the fact that many of the prayers speak of
"God of our fathers." Now his father was not a member of the
house of Israel. May he use that customary phrase when he prays?
The question of course was not a new one. It had already been
referred to in the Mishna. In Bikkurim, I.4, there is a discussion
of the declaration to be made when the pilgrim brings his first
fruits to the Temple (Deut. 26.3 ff.). This verse reads, *You shall
say in the presence of the Lord your God: "I have come to the
land which God swore to our fathers to give us."* The Mishna,
referring to this text, which must be read by every pilgrim bringing first fruits, says: "The proselyte may bring first fruits, but may
not do the reading, because he is unable to say (truthfully) *the
land which God has sworn to our fathers to give us.*" The commentator on the Mishna, Bertinoro, says that Maimonides decided that the law is not according to this Mishna, but that the
proselyte may do the reading, because the land was given to
Abraham, and Abraham is the father of all proselytes. Bertinoro,
who lived in the second half of the 15th century in Italy, and died
in Jerusalem (and, whose first name, by the way, was also
Obadiah), obviously had seen a manuscript of the responsum
that we are about to cite, since he repeated its exact argument.

TEXT

Question:

The questions which Obadiah, the righteous proselyte, asked of our teacher, Moses, of blessed memory, and his answers.

(The use of the plural in the heading for the questions and answers may indicate that originally all three questions, addressed by Obadiah to Maimonides, were joined together and this was a heading for all of them.)

Answer:

Says Moses the son of Maimon of the children of *the exile of Jerusalem in Spain* (as a compliment to Obadiah the Proselyte, Maimonides describes himself in a phrase taken from the prophet Obadiah 1.20), may his memory be a blessing (the responsum was copied after the death of Maimonides).

There has come to us the questions of our teacher and rabbi, Obadiah, the learned and intelligent righteous proselyte. May God repay him and may his reward be perfect from the God of Israel, since he came to seek shelter under His wings. You ask concerning procedure with regard to benedictions and prayers. When you pray privately or with the congregation, may you say, "God of *our* fathers, who has sanctified *us* by His commandments, and who has separated and chosen *us* and has given inheritance to *our* fathers and brought *us* out of the land of Egypt and did miracles to *our* fathers," and all such similar phrases (i.e., that appear frequently in the prayer book)? You must say all of these as they are; and you must not change a single word; but just as a born Israelite prays and blesses, so must you bless and pray whether you are praying privately or are the cantor of the congregation.

The essence of the matter is this: Abraham, our father, taught all people and brought them wisdom and told them of the true faith and the unity of God and rejected idols and made void their service and brought many under the wings of the Divine Presence; he instructed them and commanded his sons in his household

after him to guard the path of God, as it is written in the Torah
(Gen. 18.19): *For I know him* (God says), *that he will command his sons and his household after him to guard the way of
God.* Therefore, every one to the end of all generations (i.e., at
all times in the future), who becomes a proselyte and whoever
declares the name of God as One, as it is written in the Torah, is
a disciple of Abraham, our father, upon whom be peace, and
they are all children of his household. It is he who turned them
to the good path, just as he (Abraham) turned the men of his
generation by his own word of mouth and by his teachings. Thus
is he the one who converts all who are destined to become
proselytes through his mandate which he commanded his sons
and his household after him. Thus we see that Abraham our
father is the father of his worthy descendants who walk in his
paths, the father of his disciples and of every proselyte who comes
to join Israel.

Therefore, you must say (in your prayers), "Our God and
God of our fathers"; for Abraham, on whom be peace, he is your
father and you can say (in the prayers), "who has given as inheritance to our fathers . . .": for to Abraham was given the
Land, as it is said (Gen. 13.17): *Arise, walk through the land
through its length and its breadth, for to thee I give it.* However,
as to the phrases, *who has brought us out of Egypt,* or *who has
performed miracles to our fathers,* if you wish to change them and
say, "who has brought Israel from Egypt," or "has done miracles
to Israel," you may say it that way.

> (Maimonides means that the proselyte is direct kin to
> Abraham but perhaps cannot be described as being kin to
> the later generations who were in Egypt. But he does not
> stress this distinction, since he continues as follows:)

But if you do not change the phrase, no harm has been done at
all; for, since you have entered under the wings of the *Shekhina*
(The Divine Presence) and are joined with Him, there is no difference at all between us and you, and all the miracles that were
done are as if they were done for you as well as for us. Thus
Scripture says: *Let not the stranger who is joined unto the Lord*

say, *"God has set me apart from His people."* (Isa. 56.3.) There is no difference at all between us and you in any matter. There is no question but that you must read the blessing: "who has chosen us," and "who has given us as an inheritance," and "who has set us apart," because the Creator has already chosen you and set you apart from the Gentiles and given *you* the Law; for the Torah was given both to us and to the proselytes, as it is said: *As for the congregation, one statute there is for you and for the proselyte, an eternal law for your generations, for you and for the proselyte before the Lord; one law and judgment shall be for you and for the proselyte* (Nu. 15.15,16). Know thou that our fathers who came out of Egypt were, the majority of them, idolators. In Egypt they intermingled with the Gentiles and learned their ways, until the Holy One, blessed be He, sent Moses, on whom be peace, the teacher of all prophets, and set us apart from the other peoples and brought us under the wings of the *Shekhina,* for us and for all the proselytes, and gave us all one Law.

Let not your genealogy be deprecated in your own sight. If we (born Jews) trace our genealogy to Abraham, Isaac, and Jacob, you are related to Him who created the world, for thus it is said clearly in Isaiah 44.5: *One will say I am the Lord's, and another will call himself with the name of Jacob.* And all that we have said to you with regard to the benedictions, that you should not change their form (i.e., that you should not omit the words, "God of our fathers," etc.), for all of it there is a proof in the tractate Bikkurim I.4. There we learn that the proselyte who brings (first fruits) does not read the statement prescribed, because he cannot say (the Land) *which God swore to give to our fathers;* but when he prays privately, he must say, "Our God and the God of the fathers of Israel," and when he is in the synagogue, he says, "Our God and the God of our fathers." This is the anonymous Mishna and is the opinion of Rabbi Meir (this is according to the general principle stated in the Talmud [Sanh. 86a] that all anonymous parts of the Mishna are to be ascribed to Rabbi Meir). But this is not the law, as is made clear in the Jerusalem Talmud (Bik., end of ch. I), where it is said: It is taught in the name of Rabbi Judah; the proselyte himself can bring and do the reading. Why? (I.e., why is he permitted to say, "God of our

Fathers"?) For (God said to Abraham) *I have made thee into a multitude of nations* (Gen. 17.5). In the past you were father to Aram (as in the Palestinian Talmud text); from now on you will be father to all living creatures. Rabbi Joshua son of Levi says, the law is according to Rabbi Judah (i.e., that a proselyte may say "God of our fathers"). An actual case came before Rabbi Abbahu and he decided it according to Rabbi Judah (thus far the quotation from the Palestinian Talmud).

(Maimonides then concludes as follows:)

Hence it is made clear to you that you must say, *which God swore to our fathers to give us,* that Abraham is your father and ours, and of all the righteous who walk in his way. The same applies to all the other benedictions and prayers. Do not change any of them at all.

Thus writeth

Moses the son of Maimon

The second responsum to the same proselyte is no. 345 in Freimann's edition and deals with a theological question, namely, what is meant by the statement in the Talmud (Ber. 23b) that everything is predetermined by God except our reverence for Him.

The final responsum to Obadiah the Proselyte is no. 369 in Freimann's edition. Some teacher had insulted him by declaring that the Mohammedans (from whom Obadiah sprang) were really idolators. Maimonides proves that the Mohammedans are pure monotheists and rebukes the teacher for having insulted Obadiah.

6

✡

DIVORCE FROM AN APOSTATE

Jacob ben Meir, Rashi's grandson (born in Ramerupt, 1100; died in Troyes, 1171) was known as Rabbenu Tam, "Our Perfect Teacher," a reference to the fact that the patriarch Jacob was described as *Tam,* "quiet," or "perfect" (Gen. 25.27). He lived during the worst times of the Crusades in France, and suffered personal violence from a group of Crusaders, who wounded him and would have killed him, had he not been rescued by some noblemen. He was the greatest of the tosafists, the Franco-German analysts of the Talmud whose critical, analytical notes are published on the outer column of every talmudic page, the inner column being the commentary of his grandfather, Rashi. He was the prime developer of this method of study of the Talmud, which consisted primarily of comparing passages from all over the talmudic literature in order to arrive at the meaning of the passage under discussion. This was essentially the method of the Talmud itself which cited passages from all over the Mishna and contemporary works in order to arrive at an understanding of the meaning of the Mishna passage under discussion. These *tosafot,* or additional notes, thereby kept the talmudic method alive, and it has continued until this day in most of the *hiddushim,* or new notes, or insights of talmudic scholars.

Rabbenu Tam was more than a scholar. He was the leader of French Jewry and was, of course, concerned with maintaining the cruelly assailed Jewish community and organizing its social and religious life under talmudic law. He therefore summoned a number of convocations of scholars at which certain ordinances were passed, just as four or five generations earlier, Rabbenu Gershom, "the Light of the Exile," summoned a synod in Mayence to bring order into the Jewish social and religious life of his day. Among the decrees passed in the synods convoked by Rabbenu Tam was one stating that the ban should be issued against all Jews who failed to bring their disputes before the Jewish courts, but had recourse to the Gentile courts. Another decree ordained that whoever questioned the validity of a divorce on the basis of technical flaws in its text should be put under the ban. This was a vital decision in those disorderly times, when husbands might give a divorce, then perhaps disappear. If the divorce were questioned and invalidated after the woman re-married, the second marriage could be declared adulterous and the children born of it illegitimate.

In general, Rabbenu Tam's authority was so great that he and his famous grandfather were deemed of equal stature. The reverence with which both grandfather and grandson were held can be deduced from one rather minor instance. Jacob Moellin, the great authority in the Rhineland two centuries later, followed the custom of placing the *mezuzah* at an angle. This is explained by his pupil, Zalman of St. Goar, who recorded his teacher's customs, as follows: "I heard from Maharil (i.e., Jacob Moellin, his teacher) that we are accustomed to affix the *mezuzah* on a slant. This he did because Rashi thought that it should be vertical and Rabbenu Tam thought that it should be horizontal. So we make it half vertical and half horizontal, to carry out the opinion of both of them" (*Minhagei Maharil,* "Laws of Mezuzot").

Because of Rabbenu Tam's great authority, he received legal questions from all over the Franco-German world and some even from Spain. His responsa are collected in the second part of his work, *Sefer haYashar* ("The Book of the Upright," edition Rosenthal, Berlin, 1898). The responsum here cited deals with the troublesome question of obtaining a divorce for a Jewish woman from a husband who had become an apostate. Since by Jewish Law the marital rights of a husband are his by virtue of having been born a Jew (or by conversion to Judaism), the fact that he had abandoned Judaism does not diminish his power to grant a divorce to his wife. The responsum reveals a number of important circumstances. First, it demonstrates Rabbenu Tam's strong-mindedness: with characteristic forthrightness he addresses an older scholar (his kinsman, Rabbi Yom-Tov) and does not hesitate to correct him sharply. Secondly, it reveals his firm stand (which was enacted as a decree in one of the synods which he summoned) that a divorce should not be invalidated upon minor technical grounds, especially a divorce so difficult to obtain as one from an apostate. Finally, the responsum reveals the persecution which existed in those days, when many of the Jews were driven (or chose) to abandon the religion of their fathers. The responsum cited is no. 25 in the Rosenthal edition.

TEXT

The opinion which you adopted seems far-fetched to me and forced. You cause a daughter of Israel to become an *agunah* (a chained woman—a woman who, not being able to obtain a divorce from her husband, can never remarry) and rest your decision upon an exaggerated or meaningless reason. That which you, my kinsman Rabbi Yom-Tov, are doing with regard to the divorce is not good. You said that it (the writ) was signed (by the witnesses) *after* it had been placed in the hands of the woman (and therefore was invalid on the ground that it should have been signed before it was given to her). For, you see, we consider the law to be according to Rabbi Eliezer (Git. 4a). According to Rabbi Eliezer, the signing on a bill of divorcement (is not indispensable, but) is only for the sake of proper procedure (literally, for the sake of the improvement of society). Such "proper procedure" can apply both after she received the divorce document (the *get*) and before she receives it. Or, perhaps just because the husband said to the scribe, "Write a *get*," and he then said to the witnesses, "Sign it," you are inclined to invalidate the *get* on the theory that he did not mean her to be divorced until after the *get* was actually signed. Were then the witnesses who signed identical with the messengers who delivered the *get?*

> (He then proceeds to an analysis of three or four passages in the Talmud, tractate Gittin, as to the various ways in which the husband may have given the order to write the *get* and the variety of possible signatories, etc. He then proceeds to discuss the crucial objection of Rabbi Yom-Tov to the divorce, namely, that the new Christian name of the apostate was not included in the divorce. This was precisely the kind of technical objection which Rabbenu Tam abhorred, and he therefore discusses it rather sharply.)

You declare the *get* invalid because they did not write the (Christian) name of the apostate. It is evident that you are *as one who is gathering sheaves in the valley of the shades* (a verse from Isa. 17.5, by which he meant to say that Yom-Tov was making idle and worthless objections). For, in fact, had it included the present name of the convert, it would have been still more open to objection. You and I both know that these apostates are nicknamed mockingly among the Jews, Judah being called Judach (implying "recreant") and Abraham being called Abran (implying "sinner") and Asher, Ashera (meaning "an idolatrous grove"). Menahem (the apostate whose divorce is now under discussion) is nickanmed Melahem (meaning "quarrelsome"). For all who knew him from his childhood called him Menahem, but none at all recognize him by his name William (Guillaume). Even if they *did* know that (new) name, they would not (care to) mention it.

How many apostates have divorced their wives and never was there anything written in the *get* other than their Jewish names; for thus most of the Jews called them. Certainly their Jewish name is of no less standing than a nickname (which should be mentioned or recorded in the *get*). We have similar experiences every day. When (for example) my kinsman Eliezer divorced Madame Rachel, our aunt, his name was Vesselin and her name was Belle-Assez; and yet they wrote "Eliezer" and "Rachel," their Jewish names, and ignored the names which the Gentiles called them. The fact that the majority of Christians use the (new) name does not constitute a majority in Jewish Law. It is the name which is used by the majority of Jews that counts, since the man who is giving the divorce is of the children of Israel (by origin).

(Rabbenu Tam then goes into an analysis of the various laws in the Talmud dealing with the names and by-names of husband and wife, which names or by-names need or need not be used. Then he concludes with an exhortation to the older teacher to retract his decision.)

I plead with you most earnestly to reverse yourself, for many men have raised objection to a divorce and have been unable to repair the harm that they have done. Now there is really no flaw in this divorce. You are overcareful about things that have no reality. In fact, it seems to me that there is some hidden rancor in your heart against the parties. I sent to the signers of the document. They asked me to write out my arguments and send them to you. They signed my statement and are astonished at your insistence that the Christian name be written as the essential name. More than twenty divorces from apostates were made in Paris (in France) and they wrote only the Jewish names in them; so, too, in Lorraine. All these documents were prepared by great scholars. I saw with my own eyes the divorce of the son-in-law of the noble Rabbi Jacob Parnes, of blessed memory, who (the son-in-law) became an apostate. The name in the divorce was written Shemaya, surnamed Waldman, whereas his new Christian name was Gottschal, and it was not mentioned in the document at all. For God forbid that it should be mentioned (in a document written) under the Law of Moses and Israel. If (you) my relative had not told me that (this apostate's) name was William, (neither I nor any) of the men of our kingdom would know any other than his Jewish name. They nicknamed him Melahem ("quarrelsome").

(He concludes the responsum, addressing the father of the divorced wife, as follows:)

You, noble father of the girl, marry your daughter to someone worthy of her, for one should pay no attention to the words of those who mock (i.e., who object to the divorce), for they cannot find their hands and their feet (i.e., they do not know what they are doing) and they stumble in their minority (i.e., there are not enough of these objectors to matter). The arguments on which they depend are of no account. The matter is settled that she is permitted (to remarry). Also the witnesses, of whom my relative said that they testified before him (against the divorce), deserve to be banned. Let him find out who they are and I will know what the end of them will be. Peace!

7

✡

COMMUNITY GOVERNMENT

Meir ben Baruch of Rothenburg (born in Worms, 1215; died in the Fortress of Ensisheim, 1293) was referred to as the Chief Rabbi of Germany. Some scholars believe that he actually was the chief rabbi, appointed by Emperor Rudolph. Others doubt that there ever was such an office in German Jewry. At all events, the fact that he is so described indicates his widespread authority. Meir was well-known also among Spanish scholars. The great talmudist, Solomon ben Adret, directed a legal question to him. Since the days of Rabbenu Gershom in the 10th century, Rabbi Meir was the only one who was referred to as "Light of the Exile."

Meir ben Baruch studied in Germany and in France. He witnessed the tragic burning of the Talmud in Paris in the year 1244. As a result of his studies in France, he continued the writing of *tosafot* (additional notes to the Talmud), many of which are in the printed editions of the Talmud. He wrote books on various legal themes, the laws of slaughtering, of mourning, and others. He was also a synagogue poet of note and, above all, a great teacher.

He had many famous disciples. Asher ben Yehiel was perhaps the greatest. When Asher ben Yehiel left his Rhineland home and emigrated to Spain, he brought the influence of his teacher's decisions into Spanish Jewry. Another of Meir's pupils was Mordecai ben Hillel, whose great compendium, *Mordecai,* is now appended to the work of Alfasi. Still another was Meir haKohen whose *Hagahot Maimuniyot* are appended to the Code of Maimonides. The compendium of Asher ben Yehiel is found in all regular Talmud editions. In these three works of his main disciples, Meir of Rothenburg is constantly cited, and thus these works constitute a mine of information on his teachings. In addition, his responses to questions sent him from various lands exist in many collections.

Toward the end of his life, Meir and his family were traveling in northern Italy, possibly on their way to settle in Palestine. He was recognized by an apostate, arrested, and finally handed over to Emperor Rudolph, who held him for ransom. Meir refused to permit himself to be ransomed lest this start a series of similar extortions. He therefore remained in the Fortress of Ensisheim for seven years, until his death. During these seven years of imprisonment, he continued to study and many of his responsa date from this period.

The responsum cited here is from the Budapest edition of Meir of Rothenburg's responsa (1895). It deals with a question vital to the Jewry of the Middle Ages, namely, communal authority, its source and extent. Since the Jews did not belong to any of the feudal classes, they had virtual self-government. The secular government consented to this, since Jewish self-government made it easier to collect taxes from the Jews. The governments simply taxed the community and the community taxed its members. Since the Jewish community fixed the assessments for the taxes, the question of the right of an individual or a minority to protest against the assessment frequently arose. This and related questions often involved the basic question: What right had the community to impose burdens on an individual? Thus the basis of communal powers and authority was a frequent subject of discussion among the earlier authorities. Some believed that the community's authority stemmed from the fact that the community was organized initially by the unanimous consent of its members. Others held that great scholars living in the community inherited the rights of the old Sanhedrin to exercise authority over the community. For a full discussion of this matter of the community and its powers, see Louis Finkelstein, *Jewish Self-Government in the Middle Ages,* especially pages 49–55 (and Irving Agus, *Rabbi Meir of Rothenburg,* II, 448–489), where the responsum of Meir of Rothenburg, which we cite, is also mentioned.

In this responsum, Meir merges various past opinions on the authority of the community: first, that it must rest on the complete consent of all its members (not necessarily for every decision, but certainly for the choice of the leaders who make the decisions); he speaks, besides, of the special authority of "a great man." The specific question here deals with a community in which a few of the men come to a private agreement to govern the community and to assess the taxes. The responsum is no. 968 in the Budapest edition.

The responsum concerns the members of the community, a few of whom banded themselves together and appointed a presiding officer without the consent of the entire community and therefore, not legally, wished to govern the rest of the community, to impose taxes, and manage religious and civil matters, to be lenient or to be strict as they desired.

TEXT

They are not (legally) masters in this matter. They are not permitted to make any new enactments without the consent of all (i.e., the entire community). For the statement in the Talmud (B. B. 8b), to the effect that the members of a community can levy fines in support of their decisions, really means (that they may do so only) after the consent of the entire community (has been given). Then they may do so without formal contractual arrangements. They may take possession of chattels by their words alone (i.e., without "acquiring," that is, without the formal act of transference as necessary in private contracts and transfers). Thus they are permitted to impose a fine on all who had accepted their authority, but who subsequently violate their decisions. They are permitted to impose the fines in accordance with (the schedule) which the community has agreed to, i.e., to impose definite sums as fines.

Or (the alternate way of organizing the community besides that by which a general assembly determines the laws and the amount of fines) the seven leaders of the city (literally "the seven good men" of the city) who were chosen from the beginning by the votes of the entire community to oversee the affairs of the community and to fine and to punish, these (leaders) have the right (delegated to them) to impose fines in defense of their decisions (i.e., either the entire community agrees on its regulations in a "constitutional assembly," or they elect seven governors who then have the right to make the laws and enforce them).

But here, in this case, these men have appointed *themselves* as rulers. They have no such authority, especially here when there is "a great man" in this city (a scholar of such stature as may be deemed thereby to have authority). This (the especial right of a great man or scholar to institute decrees) we derive from the first chapter of the tractate Baba Batra (9a). There is mention of the case of those butchers who agreed (that each slaughter only on the day assigned to him and) that whichever one slaughtered on a day which belongs to his fellow-butcher, such a one shall be punished by having the hide of the animal he has slaughtered torn up.

> (The talmudic passage discusses the validity of this sort of small-scale self-government on the part of a group and decides that they may do so and enforce their decisions upon each other, *unless* a great scholar is present who can decide these things, not according to their private decisions, but according to Law.)

But here (in the case of this city) where "a great man" is to be found among them, it is not for them to make decisions. Even the terms that they fixed among themselves (i.e., to form this governing group), since they did not fix them with the knowledge of the great man, they have no validity (as a legal contract between them). All the more do they not have the authority to apply their decision *against* the great scholar himself in any way. Such action is simply inconceivable. Especially since Rabbi Meir Cohen (the local scholar) is quite willing to bear the yoke along with them in all decrees to be imposed or agreed upon.

He is willing that they should impose taxes by his consent along with theirs. Nevertheless, in spite of his expressed willingness to cooperate, they did not heed him, and they pledged his property to the Gentiles (that is, they used Gentiles to impose a lien on his property to guarantee the payment of the taxes which they had imposed). In this case he has full right to rescue his property from their hands in any way he can, even by entering into someone else's house to reclaim his property; even by making use of Gentiles for this purpose. For we hold to the principle that a man may sometimes take the law into his own hands (B. K. 27b). To be sure, the Talmud (B. M. 113a) places a limit on the rights of a man to take the law into his own hands, as in the following cases: If a man lends money to his neighbor (and when the debt is due, the borrower does not pay), the lender may not enter the man's house to take possession of a pledge. Even the messenger of the court may not seize (distrain) the borrower's property within his house, but only on the street. These limitations, however, apply to taking possession of a pledge; but to save his own property, a man may take the law into his own hands (or to use the word of the Talmud, "he may give a hundred strokes with a hoe-handle, or sit with a whip in his hand to guard it" [B. K. 27b, 28a]). If at the time when you (the self-appointed officers) have illegally mortgaged his property (for obtaining of the taxes you have imposed) by means of Gentiles, he takes action against you to deliver his property from your hands, he has acted rightly, according to the law, as is explained above. Therefore, cease doing this evil thing; and *if you consent and hearken,* your words will be established and you will be honored. Peace!

Meir, the son of Baruch of blessed memory

8

✡

USING THE CODE OF
MAIMONIDES

Asher ben Yehiel (born in the Rhineland, 1250; died in Toledo, Spain, 1328) was the descendant of a famous rabbinical family. Due to the persecutions in the Rhineland, he sent his son Jacob (who later became the author of the famous legal Code, the *Tur*) to Spain to study. He himself, with the rest of the family, followed later. He settled for a brief time in the Provence and then crossed the Pyrenees, where he was hospitably received in Barcelona by the leading Spanish rabbi, Solomon ben Adret. The city of Toledo then elected him as rabbi and he stayed there until his death.

He had been the outstanding disciple of Meir of Rothenburg; but in Spain he learned to appreciate the worth and the achievements of the great Spanish teachers, Isaac Alfasi and Maimonides. In fact, his own legal compendium is constructed almost exactly upon the lines of Alfasi's Code. It follows the sequence of the talmudic tractates; it omits the non-legal portions of the Talmud; it passes over those laws which are no longer applicable outside of Palestine; and he comes to a decision on the outcome of the often-inconclusive talmudic debates. This is exactly what Alfasi did; but Asher, of course, cites primarily his own German teachers.

Believing with all his heart in the correctness of the German mode of study, yet having learned to appreciate the great Spanish codifiers, he was enabled by his two loyalties to achieve a unique place in the history of Jewish legal tradition. He was the prime source for the transmission of Franco-German talmudic studies in Spain, and thus was the bond between Franco-Germany and Spain—between the Ashkenazim and the Sephardim.

Up to his time the two great sections of West-European Jewry were being drawn further and further apart by their different intellectual interests. The Spaniards were deeply interested in philosophy and general science. The Germans scorned these secular studies and concentrated on the Talmud. Because the Spaniards needed to find time in their lives for both secular-scientific studies and Jewish-legal studies, they tended to condense and simplify the talmudic studies so that their practical decisions could be quickly grasped. Therefore, it was the Spaniards who were the great codifiers. They endeavored to reduce the entire mass of talmudic learning into clear codes so that the student could master their practical teachings in comparatively little time. The Franco-Germans were not codifiers. They could hardly have become codifiers. Why would they want to shorten the time needed for talmudic studies when the Talmud and its commentaries were the sole subject of their intellectual interest? Therefore, instead of being epitomizers, they were elaborators. They expanded and developed and amplified the talmudic studies. The great codes, even up to the 16th century, came from the Spaniards, and the profound analysis and constant amplification of the talmudic text came from the Franco-Germans.

If this divergence had continued uninterruptedly, the two great Jewries would have drawn further and further apart. But Asher ben Yehiel fulfilled the historical task of bringing them closer together again. It was he who introduced the *tosafot* (the talmudic commentary notes) of the Franco-Germans as a subject of study in Spain and thus increased there the elaborate study of the Talmud for its own sake. On the other hand, it was largely through his influence that the codes of Alfasi and of Maimonides became popular among the Ashkenazim. Soon they were studied among them and they were elaborated upon as if they were the talmudic text itself.

How he aroused this new interest in detailed talmudic study in Spain is indicated in the responsum which we here cite. He demonstrated that while Maimonides' Code was learned and indeed great, the difficulty with it was that Maimonides did not give the talmudic sources for his decisions. Therefore, unless a scholar had studied the Talmud first and knew the origin of Maimonides' decisions, he could do no other than blindly accept or reject; whereas it was his duty, before deciding, to weigh all the basic opinions. Furthermore, he says in this responsum that besides failing in the duty to know the talmudic basis for decision, the student who does not know the talmudic origins of Maimonides' opinions will often misunderstand Maimonides himself. He won the Spaniards over by giving due honor to their codes, and yet convinced them that they must be skilled talmudists in order to use their own codes properly. Thus he achieved harmony between the two Jewish worlds.

The responsum starts with a discussion about a ritual bath, a *mikvah*. The Spanish teacher, Rabbi Matzliah, who offered the opinion which Asher ben Yehiel now criticizes, had based his decision upon what he understood was a ruling of Maimonides in his Code. Asher proves that Matzliah misunderstood Maimonides simply because he did not know upon which talmudic grounds Maimonides had founded his opinion.

The *mikvah* problem itself is rather complicated. The *mikvah* must consist either of water from a living fountain, or from a river or from the sea. The only water that is unfit for a *mikvah* is drawn water, water in a vessel (*she'uvim*). The water of a fountain is purified if it flows (*zohlin*). The water of a *mikvah* is purified as it settles (*eshborin*). But what happens when water which is drawn (and in itself is unfit for a *mikvah*) flows into a *mikvah* that up to now has been fit? How much of a mixture spoils the *mikvah,* and how much of the mixture can the *mikvah* take in without being spoiled? It was in such a case of the mixture of unfit waters within a *mikvah* of fit waters that Rabbi Matzliah declared the *mikvah* unfit, while Asher said the *mikvah* was fit. Asher explains Matzliah's mistake on the basis of his misunderstanding of the Code of Maimonides. The responsum is no. 31.9 in Rabbenu Asher's collection.

TEXT

Now as to what Rabbi Matzliah wrote, namely, that it happened in his city that they threw drawn water into a well and from there the (mixed) water flowed into the *mikvah* in which there was no water at the time (i.e., the *mikvah* had seeped dry). He declared the *mikvah* unfit. He gave us his reason that, when the rabbis said that the preponderance of drawn water poured into the fountain (does not spoil the fountain), they meant that only if this pouring was not done purposely. But if it *was* done purposely, the fountain (and the *mikvah* which it fills) is unfit. Furthermore (Matzliah argued), Maimonides wrote in chapter IX, in his "Laws of Mikvah," that if a pit is dug alongside a fountain, and the water then comes into the pit from the fountain, then even though the waters may stop and then resume and seep, the mixture is like the fountain itself (and the pit or the *mikvah* which the fountain feeds is kosher). But should they cease their continuous seepage, then it is like a pit (and no longer like a fountain, and therefore unfit). In the case of this *mikvah* (continues Matzliah) certainly the waters ceased their seepage.

Thus far his (Rabbi Matzliah's) words. But he did not come to the right conclusion; for the *mikvah* is quite fit for use. In fact, even if they had poured drawn water directly into the fountain, the fountain would still be fit as a source, for we learn in the Mishna (Mik. I.7) as follows: "A fountain whose waters are scanty and which were amplified with drawn water is suitable, for like a *mikvah* it becomes purified by settling; and the fountain purifies the bather by any amount (of original fountain water)." All the more is this so in the case in question (that the *mikvah* fed by the fountain is kosher). Here the water is drawn into one place, and the rule is that the fountain of any amount of water and a *mikvah* which has forty *seahs* of water are *not* made unfit by the addition of drawn water even if they throw into it a thousand measures.

As for the fact that he (Matzliah) quotes Maimonides, of

blessed memory, he did not understand his words. Maimonides
bases his opinion upon the first chapter of the Tosefta (a work
parallel to the Mishna).

(Asher then explains how Maimonides interpreted this section of the Tosefta and shows that it really had no reference
to the present problem and that it did not mean, therefore,
what Rabbi Matzliah took it to mean. Then he continues:)

Thus do all of those people err who try to base their decision
on the words of Maimonides, of blessed memory, when they are
not themselves sufficiently adept in the Talmud to know whence
he drew his words. They err, and permit the forbidden and forbid the permitted; for he (Maimonides) did not do as other authors do who quote proofs for their words and refer to the sources
of their opinions in the Talmud. When they do this, one can
(review the sources and) arrive at the essence and at the truth.
But he, Maimonides, wrote his book as one prophesies at the
dictation of God, without arguments and without proof. Whoever reads it (the Code of Maimonides) might *imagine* he under-
stands it, but it is really not so. For if he (the student) is not
adept in the Talmud, he does not understand the matter correctly
and may therefore stumble both in the law and decision. Therefore, a man should not rely merely upon what he reads in his
(Maimonides') book in judging and making decisions, as long as
he himself is unable to find the proofs in the Talmud.

In fact, thus I heard from a great man in Barcelona who was
expert in three (out of the six) Orders of the Talmud. He said,
"I am shocked at those people who never studied the Talmud
but read the works of Maimonides, of blessed memory, and yet
teach and judge on the basis of his books and imagine they
understand them. For (this great scholar in Barcelona continued) I can judge by myself that it is only in the three (out of the
six) Orders of the Talmud that I have studied, that I understand what I read in the books of Maimonides. But his books
on the laws of sacrifices and agriculture I do not understand at
all. I know that that is a fact (with regard to these scholars who
did not study the Talmud) with regard to *all* of his books (i.e.,
those who do not study the Talmud and do not know Maimonides' sources do not understand his Code)."

Thus saith the writer,

Asher, the son of Yehiel of blessed memory

Of course, the great Sephardi scholars continued their tendency to make simplified codes of the Law. The last great such Code was the *Shulhan Arukh,* by Joseph Caro, an exile from Spain. Some two and a half centuries after Asher ben Yehiel, in the middle of the 16th century, when Caro's *Shulhan Arukh* appeared, the Ashkenazi scholars of the time raised the same objections to it which were raised to the Code of Maimonides, namely, that the *Shulhan Arukh* does not contain the talmudic sources of the decisions; and that unless the scholar can independently go back to the talmudic sources, he has no right to make a legal decision. Such an opinion, for example, was expressed by Joel Sirkes (1561–1640) in his responsa (n.s., no. 42). The matter came up in a discussion with another scholar with regard to what is the proper curriculum for education. This scholar said that a person should concentrate upon the Bible and its grammar, but need not bother any more to study the Talmud, since all the laws of the Talmud were now available in the *Shulhan Arukh.* To this Joel Sirkes replied as follows: "I answered him in friendly fashion that it is impossible to decide most laws from the *Shulhan Arukh,* for its words are few and without authorities, just like the words of Maimonides, especially in civil law. We know that every day new doubts arise in the question of the laws. With regard to many of these difficulties, the great scholars are divided. It therefore needs special wisdom and knowledge to decide adequately. He who is not skilled in the study of the Talmud cannot make a proper decision."

In spite of these typical objections of the Polish rabbis, the *Shulhan Arukh* did become the standard Code; but not until their objections were largely obviated through the many commentaries giving the sources which gradually were attached to the *Shulhan Arukh* and, especially, when Moses Isserles added to the *Shulhan Arukh* the specifiic customs of the Ashkenazi Jews.

9

✡

DISTRICT AUTHORITY

Solomon ben Adret (Rashbo: born in Barcelona, 1235; died there, 1310), who was the most famous authority in Spain in his time, was renowned as the "Rabbi of Spain" (*El Rab d'España*). He was the pupil of Nahmanides (Moses ben Nahman) and, like his teacher, was compelled to participate in polemics with Christians who, under the leadership of the Dominicans, had begun to press disputative propaganda against the Jews. He wrote many books. His best known legal work, besides notes on various talmudic tractates, was *Torat haBayit* (The Laws of the Home). He wrote this book in two forms, a longer and a briefer one. His chief fame rests on his responsa. It is reported that 6,000 of his responsa were extant. About 2,000 have been printed. The fact that there was such a large number of responsa indicates the vast influence he exerted. He was called upon to answer legal questions, not only from Spain and Portugal, but also France and Germany, Italy and Asia Minor. That so many of his responsa survive reflects the constant reference that was made to them through the ages.

The responsum cited here deals with one of the crucial questions of the Middle Ages, namely that of communal authority. It is interesting to compare this Spanish responsum with one on the same theme cited above (page 43ff.) by the German scholar, Meir of Rothenburg. While it might be hazardous to generalize

on the matter, it is at least noticeable in the comparison of the
two responsa that the German authority was much more sensitive
to the danger of the authorities usurping the rights of the individual, whereas the Spanish authority seems more concerned
with protecting law and authority. This responsum really constitutes a description (based, of course, on talmudic precedents)
of the entire scope of communal authority in Jewish life. For a
full discussion of the organization and the changes in the stability
of the Spanish authorities, see Abraham Neuman, *The Jews in
Spain* (The Jewish Publication Society, 1942).

This responsum of Solomon ben Adret is from vol. III, no.
411. It is in reply to a question from Montpellier, in the Provence. Just as in the responsum of Rabbi Meir of Rothenburg,
the problem involves the right of the community to levy taxes and
imposts. Also, the direct question from Montpellier deals specifically with the relationship between a larger community and the
small Jewish settlements in its neighborhood: Can the larger
community impose assessments for taxes on these neighboring
communities without their consent? But beginning with these
specific problems, Rabbi Solomon ben Adret goes on to a description of the full right of the community to exert authority in many
fields. The question from Montpellier is quoted in full, and it is
not quite clear where the answer begins.

TEXT

Question:

Your question is: What is the custom of our place (i.e., Barcelona) in the matter of taxes and imposts? Do we include the
small towns that are around us under our decisions and bans
(for non-payment) without summoning them? Or is it our
custom that every separate place (in our district) issue its own
bans (or decisions)? Or do the rich men of these various places
come into our city in order to express their agreement with us
(i.e., to participate in the decisions and in the vote on them)?
Furthermore, you ask me to answer, on the basis of logic and

proof. You begin describing your custom and you conclude
with law, as follows:

As far as custom is concerned, we and the congregation
Villefranche and the congregation Tarragona and Mont Blanc
have one treasury and one purse in fines, in taxes, and in imposts, and in whatever is imposed on us by the government; and
whatever new decisions they (the community) desire to make
in sending memoranda or acknowledgments demanded of us
from our lord, the king. We never decree anything upon them,
even though we are the majority and the province (the provincial
council) is the head of all matters; for if we acted without their
counsel, they would not listen to us. At times we send men to
them. Sometimes delegates come from them to us, bringing their
local consent. If they do not hearken to us to do any of these
things (agreed upon), we force them by governmental power to
come to us or to agree to repeat our bans in their place. Now
there are other places among us in which the chief community
passes decrees with regard to the sister-towns and controls them
against their will. In all these matters the various localities dif-
fer according to their custom.

(The actual answer seems to begin here.)

Answer:

Thus we do always and this custom is widespread among us,
and all the more with regard to (civil) matters. For what right
or authority has one congregation over another, or even over an
individual, in matters of money or customs and agreements, except in certain well-known cases, such as, for example, if the
great court (in Jerusalem) agrees to a certain custom or prohibits something, and if the decree is one which the community
can endure (this is based upon the talmudic dictum, in Baba
Batra 60b, that we may not issue any decree against a community which the community cannot endure) such as decrees
about bread, wine, cooked and boiled food, etc., and other decrees of the court or of the king. Such was the decree of King
Saul, whereby Jonathan incurred the death penalty, even though
he, Jonathan, did not know and did not hear the decree. Jona-

than was guilty even though he was not present when the decree was made, because whatever the king decrees with the concurrence of Israel is validly decided and applicable to all. Furthermore, it is written (that Ezra decreed [Ezra 10.8]): *Whoever shall not come in three days, all his property will be confiscated.* It was so also with the decrees of the Nasi and of the Exilarch. It was so also where the Nasi gave permission to judge and whoever got permission from (the Nasi and) the Exilarch (Sanh. 5a) did not have to make good from his own purse the loss that he caused by misjudging a civil case. Judges lacking the special appointment from the Nasi of the Exilarch had to make good such mistakes. This was so because he (the Exilarch) was the ruler over them. Another source of authority is the following: If the majority of the congregation issues decrees or makes agreements as to the needs of the community even against the will of the individual, what they have done is done, provided of course it is the majority which did it and it is an "endurable decree," as is found in the Talmud, Baba Kamma 78b. For in every congregation the individuals are under the authority of the majority and they must conduct themselves in all their affairs according to their (the majority's) order; and they (the majority) stand in relation to the people of their city, as *all* Israel stands in relation to the High Court (Sanhedrin) or to the king. (This applies) whether they were of the assembly (which made the decision) or not. Even the children who will be born to them, generation after generation, must conduct themselves as was solemnly agreed upon by their fathers with regard to those matters which they (the fathers) decreed upon themselves and their seed. For thus was the original acceptance of the Torah (on Mt. Sinai; i.e., the Torah was accepted by the fathers on behalf of their descendants). So too was the later tradition, such as the Megillah and Hanukkah. In fact, even if the fathers, without formal decision, had a fixed custom to make certain vows, the sons have to follow that custom after them, as the Palestinian Talmud (Pes. 4.1) says: "Change not the customs of your deceased fathers."

(Then Ibn Adret continues with further examples from the talmudic literature, indicating the right of the community authorities to execute decrees and the duty of the people to follow them, especially when they are traditional decrees. He concludes with the statement:)

However, in other matters (than all those enumerated above), insofar as men of one city might desire to impose decrees upon men of another city, I do not see that they have permission to do so without their knowledge (of the other cities), nor to ban them, nor to compel them to pay taxes, since they are not under their authority in this matter, unless, of course, (they confine themselves to ritual matters and) make decrees and exert authority to keep people from forbidden things. That is indeed permitted (for one city to do for its entire neighborhood) and is proper and obligatory, to prevent people from doing forbidden things.

As for your question: If the assembly made a decree in general and there were some men there who were silent, is their silence tantamount to acceptance (of the decree of the majority) or not? This seems simple to me. When (the assembly issues a decree), there are (always) some who stand silent. Even if it were a minority of the congregation, all who are present there are in duty bound to conduct themselves in accordance with the decree; that is to say, all who did not object and whoever did not exclude himself from their company. I do not see that there is any difference in this rule (that silence in the assembly involves acceptance), whether it be with regard to the fulfilment of a commandment or a "free-will" matter (i.e., a matter not commanded by the Torah). Of course, if the decision is against any commandment of the Torah, he who does not wish to accept it is liable to no punishment. On the contrary, those who made the decision have done wrong and owe repentance, for one may take no oath to annul any of the commandments, and if one does, one incurs the penalties for false oath, etc.

10

✡

GOVERNMENT OPPOSITION
TO THE BAN

Israel Isserlein (born in Ratisbon, *ca.* 1395; died in Neustadt, 1460) was the foremost German authority in the first half of the 15th century. He lived most of his active life in Neustadt near Vienna. His great achievement was the revival of the study of the Talmud in Germany, where it had grown weak during the preceding centuries. He was the author of many responsa which are collected in two books, the first called *Terumat haDeshen* (Heave Offering of Ashes), which was edited during his lifetime, and the second *Pesakim uKetavim* (Decisions and Letters).

More than a century later, when Moses Isserles, the great Polish authority, wrote his notes to Joseph Caro's *Shulhan Arukh,* adding the German and Polish customs which Joseph Caro had omitted and thus making Caro's Code usable by the Ashkenazi Jews, his chief source for Ashkenazi observance was Israel Isserlein, whom he quotes constantly. The famous contemporary of Moses Isserles, Solomon Luria, also revered Israel Isserlein. In Luria's *Sea of Solomon* (Git., ch. 4, parag. 24), where he discusses various opinions on the use of by-names along with the chief name in a certificate of divorce, he defers to Isserlein's opinion and says of him: "Do not deviate from his opinion, for he was great and eminent in his generation."

The responsum cited here deals with excommunication, or the ban, which was the prime instrument available to the medieval Jewish communities for maintaining communal discipline. There were various degrees of the ban, depending upon the seriousness of the crime. Usually the ban involved isolating the culprit from business and social dealings with the members of the community. It was imposed for a great variety of offenses, e.g., refusing to obey a summons to appear at a Jewish court, insulting a prominent person, bringing a case before a Gentile court instead of the Jewish court. For a listing of the various offenses for which the ban was imposed, see the *Jewish Encyclopedia*, vol. V, page 286.

Occasionally the secular government interfered with the Jewish community's use of this instrument of discipline. Influential Jewish men sometimes would urge the government to prohibit its use, primarily against themselves. Israel Isserlein mentions precisely such a case. The government prohibited the use of the ban in the case of a certain man who had brought a dispute before the Gentile courts. The question asked of Isserlein was this: Is the imposition of the ban the sort of a religious act for which we must defy all governments and risk our lives; or should we yield to the government's prohibition? This responsum is no. 276 in *Terumat haDeshen*. In the Warsaw edition (1882), it is omitted from the main text and is published separately at the end of the book.

TEXT

Question:

A scholar banned a certain person who had haled his fellow before the Gentile courts because he did not wish to litigate with him by Jewish Law. He did this because he relied upon his personal influence with the Gentile courts, being certain that he would win if the case came before them. Now when the sage put him under ban because of this act, he, the litigant, influenced the government to decree, under heavy penalty, that whoever maintained the ban against this person (i.e., whoever refused to speak to him or do business with him) should be severely punished. (The question is:) Is the community in duty bound to risk the danger of punishment from the government by maintaining the ban, or are they not in duty bound (to risk danger to maintain the ban)?

Answer:

It appears that we are not in duty bound to risk the danger of punishment by the government under these circumstances. In fact, I saw such an incident in my youth, when even the disciples (of the teacher who imposed the ban) did not adhere to the ban which their own teacher had imposed. The teacher was in another kingdom; but the ruler of the kingdom in which the disciples lived gave orders and decreed, under threat of corporal and monetary punishment against all who maintained the ban. At that time, one of the great scholars brought proof (that the ban need not be maintained) from that statement of Asher ben Yehiel (to Moed Katan, ch. 3, parag. 8) that if a man is under a general ban, we may not eat with him or drink with him or sit within four cubits of him; but that this does not apply to his sons and the members of his household and his wife, who are permitted (to live with him in normal fashion). So said Asher ben Yehiel.

(Now follows the commentary on Asher ben Yehiel's words, quoted by Isserlein from his youthful memories.)

Here, then, we have before us the rule that the members of his household, since they have need of him and could not obtain their livelihood from anyone else, are permitted to ignore the ban. Therefore, it is clear that we are not in duty bound to harm our own livelihood because of this ban and, indeed, the (Jewish) court, when it decrees the ban, implies this precondition.

(Literally, the "heart of the court" makes this condition. Though the court does not say so, it has in "its heart," i.e., its intention, that if the ban harms the community, then the community need not maintain it.)

All the more (Isserlein continues) when we have here a definite decree of the ruler involving fines and punishments; for this is like *an antelope caught in a snare* (phrase from Isa. 51.20), for in this case we well may fear that he (namely, the sage who proclaimed the ban) would be fined so heavily that he would be in want for the rest of his life.

However, it is clear (that we may abandon the ban) only under these circumstances: when the man was put under ban because of a *financial* dispute, or because of similar matters with regard to which the government thinks it has authority to judge and to decree as it wishes, and when the matter with which he is acting so arrogantly with his neighbor does not, after all, involve violating our religion and the Torah. But if they have put him under ban because he has transgressed, or he has committed sins in public, in matters that are between him and God, blessed be He (i.e., religious matters, not civil matters which are between man and man), under those circumstances we are in duty bound to risk the probability of punishment in order to strengthen our religion and our Torah and in order to sanctify God's Name. Thus we find in the Talmud (Ber. 20a) that Rav Ada, the son of Ahava, saw a man clad in mixed garments (forbidden by law). Thinking he was a Jew, he tore the garments from him in the street. It is considered there (in the Talmud) that he risked his life for the sanctification of the Name, for he certainly had reason to fear the man who wore the garments. But he did not care and risked his life. Thus it is necessary to consider the nature of the matter involved.

What appears to my humble thoughts, that have I written.

11

✡

LEGAL PRIVILEGES OF
A SCHOLAR

Jacob Weil (died in 1456) was the chief pupil of Jacob Moellin
(Maharil). His chief rabbinate was in Erfurt and he was one of
the leading authorities of his day. All that remains of his literary
activity is his volume of responsa and, appended to it, a small
compendium of the laws of *shehita*. This compendium, according
to Jacob Z. Lauterbach (see *Jewish Encyclopedia,* XII, 492) has
been reprinted seventy-one times.

The responsum cited here concerns the special status of scholars in the medieval Jewish community. Scholars enjoyed special
privileges from talmudic times. Yet, just as the power of wealthy
citizens in the community was carefully watched lest it lead to
tyranny, so it became necessary to guard against those scholars
who unworthily took advantage of their legal privileges and tyr-
annized over the community.

Among the ancient privileges of scholars were, first of all, the
right to judge a case as a single judge; secondly, to fine anyone
who insulted them, "a golden pound," or to put under ban anyone
who insulted them; to be free of community taxation; to claim a
lost article merely by declaration that it is theirs (without needing, like others, to prove their ownership by some recognizable
sign), and such other privileges. Some scholars in the city of

Nuremberg had abused the privilege of their special status. Jacob Weil denounces them and declares: that the special status of a scholar no longer exists in our day; that the talmudic term, "the scholar," the *talmid-hakham*, is no longer applicable today as a special status.

The present status of the law with regard to the privileges of a scholar can be noted in the *Shulhan Arukh*, "Yoreh Deah," no. 243. In 243.2, especially in the note of Isserles, it is indicated that a scholar no longer has the right to fine anybody a gold pound if he is insulted. He may still put someone under ban, but *should not* do so. (See also *Pit-hei Teshuba, ad loc.*, where sources are given for the rule that he should no longer be the sole judge in any litigation.) Most of these limitations on the ancient legal privileges of the *talmid-hakham* stem from this responsum of Jacob Weil which is, therefore, a "leading case" in the law.

The responsum is no. 166. It is addressed to the leading laymen of the Jewish community of Nuremberg. It opens with flowery language, but soon becomes stern in its denunciation of those who abuse their scholarly status.

TEXT

Men of truth, seeking peace, who hold fast to the Law of God and are eager to fulfill His commandment; lovers of righteous judgment, who despise violence and falsehood, may your peace increase forever, O congregation of Nuremberg and its suburbs.

I, the humble one, who is signed at the end of this parchment, let you know for your good that *the hair of my head stood up and my flesh trembled* (phrase from Job 4.15) at the despoiling and violence and profanation of the Name that is now going on in your province, and the sinfulness that goeth forth from the hands of those (whose task it is to) maintain the Torah, namely, some of the rabbis who have attained that title. They consider themselves scholars and have taken it into their heads that the (old) law of the *talmid-hakham* applies to them; that they may, for example, judge cases alone, and that they do not ever need to enter into a case (as the defendant) against ordinary householders who protest against them. They desire to fine such people a "golden pound" and they work in devious ways to find excuses and libels against those who have money and thus snare them in their nets, to flay their skin from their flesh. Thus the Name of Heaven is profaned, for the people say (scornfully): "This is the Torah and this is its reward" (Ber. 61b).

And I am zealous for the honor of the Torah and its teachers. I desire to re-establish our world on justice and truth and peace. I *empty out my apron* (phrase from Neh. 5.13, meaning: here I will be completely frank, I will not hold any argument in reserve) to annul and to make void their thoughts that they may not carry out their intentions. For if this is not done, you will not leave a chance for a livelihood for all who have any money. So I will say my part as I have received it from my teachers and have understood it from books and have heard it from the strong-hearted who are near to righteousness. So make your ears like a grain funnel (a phrase from Hul. 89a) to hear my words and that it may be well with you and *sweet in your mouth like honey* (phrase from Ezek. 3.3). May God, blessed be He, grant me strength that I may do valiantly. May He convert my thought to action. He who knows my thoughts knows that I am not "acting for mine own honor or the honor of my fathers" (phrase from Meg. 3a), but my intention is to remove the stumbling block, that the people may not stumble and the Name of Heaven be profaned.

I have received it from my teacher, Maharil (Jacob Moellin) of blessed memory, that in these days we no longer may impose a fine of a gold pound upon anyone who insults a scholar. He brought his proof from the *Agudah* (a compendium of laws by Alexander Cohen Suesslein of Frankfort) who writes: "With regard to the statement in the first chapter of Hullin (18a) that any slaughterer (*shohet*) who does not show his knife to a scholar to be examined should be put under the ban," the author of the *Agudah* says that the gaonim have recorded their opinion that scholars should not be too touchy about this but should forgive it. Furthermore (Alexander Suesslein continues) it seems to me that, for our sins, we do not have scholars who know even the tractate Kalla. (The Talmud [Shab. 114a] gives as one definition of a scholar: If you ask him a question anywhere in the Law, he will answer—even in tractate Kalla.)

The author of *Sefer Agudah* lived before the recent persecutions and he was a great scholar; nevertheless he wrote that in his time the official status of *talmid-hakham* was no longer granted. How much the more does it apply in these days when, for our many sins, the minds (literally, the hearts) have shrunk, and many "rabbis" do not even know the shape of the Law, and have not in their hands either bread or garment, and their house is empty of all good (metaphorical for "lacking all knowledge"). Yet some of them are proud enough to act in lordly fashion and to misuse the crown of the rabbinate. Their whole intention is for their own glory: that they may sit at the head and walk at the head, and there are even some whose intention it is to amass money. They do not have the moral qualities which the rabbis enumerate that a scholar should have. Their whole purpose is to benefit themselves. Some of them are not even careful in their actions. Their reputation is bad (phrase from Meg. 25b) and through them the Name of Heaven is profaned.

So it is obvious that the law of (the status of) the *talmid-hakham* does not apply to them, neither as to judging cases alone, nor as to imposing the gold pound on one who insults them.

For this reason we no longer call *any* scholar today (legally) a *talmid-hakham*. "Because of the nettles the cabbage suffers" (A phrase from B. K. 92a, which here means: because of these unworthy men, the status of all members of the rabbinate is now lowered.)

Thus did Mahari Katz of Nuremberg (Yehiel haKohen) decide, and thus do I decide. It is law to be carried out (*halakhah l'ma'aseh*). Furthermore, the abovementioned rabbi brings proof (for this decision no longer to consider the present-day rabbi as officially a *talmid-hakham*). It is said in Baba Metzia 67b: "A scholar should not eat 'diminution' " (that is to say, when a field is given in pledge, it is possible for the lender who holds the pledge to eat the fruit of the land and thus gradually diminish the amount of the debt). The *tosafot* add (it is Rabbenu Tam who is quoted as making the statement) that although Rabina did eat "diminution," it was because in his humility he did not count himself as a *talmid-hakham*.

Clearly, then, if Rabina did not consider himself a *talmid-hakham*, how much less may we do so, orphan children of orphan parents? We surely should not consider ourselves as *talmidei-hakhamim*. I can bring a further proof from our teacher Menahem of Merzeburg, of blessed memory, who wrote so in his notes (and these are his words): "My teachers have written that the statement in Maimonides ("Laws of Injury," ch. III), that whoever insults a *talmid-hakham* must pay a gold pound, applies only to a scholar who is widely known and is renowned. This derives from the statement in the Yerushalmi (see also Moed Katan 16a) that Resh Lakish imposed a fine on someone who insulted Rabbi Yosé bar Hanina because the latter was widely known as a scholar."

(Jacob Weil then continues with other proofs that the special status of the *talmid-hakham* does not apply, and he concludes:)

So we can no longer apply the talmudic laws as to the *talmid-hakham* for the reasons that are clear to us. Nowadays, therefore, no rabbi has the right to judge a case alone. If, then, any rabbi exalts himself to proceed against any man with libelous words in your city or in your neighborhood, and desires to be a law unto himself, do not consent and do not listen to him, and do not fear and let not your heart soften before him. Think of the *eternal paths* (phrase from Jer. 6.16) and stand firm in opposition, so that this matter shall no longer be to you as a stumbling block. I will then have done my duty; and, if you do yours, you will justify the righteous and be wise in your actions.

Sayeth the humble one,

Jacob Weil

12

✡

AN INTERNATIONAL
RABBINICAL CONTROVERSY

Joseph ben Solomon Colon (born in Savoy, 1420; died in Padua, 1480) was, in his early years an itinerant teacher in Italy. This was due, possibly, to the expulsion of the Jews of Savoy. He was influenced by a pupil of Israel Isserlein of Germany (see above, p. 57) whom he met in Italy; and he thus acquired great admiration for the new German mode of study. He became rabbi in Pavia and rose to be the premier rabbinical authority in Italy. Questions were directed to him from Germany and from Constantinople. His book of responsa has been published a number of times and has had great influence in the development of rabbinic law. It is constantly quoted. (See article by Louis Ginzberg, *Jewish Encyclopedia,* IV, 170.)

He was a man with a stern sense of justice and held firm convictions. His forthrightness of opinion led him into a bitter controversy with Moses Capsali, the chief rabbi of the Turkish empire. This international dispute between the chief rabbi of Italy and the chief rabbi of the Ottoman empire engaged the attention and participation of many scholars and is of considerable historical interest. In fact, it created so much tension that, in the fanciful account quoted from earlier sources in the "History of Famous Rabbis" (*Toledot Gedolei Yisrael,* by Nepi and Girondi, pages

265 and 266), an older description of the controversy is given in which it is made to appear as an actual struggle between the secular rulers of the two states involved. The Sultan Mohammed of the Ottoman empire is described as actually demanding of the king of the Germans to send Rabbi Joseph Colon to him in chains to answer for his conduct.

From the standpoint of the development of Jewish legal litera-ture, the controversy is of especial interest. First, as to the subject-matter involved: Moses Capsali was accused of having been over-lenient in declaring a certain marriage void and allowing the woman to marry another man without getting a bill of divorce from the first man. There were also a number of analogous cases under dispute in which Capsali was said to have annulled a previous marriage bond and freed a woman for remarriage.

In matters which involve the sanctity of the family, disagree-ment could become especially bitter, particularly when as forth-right a person as Joseph Colon was appealed to for his judgment. He was not only willing to declare Capsali's judgment incorrect, but was outspoken enough to denounce him even though he was the chief rabbi of the Ottoman empire. He declared Capsali's ordination to be worthless; he put him under a ban and called him to repentance. Yet, pathetically enough, all the charges brought before Colon against Capsali were untrue. Capsali never made such lenient decisions as he was accused of making, and certainly did not merit the bitterness of the attack which Joseph Colon, in all honesty, directed against him. Colon simply did not know the facts of the cases involved; nor did he know the char-acter and the deserved status of Moses Capsali. Capsali was a revered teacher, the head of the entire Jewish community in the Turkish empire. He was highly respected by the Sultan, Moham-med II, and given a place in his Council chamber (the *Divan*) next to the Mohammedan Mufti.

What happened was simply that a party was organized against Capsali in the Jewish community. Among the leaders in the party of his opponents were Elijah Parnas, Samuel Alterni, and Asher of Cologne. This party was strengthened by a disappointed messenger who came to collect money from the Jews of Turkey for the poor of Jerusalem. For political reasons, Moses Capsali did not permit the collection to be made. Palestine was under the control of the enemy of the Sultan, the Egyptian government. But this collector, in his disappointment, joined the party of Capsali's opponents, and they brought these untrue charges against him before Joseph Colon, the great rabbi of Italy.

The responsa covering the controversy are numbers 83, 84, and 85 in the collection of Colon's responsa. We cite first a part of no. 84 that describes the first of the group of controversies, and then part of no. 83 which describes the ban that Colon issued against the chief rabbi of the Ottoman empire.

TEXT

Responsum No. 84

The sound of uproar from the city (of Constantinople) comes to my ear. I hear the bleating of the flocks, *the voice of them that cry for being overcome* (phrase from Ex. 32.18), *the sound of war in the camp* of the Hebrews.

(Here follow a series of allusive phrases based on Bible and Talmud, referring to the supposed self-aggrandizement of Moses Capsali. Colon continues:)

This man, Moses Capsali, caused *many corpses to fall* (phrase from Prov. 7.26) in the city of Constantinople, the gate of the mighty, who resolved in his heart to teach and there is no spirit within him. He is known amidst the fools. He creates corpses and illegitimacy. Therefore, I, the humble one, the young one, *have emptied my apron* (from Neh. 5.13, meaning I speak freely) and responded to those who asked me because of the neglect of the Torah. Now I come to utter my humble opinion:

Now, as I am guided from Heaven and by writers and by books, I begin to remove the stumbling block from the road, to cleanse the sacred vessels from his defilements. First, with regard to Rebecca the daughter of Enoch, who was married to Rabbi Samuel the son of Shapsi in the presence of witnesses—this is the language (of the testimony): Rabbi Samuel gave to the above-mentioned Rebecca one fig as the symbolic gift of marriage. She received it in silence and ate it.

> (The law requires that the contract of marriage be formalized by the gift of an object worth no less than a *peruta,* a penny. The Mishna in Kiddushin II.1, and the Talmud, *idem* 46a, discuss the case of a man saying to a woman, "Be thou consecrated to me by the gift of this date." She takes it and eats it. Is this valid marriage? The answer is that, if the date or number of dates which she accepts is worth a penny, a *peruta,* the marriage is valid.)

Now she (Rebecca) came before the teacher (i.e., Capsali) and she cried out; and he permitted her to be freed from this marriage without requiring a bill of divorcement. This he did for worthless reasons. He said that he had already proclaimed under the penalty of the ban that no one should marry anyone without the gift of less than ten (figs); and once he had said that the daughters of Israel are not to be married by the gift of a mere dried fig.

He, Capsali, erred in many matters which are obvious even to young children in school, as I will now begin to explain, with the help of God. We should pay no attention to his decree, nor annul a marriage because of it. His decree is no more effective than a net pulled through the sea (a pun on the word *herem,* which means "a ban," and also "a net.") Even if his *herem* (his decree) were valid, which is *not* the fact, yet surely it is not more valid than the *herem* of Rabbenu Gershom, "the Light of the Exile." Concerning Gershom's decree, Rabbi Meir (of Rothenburg) wrote that even it cannot nullify a marriage. This the *Mordecai* (a pupil of Rabbi Meir of Rothenburg) wrote in his (Meir's) name in the tractate Kiddushin.

> (Rabbi Meir of Rothenburg is quoted by Rabbi Mordecai ben Hillel, in the case of a messenger, an agent, sent by a man to espouse a certain woman for him. The agent, instead of saying to the woman, "Behold, thou art espoused to Reuben," made a mistake and said to the woman, "Behold, thou art espoused to me." Now, the messenger was already

married, and for him to marry a second woman would be a violation of the *herem* of Rabbenu Gershom against polygamy. Therefore we might expect that this marriage would be automatically void. Nevertheless, Rabbi Meir said that, in spite of the authority of Rabbenu Gershom, this marriage, though entered into by mistake, is valid enough that it must be formally voided by a *get*.)

Mordecai quotes this decision by Rabbi Meir who concludes as follows: "We do not say that, since the messenger, Shimon, being already married, violates the great *herem* of Rabbenu Gershom, 'the Light of the Exile,' therefore the marriage is voided (since all marriages are understood to be under rabbinic law and can be voided). For, consider that (we cannot void this marriage in spite of the violation of the ban against polygamy) there are many violations of negative commandments and of second degrees of consanguinity, as well as sins mentioned in the Torah which are involved in certain marriages, and yet the rabbis say that such marriages hold (and the woman cannot be freed without a *get*)."

(So Colon, quoting the above case of the agent, argues that, if in the case of so great a man as Rabbenu Gershom a marriage can be valid in spite of his decree, what worth has a decree by Moses Capsali which requires a certain minimum amount to be given to the woman for the marriage to be valid?

Colon then proceeds to give other arguments to prove the invalidity of Capsali's voiding of the marriage.

In responsum no. 83, he speaks with astonishing harshness against Moses Capsali. He begins as follows:)

Responsum No. 83

I am zealous for the Lord of Hosts against this man, Moses Capsali, who has caused the multitude to sin and who profanes the Name of Heaven. I base my judgment upon what was written and sealed with regard to him by the honored men of the great community of Constantinople (may God protect them), namely, Elijah Parnas, the aged Aaron the son of Abbaye, Isaac the son of Samuel Alterni, Asher the son of Isaac Cohen the German, and Asher of Cologne. They confirmed their signatures by words of mouth, as I have heard and seen. Therefore, I decree against him, by the power of the strict *herem* (the ban), that he shall not add iniquity to his sin by pursuing his mistakes, but shall return from his evil way and forbid what he had permitted with regard to the woman who was married with the fig, etc.

(Colon then concludes by urging the community to depose Moses Capsali and to appoint someone else in his place. These are his final words:)

I decree, by the force of this ban, upon all who see my writing or know of it, that they shall no longer call this Moses Capsali "Rabbi," nor *Haver* (comrade, equivalent to our academic use of the word "Fellow"). He does not deserve the title at all. Therefore, take away his turban and remove the diadem from his head, for he shall no longer be called Rabbi or Sage.

In later years, Joseph Colon learned that the charges that were brought to him were libelous. He then repented of what he had said and done against the great Turkish rabbi. When he was on his deathbed, he sent his son Perez to Constantinople to ask pardon of Moses Capsali. Capsali received Perez favorably and assured him that he respected his father, that his father was simply misinformed as to the facts, and that it was his (Colon's) great zeal for the Torah which had led him to react so violently.

13

✡

ARISTOTLE OR THE TALMUD

Isaac bar Sheshet ([Perfet] born in Valencia, Spain, 1326; died in Algiers, 1408) held the high authority in rabbinic law which less than a century earlier had been the place of Solomon ben Adret of Barcelona. Many responsa were addressed to him even before he was a rabbi, for he was a businessman until the age of fifty. At that time, he and other Jewish notables were imprisoned on some false charge. After he came out of prison, it may well have been that his business was in ruins and that, therefore, he decided to serve as rabbi. For a time he served in Saragossa. Then, after some communal dispute, he left Saragossa and completed his Spanish career in the city of Valencia. His rabbinical career continued after his exile from Spain. This was the period when Fernando Martinez provoked anti-Jewish riots in many of the Spanish cities and actually started the bloody sequence of persecutions which did not end until the final expulsion, almost a century later, in 1492. Isaac bar Sheshet fled to Algiers, where a number of Spanish exiles had preceded him and many others followed. The king appointed him chief rabbi of Algiers. This official status provoked the hostility of another great scholar, Simon ben Zemah Duran, who had fled to Algiers from the Balearic Islands.

Isaac bar Sheshet's outstanding work is his volume containing 517 responsa. These were highly valued by succeeding scholars.

In fact, Joseph Caro, the great 16th-century codifier, quotes him constantly and cites his own teacher, Jacob Berab, as saying that Isaac bar Sheshet's opinions are to be preferred over all his contemporaries. A thorough study of the responsa of Isaac bar Sheshet was made by Abraham M. Hershman in his work *Rabbi Isaac ben Sheshet Perfet and His Times,* Jewish Theological Seminary, New York, 1943.

The responsum cited here is no. 45. It represents a stage in the history of Jewish thought. A century earlier, in the time of Solomon ben Adret, the great controversy over Maimonides' philosophic teachings and over the study of philosophy in general was at its height. Stirred up chiefly in the Provence, it reached a climax with a ban issued by Solomon ben Adret and his court against anyone studying philosophy before the age of thirty, up to which time, presumably, he would be studying the Talmud and other Jewish literature. The controversy had been so bitter that, at one time, the secular government was persuaded to burn the works of Maimonides.

Of course, neither the book-burning by the government nor the ban by Ibn Adret could halt the study of philosophy and science, especially in Spain; so a century later, the question again was asked, this time of Isaac bar Sheshet, whether it was right to study the works of Aristotle. Bar Sheshet's answer reveals that the controversy had died down; at least it proves that Isaac bar Sheshet himself was of calm and reasonable mind. In fact, he demonstrates in his responsa that he himself was well-acquainted with philosophic problems. In his responsum no. 118, he discusses the difference between the two Jewish philosophers, Levi ben Gershon (Gersonides) and Abraham ben David, as to how to harmonize God's omniscience and therefore His foreknowledge of events with man's freedom of will. He describes both points of view and gives his own solution of the problem. Because of his own appreciation of philosophy, he does not, in his answer to the question asked in responsum no. 45, condemn the study of it, but he calls attention to the danger involved in studying it to the exclusion of talmudic lore. He indicates that even men as great as Maimonides and Levi ben Gershon, who are to be revered and who are great scholars in Jewish Law, nevertheless were in some of their opinions misled by their philosophic study. How much greater then is the danger for average people? Better study the Talmud and Jewish Law; it is the road to true faith and to God and His commandments.

TEXT

You ask what is meant by "the wisdom of the Greeks" from which (according to the Talmud) a man must keep himself far away? Does this refer to those world-famous books (Aristotle's) *Physics* and *Metaphysics?*

> (The questioner refers to the fact that the Talmud, in a number of parallel passages [B. K. 82a, etc.], prohibits the teaching of "Greek wisdom." In the first part of the responsum, Bar Sheshet indicates that this "Greek wisdom" which the Talmud prohibits, does not refer to philosophy, but is a special prohibition of certain secret allusive slang which the Greeks used to conceal thought. He cites Rashi, who has a different though similar interpretation of "Greek wisdom." Rashi says that it refers to a secret method of communicating thoughts by winks and gestures. Having explained the talmudic prohibition of the Greek wisdom in this special way, he proceeds with the main intent of the question.)

The famous (Aristotelian) books on Nature are therefore not meant (to be prohibited). Nevertheless, it is better to avoid them, because they strive to uproot the essentials of our holy Torah, especially the two central pillars upon which the Torah rests, namely, the creation of the world (out of nothing) and God's providence over individual human beings. These books bring what they believe is proof to demonstrate the (uncreated) eternity of the world, and that it (the world) is a necessary (i.e., an automatic, an unwilled) derivative from God, just as light comes automatically from the sun and shade from a tree. Therefore (they say that) God, blessed be He, could not change a single thing of Nature, neither to lengthen the wing of a fly nor shorten the leg of an ant, just as the sun cannot change the light which comes from it, nor the tree its shade. So God's providence cannot apply to anything below the sphere of the moon.

They write further in their books that there is no perfect knowledge (attainable by man) except through investigation; but (it does not come) from tradition. Whereas we, who are the recipients of the truth, believe that our Torah is perfect, that it came to us from God when we stood at Mount Sinai, through (Moses) the chief of the prophets, upon whom be peace. We believe that it is above all other knowledge and that all their "investigations" are as nothing compared to its value.

In chapter 10 of Mishna Sanhedrin, we learn as follows: Among those who have no portion in the world-to-come are those who say that resurrection is not proved in the Torah, those who say that the Torah is not revealed, and the Epicurean. To which Rabbi Akiba adds: also he who reads the external books; and the Talmud says that that means the books of the *minim* (i.e., of the sectarians and the unbelievers). Now can there be (continues Isaac bar Sheshet) books of greater heresy than those that bring proofs to deny the fundamental doctrines of the Torah? Note, too, that Rabbi Akiba did not say those who *believe* in the "external books," but even those who *read* them, lest they (the books) lead his heart away to credit their words. This indeed happened to Elisha (ben Abuya, the famous heretic in the Talmud). They say of him (Hag. 15b) that when he (Elisha) stood up in the house of study, many heretical books dropped from his bosom.

> (Bar Sheshet then cites a responsum sent by the Gaon Hai to Samuel haNagid, the famous 10th-century Spanish statesman and scholar, declaring that it is not proper to study these "external books." Then he also quotes the older opinion of Solomon ben Adret against the study of Greek philosophy. And he continues:)

Now you cannot cite the case of Maimonides (who did study Aristotle) as a proof to the contrary. He (before he began to study Greek philosophy) had learned first of all the entire Torah completely, the laws and the narratives, the Tosefta, the Sifra and

the Sifre, and the whole Talmud, Babylonian and Palestinian, as
can be seen from his book *Mishneh Torah*. Furthermore, in order
to answer the non-believer, he wrote his book, *Guide to the
Perplexed*. His purpose was to refute the arguments and the
proofs adduced by the philosopher (Aristotle) who tried to
prove the eternity of the world and to deny God's providence.
(Maimonides wrote his *Guide*) because in his time there were
many Jews perplexed over the essential doctrines of the Torah,
because of what they had learned from Greek wisdom. We can
say (of Maimonides) as the rabbis said of Rabbi Meir (who was
a friend and disciple of the heretic Elisha ben Abuya): the rabbis
asked (Hag. 15b) how could Rabbi Meir learn Torah from his
(Elisha's) mouth?

> (He then cites the Talmud quotation of the verse in Prov-
> erbs 22.17, *Incline thine ear, and hear* the voice of the wise,
> and shows that the Talmud decided that a great man like
> Rabbi Meir is permitted to have contact with these heresies
> because he is able to select the "fine flour and throw away
> the bran"; as they say in the Talmud, "Rabbi Meir found a
> pomegranate. He ate its pulp and threw away the shell.")

Therefore the teacher Moses son of Maimon, blessed be his
memory, cited this very verse at the beginning of his *Guide:
Incline thine ear*, etc. (i.e., to study these matters critically and
throw away what is not worth keeping).

Nevertheless, this great teacher did not escape entirely from
being drawn after the Greek wisdom in some of the proofs that
he brings.

> (Then Bar Sheshet considers another great rabbinic scholar,
> Levi ben Gershon [Gersonides], who also had great rabbinic
> knowledge and therefore could be trusted to study the Greek
> wisdom selectively. Yet even he was somewhat misled by
> what he studied.)

The sage Rabbi Levi (Gersonides) of blessed memory, even
though he was a great scholar in the Talmud and wrote a beautiful commentary to the Torah and the prophets, and followed in
the footsteps of Moses ben Maimon, even his heart was somewhat
led astray by those wisdoms.

(Bar Sheshet cites some of the rationalistic explanations which Gersonides gives for the sun's standing still for Joshua, and such others. Then Bar Sheshet concludes:)

Now, then, let every man draw an argument *a fortiori* (*kal vahomer*) with regard to himself, since those two monarchs of the mind could not keep their footing in certain matters (because of the influence of their Greek studies), nevertheless their honor is unimpaired. But if the great ones of the world had this happen to them, how can we keep our footing, who never saw the light as they did? In fact, many (because of their studies of Greek philosophy) have broken off the yoke of regular prayer and of the Torah and the commandments, because they studied these wisdoms, as the Gaon Hai wrote (in the responsum to Samuel haNagid referred to above).

14

✡

THE RABBINATE AS A PROFESSION

Simon ben Zemah Duran (born on the island of Majorca, 1361; died in Algiers, 1444) studied in Spain and became expert in all the Jewish disciplines. He was also learned in the scientific subjects of astronomy, mathematics, medicine, and, in fact, earned his living by the practice of medicine. The same persecutions in Spain, in 1391, which drove Isaac bar Sheshet from Valencia to Algiers, also compelled Simon Duran to leave Majorca and likewise to settle in Algiers. He had no opportunity there for the practice of medicine and so he entered the active rabbinate. Isaac bar Sheshet was already the chief rabbi and, although Simon was younger, he associated Simon Duran with him in drawing up a list of regulations for the governance of the community of Algiers. After Isaac bar Sheshet died, Simon Duran succeeded him as chief rabbi of Algiers. He was a prolific author. He wrote commentaries on the Mishna and the Talmud and the Code of Alfasi, and a number of works on philosophy. His great fame rests on his collection of responsa (*Tashbetz*) which was printed a number of times.

The responsum which we cite here had great influence on the development of Jewish religious life. It concerned the development of the rabbinate as a separate professional livelihood.

Hitherto rabbis were scholars who served their communities largely without pay. They earned their living from their own businesses. Many did, indeed, receive fees for certain specific religious functions; but they were not regularly salaried officials of the community. Simon ben Zemah Duran lived at the time when the rabbinate was making its transition to professionalism. This was due to a large extent, as Duran himself explains, to the fact that the increasing persecutions in Spain sent many great scholars into exile. The opportunities for a livelihood in business or in medicine were scant, and at the same time the new half-organized communities of refugees needed the full time of a rabbinical leader. Therefore Simon ben Zemah Duran devotes a large section in his responsa, from no. 142 through no. 148, to dealing with the whole question. He reverts to the discussion in his commentary to the Ethics of the Fathers. He there summarizes his arguments in the responsa when he comments on the statement (IV.5), "One should not make the Torah a spade to dig with." He explains the reason why it was necessary now for a rabbi to take regular pay; and he concludes with a picture of the social conditions in the newly-expanded community of Algiers.

TEXT

(The question which he answers is given at the beginning of responsum no. 145. He phrases the question himself and refers to the fact that, in the past generations, some fees and advantages were always given to rabbis. He then concludes, in effect, that since various fees and honors were always permitted, a regular salary should likewise be permitted.)

Since I have noted that many people grumble at the fact that it was customary in all the congregations of Israel for many generations to give some reward to their sages, and that (these complainers) base their argument on what Maimonides said in his commentary to the Ethics of the Fathers, IV.5 (i.e., not to make the Torah a spade to dig with), therefore I shall set forth my thoughts in this matter, insofar as they will enlighten me from

Heaven, and my researches in the Talmud and other places. I shall discuss whether this matter (to give rewards to the scholars) is merely a permissive one, or a commanded one, or an actual obligation, and whether there is in it the slightest scintilla of sin. I am confident that, with the help of the earlier scholars who permitted themselves (to receive such fees), I shall not stumble in the Law and that the matter of this moot subject will be clarified.

> (In six responsa he then analyzes all the talmudic references that have to do, first, with the rewards and privileges of priests [kohanim]; secondly, of sages and of scholars and of teachers, their right to receive pay for teaching their pupils, their right to be freed from taxes, their right to receive respect and honor. After all this careful analysis, he sums up the matter in his responsum no. 148, which we will now cite:)

Having removed from the sages ancient and recent, of blessed memory, the complaints of the children of Israel, and of the great teacher Maimonides and those who followed him, I shall sum up the matter as it has come into our hands from the scattered places in the Talmud.

The community of Israel is in duty bound to elevate anyone who is most worthy in his generation, as Rab Ami was in his generation; but also the sage can take these privileges on his own initiative, as is proved in the Talmud in Hullin 134b.

> (This first reference deals with the rights of a priest [kohen] to take what duly belongs to him. Rab Ami was not only a great sage, he was also a kohen.)

If he is a sage, of whom they can ask questions from the *entire* Talmud, and he can answer, it is proper to appoint him chief of all Israel and the head of the yeshiva, and all Israel must exalt him.

If they ask a man the law in a specific tractate (not in the whole Talmud) and he can answer, he may be appointed chief in his own city, and he must be treated with respect. If he is not even at that level, but he engages in studies and neglects his own business affairs, the people of his city are in duty bound to help him gain his livelihood, as is shown in the Talmud (Shab. 114a). If there is already a rabbinical head in the city who merits all this honor but he happens to be rich in his own right, but there is in the city another sage who needs to be elevated (to the position of the rabbinate), he must in modesty and goodness say that that other (the poverty-stricken sage) should be the one who should teach in the yeshiva until he is elevated, as is proved from the Talmud (Sota 40a).

(Duran then proceeds to speak of the other privileges of the rabbis: to be free from taxes, and the like. Then, after completing an enumeration of the duties of the community to the scholars, he continues with the duties which the individual members of the community owe him.)

Thus it is a duty incumbent upon every individual to benefit the scholar from his possessions; and if such persons help him and create business for him, there is no greater virtue than this and they merit a place in the heavenly academy. This is the duty of the individual. Of course, if the sages refrain from accepting such benefits, except what they receive from their pupils, their action is right and proper, as is proved in the Talmud (Ket. 96a). Also, if a donor desires to be honored by contact with the sage (see Hul. 7b) or (helps the scholar) in order that the sage can engage in Torah and not have to neglect it because of his livelihood (he should do so), as Simon the brother of Azariah and Rabbi Yohanan did, who were supported by the Nasi (the patriarch) in order that they might engage in the study of the Torah. Thus Issakhar did with Zebulon his brother (i.e., Zebulon did business so that Issakhar might have time to study the Torah, Ber. Rabbah 99.9); and Zebulon merited to be blessed along with Issakhar; not only that, but Zebulon is mentioned first in Scriptures, for it is said (Deut. 33.18): *Rejoice, O Zebulon, in thy going forth, and Issakhar, in thy tents.*

This is what occurs to me on this subject. May He who has given me the merit to defend the earlier scholars, of blessed memory (for accepting the fees and privileges), give me the merit of those who are worthy of the crown of the Torah and the crown of a good name as they (the earlier scholars) were. Thus writeth

Simon, the son of Zemah of blessed memory

(In his commentary to the Ethics of the Fathers, IV.5, he refers to the long treatise which he wrote on the subject, i.e., the one which we have just summarized. He reviews the same arguments, and ends with a biographical note in which he says that he is justified in accepting the position of rabbi and taking a salary. Although justified, he feels the need to explain that he was forced to do this by the necessity of his exile which prevented him from practicing medicine. His words are:)

For all these reasons we resolved to make a practical decision with regard to ourselves (i.e., myself) to take a salary from the congregation and to be appointed as rabbi and judge over them. We did not permit ourselves to do this before we had debated this matter, as we wrote in our long treatise, and before the great scholars of our generation saw it and said it was correct. Thus we have seen that this permission (to take rewards) was customary with the great scholars before us, the highest men and men of action, scholars and rabbis who are far greater than we.

(Then he explains that, of course, he holds to the talmudic principle that a man must not study in *order* to obtain honor or reward. He must study for the love of it.)

But let it be known that the aim of our studies with the sages (his teachers) was not for this purpose, namely, to sit at the head (of the community). Because we owned property and we had learned the art of medicine. Medicine is a wisdom which honorably supports its practitioners in the Christian lands. But for the sins of this generation, persecution was decreed in all those lands, and we were left with only our lives. We abandoned all our possessions there, and whatever we could save we gave to the idolators in order that we might survive (literally, *that our taste remain in us*, a phrase based upon Jer. 48.11) and not come to harm. It is enough for us to have this door of permission (the talmudic arguments cited above) which we have used in order

that Torah shall be our work and we will *not cease from it day
and night.*

If the profession of medicine could have supplied us a livelihood, in this land in which we have settled (i.e., Algiers), we
would not have come to this state. But it is of low status here;
and we do not wish to return to the Christian land because of the
confusion in those places where every day new persecutions are
decreed; and, as the Midrash says: "Whoever was once bitten by
a snake, is frightened by a rope."

15

✡

KADDISH FOR THE MARTYRS

Jacob ben Moses Moellin (Maharil: born in Mainz, 1365; died in 1427) was the teacher of Jacob Weil (compare responsum no. 11, above), who became the leading authority in his generation. Maharil lived at the time when the Hussite wars created great disturbance in central Europe and disrupted many Jewish communities. His great achievement was his preservation of the *minhagim,* the inherited customs of the various communities, thus maintaining the continuity in the towns whose communities were alternately broken and re-established. He is one of the chief sources of all the Rhineland and central European traditional customs (*minhagim*) which Moses Isserles, a century and a half later, appended to Joseph Caro's *Shulhan Arukh.* Isserles, in his notes to "Orah Hayyim" 619.1, cites Maharil (who was also a cantor and a synagogue poet) as the source for the mandate that one should not change the melodies or the synagogue poems of his community. Interestingly enough, in the same section of the *Shulhan Arukh* (619.6), where the Day of Atonement services are being discussed, Isserles cites some good advice given by Maharil to the cantors. There the custom is recorded that pious people stay in the synagogue for extra devotions all through the night of Yom Kippur. Maharil says that cantors, however, should not do so, since they must conduct the services the next day and, if they do not get enough sleep, may lose their voices.

Maharil's most famous work is his book of customs, *Minhagei Maharil*. He describes, for example, funeral and marriage services as he conducted them. He does so with such full detail that we have a vivid picture of much of the life of Rhineland Jewry. Besides his book on customs, his responsa have been widely used. They, too, reveal the life of German Jewry in those troubled times.

The responsum cited (no. 99 in his collection) throws a somber light on the unhappy past. It deals with the strange-sounding question of whether or not *kaddish* should be recited for martyrs. One would take for granted that martyrs are reverently remembered. Furthermore, they should surely be remembered by the recital of the *kaddish* in their honor since the *kaddish* had such rich emotional associations. Originally the *kaddish,* as referred to in the Talmud, refers primarily to its opening paragraph and is a doxology in praise of God. It was recited after study or after public sermons. The Talmud says, in B. Sota 49a, that the world rests upon the recitation of this praise of God after the sermon. And in Berakhot 3a the thought is expressed that when the people of Israel enters into the synagogue and schools and recites, "May God's great name be blessed" (i.e., the opening phrase of the *kaddish*), God Himself says, "Blessed be the King who is thus praised in His house." Then why should there be any question as to whether the martyrs deserve this noble prayer in their memory? The question, however, which is asked is not based on the true meaning of this exalted praise of God after study and sermon, but rests rather upon folkloristic ideas which have clustered around the *kaddish*. The reciting of the *kaddish* by orphans rests to some degree upon a folkloristic idea that the purpose of the *kaddish* is to redeem the dead from the torment of hell. The story is told in a number of sources (for example, *Or Zarua,* ed. Zhitomir, II.11d) that Rabbi Akiba saw a man who suffered torments in the netherworld. He sought out the man's son and taught him to say *kaddish,* and thus the man was delivered. This folk idea was connected with the statement in the Talmud (Ed., end ch. 2) that the wicked are punished in hell for twelve months. Therefore *kaddish* is said for only eleven months in order that the mourner, by a twelve-months recital of *kaddish* shall not seem to declare that his father is wicked.

This folk notion, that *kaddish* was for the purpose of redeeming souls from torment, ran counter to the concept of the high status of the martyrs. The martyrs were deemed to be pure, sanctified (i.e., saints). Then why should they need any such redemption? Of course, special notice was taken of the martyrs during prayer. The Rhineland cities kept careful lists of all their martyrs and read out the lists at certain intervals during the year. In these lists the martyrs are always described in terms such as this: May their soul "be bound in the bundle of life" with other righteous men and women in the Garden of Eden. The term for "martyrdom" is *kiddush haShem,* sanctification of God's Name, and the martyrs themselves were called *kedoshim,* "saints," or "holy ones." Certainly a strong sentiment would require that every prayer, including the *kaddish,* be recited for them. Yet many worried that reciting the *kaddish* would imply their need to be redeemed from the punishment for sin. Maharil's answer is that they are indeed exceedingly holy. They *are* saints. But all saints have some sin, and the *kaddish* should therefore be recited.

TEXT

As to whether the *kaddish* should be recited by orphans of the martyrs, I have not heard what you have written in the name of my sacred teacher (that *kaddish* should not be recited), but I have heard other people say so. Yet I have paid no regard to their opinion because it seems to me obvious that it should be recited. My reason comes from the laws of mourning which Meir of Rothenburg wrote based on the statement in the Talmud (Ed., end ch. 2) that the wicked are judged for twelve months; and Isaac Or Zarua (the son of Moses) said that we must mourn for the holy ones. He writes a long responsum on the subject and ends with the statement that whoever says that we should not mourn for them will need to make atonement for his words.

Thus did I hear from my teachers that in fact this matter was decided during the persecutions in Prague (during the Hussite era) where there were some who did not want to mourn for the holy ones (the martyrs). But in the end the great scholars of those days decreed that we should mourn for them; and this seems right to me.

Although they are the sacred ones of the Most High and are so greatly exalted that no human can be at their level, nevertheless, who can judge whether or not they may have been guilty of some sins which led to this violent death and even to the pain of the grave, as Rabbi Simha wrote. So also said Nahmanides, that the punishment of shortened life comes even for a few sins. For were it not so, then if there were anyone who had a father known and widely respected for scholarship and from his youth, should we argue that he should not say *kaddish* for so noble a man?

As for the fact that we believe that death purifies, even as the Day of Atonement and repentance purify from sin—and indeed there are times when all three (modes of purification) come together for one man—nevertheless, we must pay attention to the possibility that perhaps he neglected (literally, "pushed aside") atonement. Thus we see that Jesse (the father of David who was deemed totally without sin) died at the instigation of the serpent and was killed (the Talmud, Baba Batra 17a, speaks of four biblical characters who were so righteous that there was no sin for which they could have deserved death. It must, then, have been the serpent, who had brought sin to Adam, who urged their death). This idea might seem difficult to a wise person like you, but Job (the righteous man who suffered) will prove (that this can happen) and Saul and his sons who fought the wars of the Lord, blessed be He, nevertheless, even they needed the Divine promise (given by Samuel, I Sam. 28.19): *Tomorrow thou and thy sons will be with me.*

(Thus the sense of reverence overcame folkloristic apprehensions; and Maharil confirmed and spread the custom of saying *kaddish* for the martyrs.)

16

THE JEWISHNESS OF THE
MARRANOS

Solomon ben Simon Duran (born in Algiers, *ca.* 1400; died there, 1467) was the son of Simon ben Zemah Duran (see responsum no. 14, above) and his father's successor as rabbi of Algiers. His volume of responsa was published in Leghorn in 1742. Until then, his responsa had circulated in manuscript and, judging by the quotations from his opinions by later authors, had exerted a wide influence. The responsum which we cite is no. 89 and constitutes a "leading case" in Jewish Law. It is one of the key responsa dealing with the problem of the marranos of Spain and Portugal.

Although the final expulsion from Spain did not take place until 1492, after the death of Solomon Duran, the great persecutions of 1391 which had sent his father to Algiers created vast numbers of marranos in Spain. These apostates constituted a somewhat different social and religious problem from the apostates, for example, in the Franco-German lands. (See the responsa of Rashi, p. 17ff.) In northern France, in the Rhineland, the problem concerned chance individuals who had become Christians. The marrano problem involved entire communities and eventually the whole Jewish population remaining in Spain and Portugal. The attitudes of condemnation or rejection, which might have been comparatively easy with regard to individual apostates, became very difficult when the problem concerned an entire population of converted Jews. Furthermore, the apostates in France and the Rhineland constituted a problem only during a certain limited period, chiefly in the time of the Crusades; whereas the marranos of Spain and Portugal continued to escape and seek admittance to Jewish communities up to the dawn of modern times. Hence, the Jewish scholars, dealing with the problem of the marranos, needed to pass judgment upon tens of thousands of Jews under the changing conditions of many centuries.

It was therefore difficult for the Jewish authorities to maintain a fixed attitude toward the marranos. For example, in judging the validity of a marrano marriage which took place in a church (the marranos were compelled to have their marriages in church), the decision might be different from century to century. During the 14th and early 15th centuries, when there still were Jews in Spain, one might still assume that the marranos had had a regular Jewish marriage secretly. But such an assumption could no longer be made when there were no professing Jews left in Spain. Or, in the early centuries, when one could assume that marranos married only marranos, one might make a different decision about them than in later centuries when it might be assumed that there was increasing intermarriage with Gentiles.

However, as to the basic status of the marranos, Solomon ben Simon Duran's decision, which we cite, became classic. He established their essential Jewishness.

TEXT

Solomon, the son of Rabbi Simon son of the sage Zemah, of blessed memory (gives the following answer with regard to) the uncircumcised children of those apostates who are called *anusim* (i.e., marranos) who come to return in repentance. It is necessary to make the law with regard to them clear in the matter of their repentance and their circumcision and their ritual bathing. (A proselyte who enters Judaism must take the ritual bath and, if male, must also be circumcised.) He says (he begins in the third person) that their status is Jewish in all their relations. It is a basic law (literally, a far-reaching law) in Israel that a Jewish apostate, even though he has sinned, is still a Jew, as the Talmud says (Sanh. 44b) and his marriages are valid marriages. His children have the same status as he has, provided, of course, the children are born of a female apostate (i.e., not of a Gentile mother) as the Talmud says (Kid. 68b).

Now do not say that (the enduring Jewish status) applies only to a Jewish-born apostate. It applies also to a (Gentile-born) proselyte who returns to his original religion, as the Talmud says (Yeb. 47b). This is so even for many generations: to the end of time (literally, to the end of the world) we count him a Jew. Do not say that this applies only to an apostate Jew who marries an apostate Jewess (that their children are Jewish); but even if a Gentile marries a Jewess, or a Jewish woman apostate, the children are counted as her children (not the Gentile husband's children). To the end of all generations, he is a Jew, for Scriptural law declares the seed of a Gentile in the womb of an Israelite to be hers.

> (Then he gives a proof of this from the talmudic discussion in Yebamot 16b, in which the Talmud discusses the status of the children of the Ten Tribes. The Ten Tribes disappeared among the Gentiles. Yet theoretically the children of their daughters would be Jews for all generations. Therefore if a Jew married any Gentile woman, it might be theoretically possible to say that this woman is one of the Ten Tribes and therefore the child may be Jewish. In that case, the marriage with any Gentile woman might, perhaps, be a Jewish marriage, at least valid enough to require a bill of divorcement. Therefore, to avoid this possible confusion, the rabbis in the Talmud formally declared the descendants of the Ten Tribes to be Gentile. But it is clear that it was only the Ten Tribes whom the Talmud, to avoid confusion, declared as Gentiles; their declaration does not apply to these marranos who are descendants of the tribe of Judah.
>
> He continues as follows:)

Therefore children of these apostates (the marranos), as long as their mother is of Israel, even over many generations and even if it was a Gentile man who married this apostate Jewish woman, are, to the end of all generations, Jewish.

(He then continues to discuss the Jewish rights of these descendants of marranos; for example, that one may not take from them interest on loans, since they are Jews. He continues that, since they are Jews, it is wrong to put them through the process of conversion when they seek to return to the Jewish community.)

Since it is now clear that these (marranos) are not to be considered proselytes, we do not need therefore to enumerate to them all the commandments and their punishments (as must be done to a Gentile who wishes to become a proselyte—Yeb. 47a). This is obvious, since, if you were to say to him that (as you might with a Gentile candidate for conversion), should he (the marrano) not wish to accept the commandments, we would dismiss him and he would be free of them as if he were a Gentile —God forbid that this should even come into your mind. Because he is already in duty bound to fulfill them just as we are. Therefore, we must not terrify him or confuse him, but draw him to us with kindness, for he stands (as we do) under the oath taken at Mount Sinai.

(He continues this thought to indicate that none of the ritual of conversion should be applied to marranos, and continues:)

Since he is an Israelite, he does not need the ritual bath nor formal acceptance, for he is already in duty bound to obey all the commandments. Therefore, just as the father at the circumcision of his son is in duty bound to pronounce the blessing "to induct him into the Covenant of Abraham, our father," for (circumcision) is a commandment that is incumbent upon him (namely, the father), so here, too (in the case of the marrano), when he has himself circumcised, he must pronounce the blessing, "who has sanctified us, etc. to enter into the Covenant of Abraham, our father." For the commandment is incumbent upon him (the marrano), since it is the law that, if a Jewish child was not circumcised by his father (or his father's agent), he must arrange for his own circumcision (when he grows up).

(Since he speaks of the adult marranos arranging for their own circumcision, he goes into the medical question of the proper hygiene to be observed in the fulfillment of this commandment in the case of an adult, and ends with this blessing:)

"Our God and God of our fathers, bless Thy servant whose name is now called X and send him Thy mercy. As Thou hast already moved his heart to return in perfect repentance to Thee, so mayest Thou now implant in his heart the love and fear of Thee. Open his heart to Thy Law and guide him in the path of Thy commandments, that he may find grace in Thy sight. May this be Thy will. Amen."

This legally sound and nobly motivated responsum became the standard opinion as the status of the marranos in all the centuries that followed. The responsum was frequently referred to and played an important part, therefore, in the brotherly and merciful reception which these heroic refugees were given in all Jewish communities.

17

✡

COMMUNAL DISPUTE IN TREVISO

Judah (ben Eliezer) Minz (born in 1408; died in 1508) was the rabbi of Padua for forty-seven years and is said by tradition to have been also Professor of Philosophy at the University of Padua. Whether or not the tradition is reliable, there is no doubt that he was the leading authority of his day in Italy. Unfortunately, during the sack of Padua, all his manuscripts were burned; but his grandson found fifteen of his responsa, which were published together with responsa of his son and of his son's son-in-law, Meir Katzenellenbogen. As Minz's name indicates, he was of German extraction and may himself have been an immigrant from Germany. There was a constant immigration from Germany into Italy, and many of the north Italian communities were largely German. This fact explains the sources quoted in the responsum of Judah Minz which we will cite. It deals with a dispute in the Jewish community of Treviso. This community, likewise, was largely settled by German Jews and therefore, in dealing with their communal dispute, he cites as his chief authority the great German teacher, Meir of Rothenburg (see page 41) as quoted by Meir's disciple, Meir haKohen.

It is also of interest to note the matters about which members of the community of Treviso fell into dispute with their leaders. The new synagogue being built was costing too much money.

Some did not want to build a new *mikvah* nearer the Jewish quarter. They also found fault with the kindly manner used by the officers when dealing with mendicants. They wanted the wanderers and mendicants treated less politely so that they would be discouraged from coming. The responsum is no. 7.

TEXT

Peace unto you, my friends, the enlightened ones who dwell in the congregation of Treviso; great and small, may God preserve you. I wish to tell you that, since you are wrought up about the three matters, I will give you my humble opinion from the point of view of truth and the good order of the congregation and peace.

Questions:

These are the subjects under dispute: one, with regard to the building of the synagogue, the house of our Lord, "the small sanctuary": according to the way the building is arranged and being erected at the command of the officers of the community or those appointed especially for the building, there is lacking a little money to complete the building in a proper, worthy way. Because of this deficit, there are attacks and quarrels with the officers, (with some people) saying, "You should not have built thus and thus." (All these complaints) are really for the purpose of finding an excuse to withdraw from giving enough money to make up the deficit in the building costs. Second, about the matter of the *mikvah:* there is dispute over the proposal to build the *mikvah* in the Jewish quarter, etc. Third, there is the question of the reception of travelers, or itinerants, by means of tickets (for food and lodging) which are distributed from an urn as they happen to be picked out. Some say let the itinerant himself, and not the head of the community (step up and) take the ticket from the urn. This is proposed in order that the poor man shall be embarrassed and not want to come (to Treviso) any more. But those who disagree with this proposal say that such embarrassing treatment is not a true fulfilment of the commandment to welcome strangers, but can be more properly called expelling strangers, and that the custom wherein the officer takes out the tickets and gives them (unostentatiously) to the itinerant strangers (is better). This custom should not be changed, and the poor should not be embarrassed. This is the statement of the quarrel within your gates.

Answer:

Since writing is difficult for me, I choose to be brief. In fact, I will transcribe one of the *Maimuniyot* responsa (by Meir haKohen, now printed with the *Yad* of Maimonides. It contains responsa by Meir of Rothenburg, the author's teacher). You must read this and not deviate from its decision. You should, moreover, know the source of (the answer to) what you are seeking: it is one of the responsa of Meir of Rothenburg (which I quote from the *Teshubot Maimuniyot*). Most of our customs, especially the customs of the Ashkenazim, follow his opinion. He is one of the later teachers and knew the opinion of all his predecessors. Thus it says (of Meir of Rothenburg's authority) in the *Maimuniyot,* in chapter 8 of the "Laws of Passover," that even where most of the gaonim disagree with Meir of Rothenburg, we follow him. All the more (should we follow him) in a case where no one disagrees with him.

Now this is the wording of his (Meir of Rothenburg's) responsum: "As for your question, dear friend, Abraham haLevi (about what to do), if there is a quarrel in your community and they are unable to come to an agreement in choosing officers with everyone's consent, one saying one thing, the other saying the opposite, and because of this division of hearts, study of the Torah is neglected and there is no truth and judgment and peace in your city, nor in the whole kingdom (district) which is attached to your city—you ask me how then shall they proceed (in this impasse)? It seems to me that they should gather together in a meeting all the taxpayers of the community, who should promise on oath (literally by "blessing") that everyone will give his opinion in the Name of God and for the good of the community; and that they should follow the decision of the majority as to choosing officers, appointing cantors, and fixing the treasury for charity, and in appointing charity officers, building or dismantling the synagogue, adding to or diminishing or acquiring a wedding-house, building or destroying it, acquiring a bakery, building or destroying it. In brief, all the needs of the community shall be decided by the majority. If the minority refuse and stand off at a distance and do not do everything as I have said, then the majority shall have the power to appoint heads, to compel and to exert pressure, either by the laws of Israel or by the Gentile laws, until the minority gives their consent. He concludes: And thus will peace be attained. Signed, Meir the son of Baruch (of Rothen-burg)."

Now, my friends (continues Judah Minz to the community of Treviso), set your hearts on the pathway that goes up to the house of God. Do not swerve from the road which this great teacher has taught us. Do not deviate to the right or the left, *for his paths are paths of pleasantness and all his roads peace.*

(Then Judah Minz reviews for them the opinion of Meir of Rothenburg in greater detail. He applies it to each of the three quarrels in the community, and ends as follows:)

What appears to my humble mind and knowledge have I written. But I have made no comment on the statement about the old custom (*minhag*) which you say is prevalent in your community (about the distribution of food tickets). If you have a fixed custom of which we can say that it was established by worthy scholars of the past, then you must follow it. In these matters it is the custom (*minhag*) that counts, provided it is a custom established by worthy predecessors. Also, if you have arguments and rejoinders against what has been said above, bring your answers and your witnesses to me and justify your words. I will continue to take trouble to discuss the matter for you, in order to bring peace among you, for great is peace.

Therefore may your peace grow great, as is the wish of him who loves you, the burdened

Judah Minz

18

✡

RESTORING THE SANHEDRIN

Jacob Berab (born in Moqueda, near Toledo, 1474; died in Safed, Palestine, 1546) had fled from Spain to Tlemcen, in North Africa; and though he was a youth of eighteen, this large community chose him as their rabbi. He moved to Jerusalem and finally settled in Safed, which was the great Jewish center, Jerusalem being then only a minor community.

Levi ibn Habib (born in Zamora, Spain, 1480; died in Jerusalem, *ca.* 1545) was compelled at the age of seventeen, in Portugal, to undergo baptism. He fled to Salonika, where he could return to the Jewish faith. His responsa are often quoted; and fortunately for us, the correspondence with Jacob Berab is preserved at the back of the book of his collected responsa.

As the exiles from Spain and Portugal sought new homes, chiefly in the lands of the eastern Mediterranean, they were concerned, first of all, with physical safety. Having found a fairly secure residence, they began to think of strengthening their personal religious life and rehabilitating and reconstructing the Jewish community. The inner mood of that vast exile was never adequately described by historians of that day; it was, after all, before the age of socio-psychological studies. Yet we can get an insight into some of their prevailing ideas and attitudes from the problems presented and the proposals discussed in the responsa of that day.

Tradition taught that the messianic time would be preceded by a period of general agony. On the one hand, the exiles naturally believed that their widespread sorrows were the sufferings preliminary to the coming of the Messiah. But on the other hand, if the Messiah was to come, the people of Israel had to be worthy of his advent. Now these tragic exiles felt deeply unworthy. Many of them had been forced to adopt Christianity. How could they do adequate penance for their apostasy?

Apart from this personal problem of the individual and his sense of guilt, there were new problems for the Jewish community. The refugees settled in the communities in the east, where they encountered *minhagim* (customs) different from their own. The new settlements were therefore disunited, disorderly, and quarrelsome. Was there no central source of authority that could bring order into Jewish life?

The desire for personal atonement in preparation for the Messiah and the hope for an overall authority to bring order into the communities were united in the plan evolved by a group of Spanish exiles in the city of Safed to re-establish the ancient Sanhedrin.

The ancient Sanhedrin, which had ceased with the destruction of the Temple by the Romans, was held to have been the last in an unbroken sequence of authoritative bodies going back to the seventy men assembled by Moses. It had enjoyed supreme authority. If such a Sanhedrin could possibly be revived, order and system could easily be restored to all the Jewish communities. But this restoration seemed impossible because membership in the Sanhedrin needed a special type of ordination: Just as the Sanhedrin as a body had been in unbroken sequence from the days of Moses, so the individual members of the Sanhedrin had received special ordination, each pupil from his teacher, back to the days of Moses. Though the Sanhedrin had been dispersed at the time of the destruction of the Temple, its ordained members still retained their individual authority. They continued to ordain their disciples. Thus continuous ordination had existed down to the time of Hillel II (4th century), when the chain of ordination broke.

What we call "ordination" today is not the classic, unbroken, spiritual ordination of the past. It is merely *hatarat hora'ah,* a certificate permitting a disciple to teach independently of his teacher. It is a scholar's license and not a spiritual ordination.

Now, since the true ordination had ceased finally in the 4th century, and since no one could be ordained unless his teacher himself had been ordained, there seemed no way of reviving ordination, and hence no way of re-establishing the old Sanhedrin.

In spite of this seemingly insuperable difficulty, the emotional need to re-establish the Sanhedrin persisted. It was rooted in the sense of personal guilt borne by the refugees, so many of whom had been converts. The punishment for apostasy was *karet,* literally, a cutting-off, a shortening of life, as a punishment from God. For a sin which involves *karet,* repentance seemed an insufficient atonement. From their Catholic life they had observed that atonement was made for certain serious offenses, by physical penance, as well as by repentance. Was there not some physical penance in Judaism which could save them from the punishment of *karet?* Yes, there was: The Law (M. Mak. III.15) says that those who are flogged are freed from the punishment of *karet.* But no judge could inflict flogging unless he were duly ordained. Thus the yearning for such expiation was, perhaps, the chief motive for the attempt to restore the old ordination.

But how could ordination be established? Only a man, himself ordained, could ordain others; and there had been nobody for centuries who had been duly ordained. A way was found out of the impasse by one of the great exiles from Spain, Jacob Berab, the rabbi of Safed.

Jacob Berab noted that Maimonides (whose authority was, of course, supreme for the Spanish Jews) had made clear (in his commentary to the Mishna, Sanh. I.3, and in his Code, *Hilkhot Sanhedrin* IV.11) that there must surely be a method for restoring ordination, for God had promised: *I will restore thy judges as of yore* (Isa. 1.26). Since, according to the Law, the Messiah will not innovate anything, the restoration must occur by human means before the Messiah comes. Hence there must be a practical method provided by Law for re-establishing ordination. Such a method is available, said Maimonides: If the scholars of Palestine (the classic ordination could take place only in Palestine) would agree to ordain one of their number, that man would thus be duly ordained in the ancient, classical sense. He, in turn, could then ordain others and so the old Sanhedrin would be re-established.

Thereupon the scholars of Safed issued a public statement through which they ordained their teacher, Jacob Berab. Jacob Berab ordained his famous disciple, Joseph Caro, and three others. But a difficulty arose. At that time, Jerusalem was a small community compared to Safed. Yet it had the sanctity of its name and was led by another famous Spanish exile, Levi ibn Habib.

Berab sent an ordination by messenger to Levi ibn Habib, and the sages of Safed sent him a copy of their proclamation. Ibn Habib, however, declared the whole procedure invalid and explained that Maimonides in this case was not properly understood. The famous dispute between the two men followed.

We cite the chief letter of Jacob Berab defending the new ordination, and then the preliminary part of the pamphlet in which Levi ibn Habib sums up all his arguments against the ordination.

TEXT

Statement in Letter of Jacob Berab:

Our sins have brought it about that ordination ceased at the end of the days of the sages of the Mishna, when the alien government decreed that both the ordained and the ordainer shall be put to death. No regular court of ordained judges was therefore left in the Land of Israel. This was about three hundred years after the destruction of the Temple. At that time the sages of Israel and the elders of that generation gathered and agreed upon a sound plan to remove disputes and disagreements that had existed until then on the method of settling the dates for the New Year, the Day of Atonement, and the other holidays. The dispute was whether to continue the old method of witnesses who see the new moon or to adopt the (newer) method of settling the calendar by calculation. With great wisdom, and by using the calendar tradition that they had possessed since the days of the prophets and ancient sages of Israel, they then agreed to establish for us the proper calculation which they bequeathed to us: namely, how to intercalate the years (i.e., how to determine which is a leap year) and to fix the months of the festivals, etc. This they did so that the children of Israel, who from then on would be scattered to all the ends of the earth, might be able to follow these rules for the years and the months and the festivals every year.

(Berab begins with a discussion of the question of calendation because Levi ibn Habib, in a previous responsum objecting to the new ordination, expressed the fear that if men were newly ordained, they might restore the ancient method of determining the calendar by witnesses and thus throw the whole calendar into confusion. Berab indicates that this will not occur because the patriarch, Hillel II, and his court, who fixed the mathematical determination, were themselves ordained with the old ordination and that, therefore, their mathematical determination would remain sacred until the time of the Messiah. There is no fear, then, that the restoration of ordination would upset the calendar. Then Berab, having disposed of this objection, goes into the central problem: whether it is legally possible to restore the old ordination after the lapse of all those centuries, when there is no longer an ordained rabbi. He proceeds to examine the texts of Maimonides upon which his plan is based.)

I found that Maimonides wrote in his "Laws of Sanhedrin," ch. IV.11, as follows: "It seems to me that if all the sages in Israel agree to appoint judges and to ordain them, these will be ordained (truly ordained with the ancient ordination); and they will have the authority to judge laws of fines (only ordained judges of the ancient ordination could impose fines and such punishments as flogging, etc.). They will have the right to ordain others. If so, why were the rabbis (in the Talmud) worried lest the ordination disappear? Because Israel was scattered and it was impossible to obtain unanimity. Of course, if there were one man ordained by a teacher who had been previously ordained (i.e., by an unbroken ordination back to Moses), such a person would not need unanimous consent but could judge laws of fines for all. *But the matter needs further consideration."*

(The closing phrase in the statement of Maimonides is the crucial one—"the matter needs further consideration." Levi ibn Habib, as we shall see, bases his chief objection to the new plan for ordination on this phrase. He says that Maimonides, in his commentary to the Mishna, gives his plan for renewing ordination, but he wrote his commentary in his youth. When, however, he wrote his great Code, he ended with the words "the matter needs further consideration." According to Ibn Habib, this cautionary statement is, in effect, a retraction of the entire plan. He takes it to mean that when Maimonides was mature and wrote his Code, he no longer believed in the possibility of restoring ordination by the agreement of the sages in the Land of Israel. Therefore, Berab now tries to prove that the phrase, "the matter needs further consideration," was not to be understood as applying to the whole paragraph, but only to the last sentence. That is to say, what needs further consideration is only the concluding statement, whether or not an individual scholar who is ordained can judge alone without needing other ordained judges. Berab then reverts to the question of the calendar and adds further proof that there will be no possibility of upsetting the calendar if ordination is restored.

He concludes his long responsum with a discussion of the personal motives which impelled many of the exiles, namely, the need of having an ordained court which should have the right to impose flogging as a complete penance for the sin of apostasy. He continues as follows:)

Now there remains for me to explain the matter of flogging. If a penitent comes before an ordained court and he had not been warned previously as to his sin and there are no witnesses that the sin occurred, are they able to impose the flogging prescribed by the Torah or not? (In other words, can a man demand such a penance when his sin is not even legally proved?) We are not speaking here of compelling the man (against his will) to be flogged, for under those circumstances (compulsion), we may not flog a man unless there are witnesses and previous warning. The question before us is, however, this: If a man comes as a penitent to the court and says, "I have committed a sin that incurs *karet*, and I wish to receive flogging to be freed from *karet*, as the Mishna says in Sanhedrin" (can the court order the flogging?).

> (Then the question is, can an ordained court inflict flogging when there is no other proof except the statement of the repentant sinner? He cites and refutes a number of opinions to the effect that the court cannot allow a man on his own statement to declare himself a wicked man; and he continues:)

Nevertheless, if he wishes to do penance, we flog him and thus give him atonement; for this is the atonement, namely, that the flogging takes the place of death (*karet*). As for the maxim of Rava (Yeb. 25b) that a man may not declare himself wicked, that maxim applies only to the death penalties inflicted by the (human) court, but not to *karet* (shortening of life at the hands of Heaven). . . . Thus, if a repentant man comes before a court and asks to be put to death, they may not put him to death. But in the matter of flogging in place of *karet*, a man may of his own choice accept the punishment of flogging.

> (Having thus disposed of the various objections, he concludes his responsum as follows:)

This is what seems to me to be the case with regard to ordination in our time. In the year 5298 (i.e., 1538) the Lord aroused the spirit of the sages of Israel. There were one or two exceptions, who can be ignored because they were so few, who were in doubt and confused by the phrase of Maimonides, "the matter needs careful consideration." They (the minority) believed that this referred to the whole matter of ordination. Therefore they thought that we have no power to re-establish ordination in these days. They also feared that it would enter our minds to tamper with the calendar, with the result that we will consume leaven on Pesah and eat on the Day of Atonement. But, thank God, we have disposed of all these doubts and have explained to what the phrase of Maimonides refers. Also we have written above that, even if we have many newly ordained men, we will not have the power to fix the calendar until the Messiah comes, for only then will there be a court equal in standing to the court of Rabbi Hillel (Hillel II, who fixed the calendar in the 4th century). So they (the scholars) came to an agreement and they ordained me, the humble one among the tribes of Jacob, Jacob Berab. After two or three months, there almost happened to me what happened to Rabbi Judah ben Baba (Sanh. 14a), whom the Romans put to death for ordaining his disciples. Two informers rose up against me for no sin of mine—may God punish them for their evil work—and forced me to leave Palestine (he went for a time to Damascus). Then I thought that perhaps, God forbid, the opportunity would be lost when I leave Palestine; for no one can ordain anybody outside of Palestine (Sanh. 14a), so the result would be that all our labors would have been in vain; for it had already become clear how difficult it is to weld a multitude of opinions into a joint agreement. Therefore I ordained four elders, the best of the colleagues there at the time.

God knows that my intention was only for the sake of Heaven, and not to lord it over anybody. I saw Maimonides wrote in his commentary to the Mishna, as I mentioned above, namely, that when God shall prepare the hearts of men and their intentions become pure, the children of the Land of Israel will agree to appoint over them the head of a yeshiva; and he (Maimonides) came to this conviction because of what the prophets said: *I shall restore thy sages as of old* (Isa. 1.26). May God fulfill among us the verses which the prophets spoke: *And the redeemed of the Lord will return and come to Zion with joy* (Isa. 51.11). Amen. May this be God's will.

Jacob Berab

Levi ibn Habib's objections to the plan are clearly stated in the correspondence published at the end of his responsa. At the beginning of that section, he summarizes all his arguments in answer

to those of Jacob Berab. It is from this summary that we cite
relevant excerpts. He begins as follows:

Statement in Correspondence of Levi ibn Habib:

A short booklet on the dispute and the legalistic discussion of law leading to action (*halakhah l'ma'aseh:* the rabbinic
literature makes a distinction between Halakhah which is merely
the clarification of the law and *ma'aseh,* the definite direction to act on the matter. The phrase implies that there is no
further doubt) passed between the sages of Safed and the sages
of Jerusalem in our day. The sages of Safed saw fit to take action
on the basis of the teaching which our teacher, Moses ben
Maimon, of blessed memory, made in his commentary to the
Mishna, Sanhedrin I.3, and in his law book, chapter 4 (*Yad,
Sanh.* IV.11), namely, that the sages of the Land of Israel have
the power to ordain even if there is no teacher left who had
himself been ordained. So they (the sages of Safed) ordained the
greatest among them, the sage, Jacob Berab. Then they sent to
us who dwell in Jerusalem a letter describing their decision which
began with the words: "Behold, one people!" (Farther along in
his epistle, Levi ibn Habib gives the full text of the letter.) Also
they ordained me, the humble one, Levi ben Jacob ibn Habib,
and this by the hand of the messenger who brought the abovementioned letter; through him they sent the document of ordination, signed by all of them.

When I saw, after careful thought, that there is no legal validity in the ordination, I answered them with a long pamphlet (the
Hebrew word is *kuntrus* from the Latin *commentarius*) to stop
them. It begins with the words: "I have seen what is written."
Also the abovementioned sage who is responsible for all this action, before he saw my pamphlet, himself composed a pamphlet
in support of the ordination. It begins: "Inasmuch as." (This is
the legal opinion which we have just cited.) This too came into
my hands and I composed a second pamphlet against it. Mean-
while, the sage received my first pamphlet and composed one
against it. . . . may the God of justice not judge us harshly for
the unfair inclusion of other matters. May He soon redeem Zion
in justice and establish the throne of David. Amen.

(After some general considerations and after citing the proclamation of the rabbis of Safed, he continues as follows:)

. . . It was clear to them that this agreed proclamation of theirs cannot stand without our agreement, namely, ours the humble ones of the flock in Jerusalem. For though we are few in number compared to them, nevertheless, we are not mere reed-cutters (a phrase from the Talmud, Sanh. 33a, here meaning ignoramuses). Besides the sanctity of this place (Jerusalem), there is an added consideration, in that the matter of ordination is in the hands of *all* the sages of the holy land, as Maimonides has written. That is why they sent to us their agreement, sealed by their hand, through the messenger, the sage Solomon Chasan, in order that we should uphold their hands by signing our name too. But with all due respect to their learning, it seems that in this matter they have veered off the road of decency and right. The proper procedure would have been for them not to sign this agreement until they had learned what we thought, after they had told us their arguments.

It entered my mind to forgive them for this and to say that their intention was a worthy one. They meant to hasten and achieve the desired end. For that reason they did not wish to prolong the matter. So they decided on action, since they thought that I also would agree with them. But this excuse (for their procedure) is not sufficient. With due apologies, I would say that even if this was their intention, they made a mistake. On the contrary, through their very desire to hasten the matter, they have pushed it off. Certainly they should have sensed that perhaps I could not agree to their plan as long as I did not know their arguments. Then, if we had any doubt as to their arguments, we would have let them know. After that, if they persisted in their opinions and their arguments, and then took action contrary to our opinions, it might have been possible to say that their agreement would have validity (since they gave us a chance to express our opinion, and) since they are a majority, and it is a commandment of the Torah to follow the majority, as long as the agreement of the majority follows discussion by *all*.

This is clear in the prelude to what Maimonides wrote in his commentary to the Mishna and in his decision on this new law when he said: "It seems to me that if all the sages agreed, etc." Of course, that does not mean that they must be unanimous. It means the majority of them, for the majority has the authority over all of them, as is explained in many places in the Talmud. I shall discuss this matter later. But when the agreement of the majority takes place without the chance being given to everybody to debate it, it is not a valid agreement at all. For if the majority had had a chance to hear the arguments of the minority, they might have agreed with them and changed their minds. For thus wrote Solomon ben Adret in his responsum.

(Ibn Habib cites this responsum to prove that the validity of the majority decision depends upon the participation of the entire assembly.)

Therefore, not only is that agreement of theirs invalid as to a majority, but now (even though) they wish to debate it with us and hear our arguments and let us know their arguments, if it seems to us that their arguments are invalid, they are not going to change their minds. Therefore their agreement has no validity.

This is the essence of Ibn Habib's objection. He later goes into additional objections, but the heart of it is that the sages of Jerusalem were not consulted before the action was taken. Jacob Berab ordained four disciples. These four ordained another generation, and these still another. Then this new ordination lapsed completely.

The subject of ordination and Sanhedrin has come up since. At the turn of this century, Rabbi Mendel Cohen of the Ashkenazi congregation in Cairo attempted to organize a society whose aim would be to re-establish ordination in Palestine. Recently the subject has come up once more. In all modern discussions, as probably in all future discussions, the debate rests upon the arguments advanced pro and con by Jacob Berab and Levi ibn Habib in the days when the exiles from Spain and Portugal sought to recover their own spiritual self-respect and to re-establish Jewish religious life.

19

✡

THE EMBROIDERED ARK
CURTAIN

Joseph (ben Ephraim) Caro (born in Spain, 1488; died in Safed, 1575) was the greatest of all Jewish codifiers. No code, neither the famous one of Maimonides nor that of Jacob ben Asher, ever attained the authority of Caro's *Shulhan Arukh*. Caro was brought as a refugee, when a child, out of Spain. His family settled in Turkey. His father was his first teacher. In his twenties he met Solomon Molcho, the famous marrano enthusiast, and was influenced by him to a sort of mysticism. It is strange that this clear-minded legalist was also a mystic. He believed all his life that the Mishna appeared to him as a living spirit to advise him, to guide him, and to rebuke him. His book, *Maggid Mesharim,* published after his death, was a sort of a mystical diary, telling of his encounters with the personified Mishna all through his life.

Perhaps it was due to his mystical leanings that he left Turkey and settled in Safed, the center of mysticism. There he came into contact with Jacob Berab, whom he counts as his teacher, and whose efforts to revive the old *Semikhah* (ordination) he seconded with all his strength. None of these strange moods or enthusiasms affected his sharp mind or slowed the growth of his enormous learning. His greatest legal work, *Bet Joseph,* is a monument of learning. It is written in the form of a commentary on Jacob ben Asher's Code, the *Tur.* It contains an analysis of all the important legal opinions up to his time.

Towards the end of his life he published a simpler Code, the *Shulhan Arukh,* in which he simply gives his decisions without any of the learned arguments in support. When Moses Isserles of Cracow added to the *Shulhan Arukh* the customs (*minhagim*) of Ashkenazi Jewry, this book started on its way to greatness. In spite of strong opposition to it by many scholars (primarily because he did not give authorities and argumentation), the *Shulhan Arukh* found adherents until it became, as it is today, the premier Code in Rabbinic Judaism.

Caro's responsa were published after his death. The responsum which we cite is from the collection called *Avkat Rokhel* ("The Powders of the Merchant," a phrase in Song of Songs 3.6). It deals with a question of perennial interest: to what extent is art work permitted in the synagogue? The prohibition in the Ten Commandments against graven images is elaborated upon in the Talmud. The relevant questions are: whether all sorts of images are prohibited or only those that might be images of god or objects actually worshiped as god. Is a painting to be considered an image, or is an image only three-dimensional? These and related questions have been frequently revived, especially in times such as the Renaissance, when the art impulse grew strong. Yet it happens that the prime post-talmudic source frequently quoted in the debates over these questions is from the 11th century in the Rhineland concerning the synagogue in Cologne. Here Caro also quotes this source. The responsum cited is no. 66.

TEXT

Question:

I have been asked concerning a silken cloth into which were woven various figures, among them images of birds. Is it permitted to use this embroidered cloth as a hanging before the sacred Ark? The question is asked because there are those who object to the matter on the ground that when the congregation stands up to pray, they bow down towards the Ark and it would then appear as if, God forbid, they are bowing down to these images.

Answer:

It seems to me that this curtain is completely permissible. There is no ground for concern. Even if this were a picture of a man (not of birds) it is possible that this, too, would be permitted. As it appears in the Talmud (R. H. 24b) where the question is asked and answered: Are we concerned whether some might suspect (that the people are bowing down to the art object)? In the synagogue called Shaf veYatib, in Nahardea, they set up a statue. Yet the father of Samuel and Levi went there to pray and no one concerned himself with suspecting that people bowed to that image.

> (This synagogue was deemed to be especially sacred. The name of the synagogue means, "It slipped away and settled down," implying that the sacredness of Jerusalem slipped away into the exile and settled down in this synagogue in Nahardea.)

But (this unconcern with possible suspicion of idolatry is explained as follows:) we were unconcerned because there was a multitude present in the synagogue (therefore no one individual would dare to worship an idol in their presence). Therefore, wherever there is a group of people, we need not be concerned with the suspicion (of bowing down) at all.

Asher ben Yehiel cites this (in his compendium) and, while Alfasi does not cite it in *his* compendium, that does not affect our case because that (in the synagogue of Nahardea) was the image of a man (and here it is of birds). So it was with the images of phases of the moon which Rabbenu Gamaliel had in his chamber (he would point out these various images of the moon when he questioned witnesses who had come to testify that they had seen the new moon. He would say, did you see it in this shape or in that shape?) Now moon images are forbidden by the Law. But

other images, even without the presence of a multitude (to discourage an individual from idolatry) are certainly permitted.
There is nothing to suspect with regard to them.

Now it may be that the opinion of those who object (to using
that embroidery for the Ark curtain) is based upon what is cited
in the notes to Asher ben Yehiel's compendium (Ab. Zarah, chs.
3, 5), namely, that Rabbenu Eliakim (11th century in the Rhineland) gave orders to remove the pictures of lions and serpents
which had been painted in the synagogue in Cologne. These
objectors (on this ground) ought to keep in mind that one must
never rely upon any decision that one finds written down until
one has searched out whether it is an individual opinion or
whether there are other scholars who agree with it. Also, one
must understand the full contents of the words of that decision.

For note that in the very passage that they cite, Rabbenu
Ephraim sends an answer to Rabbenu Joel with regard to images
of birds and horses that were painted in the synagogue. He said
that it is permitted to pray in that synagogue for the Gentiles do
not worship these images, even when they are in separate form;
and certainly not when they are painted upon cloth. Even the
image of a man is permitted by the rabbis if one finds it already
made (it is forbidden by the rabbis only to make it oneself).

Rabbenu Nissim wrote in the same chapter (to Alfasi, end of
Mishna 3) as follows: It seems to me that they did not concern
themselves with possible suspicion of worshiping (such objects or
pictures) unless it was the custom of the Gentiles to worship
them. It is permitted to make such images as long as it is unknown and unheard of that they are worshiped at all. Therefore
it is the custom to keep even three-dimensional images of those
objects which the Torah does not expressly prohibit, and we have
never heard anyone objecting to it. These are the words of
Rabbenu Nissim, and they agree perfectly with the words of
Rabbi Ephraim.

> (Then Caro goes on to discuss other possible objections,
> namely, that the worshipers might be distracted from their
> worship, or that an object should not be interposed between
> the wall and the worshiper, and he ends as follows:)

Thus it seems to me that we may put up this curtain. It is like any other curtain, since we have demonstrated that there is no prohibition because of the pictures on it. Therefore it is all right to place it up before the Ark. I have written my humble opinion. But in the city where this question has come up, there is an ordained rabbi; if he agrees with my words, then I will declare that it is permitted on the above grounds. But if my opinions do not seem right to the rabbi, then his words must be listened to.

Sayeth the youth,

Joseph ben Ephraim (of blessed memory) *Caro*

However, in a previous responsum (no. 63) Caro objects to a sculptured stone lion being put upon the Ark. The lion is one of the four animals whose image is specifically forbidden (Ab. Zarah 43b) as idolatrous. The other three are the eagle, man, and the ox; besides, that stone lion was three-dimensional.

20

✡

A RADICAL DECISION

Moses (ben Israel) Isserles (born in Cracow, *ca.* 1520; died there, 1572) studied under Shalom Shachna, one of the leading developers of the pilpulistic method (of minute and subtle analysis of the Talmud). He married his teacher's daughter and moved back to his native city of Cracow, where he established a yeshiva which he, being a rich man, maintained at his own expense. He was not only a great talmudist and codifier; he was a student of philosophy, astronomy, and history. It was he who induced his pupil, David Ganz, to write the history, *Zemah David.* He corresponded with scholars far beyond his native Poland—with, for example, Meir Katzenellenbogen in Padua and Joseph Caro in Safed.

His most enduring achievement was his addition to Joseph Caro's *Shulhan Arukh,* wherein he cited all the historic *minhagim* (the inherited customs) of Ashkenazi Jewry, and thus made it possible for this great Code to be honored equally by Jews everywhere. He likewise wrote a commentary, of the same sort but of more critical nature, to Jacob ben Asher's *Tur.* He was so revered by Polish Jewry that, for many generations, pious people made pilgrimages to his grave.

This great codifier and leader of rabbinic Jewry, nevertheless, had the courage to make a decision which was counter to the overwhelming opinion of his predecessors. It concerned the marriage of a poor orphan girl which he performed late on Friday night, long after the Sabbath had begun. In his note to the *Shulhan Arukh*, "Orah Hayyim" 339.4, he admits that marriages should not take place on the Sabbath, but that it is nevertheless a fact that one or two exceptional authorities permit it (Rabbenu Tam and Moses of Coucy). He says: "Although it is not the law (that we may hold marriages on the Sabbath) we have these two exceptional opinions to rely upon in times of emergency; for great is the principle of protecting the honor of human beings, and at times the parties are unable to agree on the dowry until Friday night and the wedding is then held." This statement of the special circumstances under which an exception to the general rule may be made is a reference to his own responsum in which he tells that he actually performed such a marriage. He defends his point of view with great analytic skill and with deep sympathy for the poor orphan girl involved. The responsum indicates how a very great and pious scholar could have the independence of mind to reason out and to act in such a way as to protect the unfortunate. The responsum is no. 125.

TEXT

(The responsum is headed with a humble and pious wish, expressed as follows: *"My help is from the Lord, who maketh heaven and earth. May He deliver me from error."* It begins with a description of the excitement which his decision created and with a picture of the pathetic situation which impelled him to formulate and maintain his unusual decision.)

I heard behind me the sound of a great noise. Voices passed through the camp saying, "Look at that man Moses" (a reference, of course, to himself, but based upon the verse in Ex. 33.8). It concerned the action taken by me recently when I arranged a marriage under the *huppah* in the usual way. All knew the state of the bride as she entered under the *huppah*. It was in the dark of night on Friday evening, an hour and a half after night had fallen. The circumstances which impelled me to this action are clear. It is known to all who live in our city and this is what happened:

There was a poor man in our land who had betrothed his elder daughter to a suitable mate. During the period of the betrothal, which was of considerable duration, the girl's father died. (Isserles uses the classic phrase: the father went to his world and left life to all of Israel.) The daughter was left bereaved, without father and mother, except for relatives who lived far from her. They shut their eyes to her plight, all except one relative (literally, one redeemer), the brother of her mother, who brought her into his house, for she had no relative nearer than he. Then when the time came for her marriage and it was time to prepare for the feast and the requirements of the *huppah,* she did not see anything of the dowry and the other needs (which the relatives had promised her). But she was told to take her ritual bath and prepare herself for the marriage, and that the dowry would be forthcoming. This maiden then did as the women neighbors commanded her. They decked her with the veil on the sixth day, as virgins are decked. When the shadows of evening began to fall and the Sabbath was approaching, her relatives who were to give the dowry closed their fists and refused to give a sufficient amount, so that at least a third of the dowry was still lacking. Then the groom absolutely refused to marry her. He paid no attention to the pleas of the leaders of the city that he refrain from putting a daughter of Israel to shame for the sake of mere money. He refused to listen to them, *as a deaf serpent does not hear the voice of a charmer* (phrase from Psalms 58.5). Nor did the voice of the rabbi move him. Because of these quarrels, time drew on; as the saying goes, "There is no marriage settlement (*ketubah*) without dispute," and the work of Satan prompted them until the time mentioned above came. Then they finally agreed and the groom consented to enter under the *huppah* and no longer to shame a worthy daughter of Israel. Thereupon I arose and conducted the marriage at that hour.

Now, since people are complaining against me, I have come now to remove their complaints from me and to bring the proof and the reasons upon which I relied in this matter, saying: In this way behold and sanctify. (The phrase originally means, when you see the moon in this shape, sanctify the new month. Isserles plays on the phrase so that it means here, for this reason, officiate at this marriage.)

We learn in the Talmud (Betza 36b) that certain things forbidden on the Sabbath are also forbidden on the holidays. Some of these things are called *reshut,* i.e., permissible things which are nevertheless forbidden on the Sabbath and holidays. The two things mentioned (first in the Mishna and then discussed in the Talmud which are classed as *reshut*) are trying a case at law and conducting a marriage ceremony. The Talmud raises an objection to calling these two activities *reshut,* permissible. Should they not be called *mitzvot?* For it is an obligation to carry out justice and to marry people? The Talmud answers that to act as judge is no obligation on anyone if there is a better judge than he in the city; and to marry is no obligation if the man already has a wife and children (in the days when polygamy was permitted, a man could marry a second wife, but it was no obligation to do so if he already had children by his first wife).

(Isserles then analyzes in great detail various interpretations of the talmudic statement. He weighs against each other the opinions of Rashi and his grandson Rabbenu Tam, and the opinion of the tosafists and that of the Jerusalem Talmud. Having evaluated the various opinions and their implications, he concludes that in time of emergency such a marriage would be permitted, and he says:)

Thus wrote Rabbenu Tam in his responsum, and Moses of Coucy quotes it, that in times of great emergency marriage is permitted on Shabbat, but he, Rabbenu Tam, never declared this to be a rule which should be observed (literally, a decision leading to action, *halakhah l'ma'aseh*). So at least (Isserles continues) it is clear that, in a great emergency, we may permit such a marriage. There can be no greater emergency than this case in which a grown orphan girl was being put to shame. It would be a lifelong disgrace for her, enough to set her apart from all other girls. Great indeed is the commandment to be considerate of the honor of human beings. It sets aside the negative commandment (Deut. 17.11): *Turn not aside from all that they teach you* (i.e., the injunction not to ignore the ruling of the rabbis). After all, the prohibition (against marriage on Sabbath) is only a rabbinic decree to keep us from writing the marriage documents (*ketubah*), on the Sabbath, as is explained in our (the Babylonian) Talmud; or because such a marriage might be deemed to be the acquisition of a possession on the Sabbath, as explained in the Palestinian Talmud. (The statement in the Palestinian Talmud means that a man marrying a woman acquires the right to the profits from her weaving, etc.)

(Then Isserles goes on to show that there are a number of such rabbinic decrees which we no longer observe; for example, the decree against dancing, which was to guard against the chance of having to repair a broken musical instrument.) We permit dancing nowadays. So also (he says) nowadays no groom writes his own wedding document. The scribe writes it during the day, well ahead of time.

(After discussing these various ways in which old rabbinic restrictions were set aside under changed circumstances, he concludes as follows:)

But the truth is that the need of the hour leads us to be lenient in such matters which are only an additional prohibition of the rabbis. The rabbinical prohibitory decrees were not meant to apply in times of emergency, and on this we stand (literally, "On this I go down and on this I come up," a familiar talmudic phrase found in Pes. 87b). To be sure, one must be strict in urging people to be energetic (efficient) before the Sabbath, so that they should not have to face such an emergency. But when it has occurred, what can be done if the hour has moved along until darkness, and there is ground for concern that the match may be broken or the maiden put to shame? Under such circumstances, he who relies on the above arguments to be lenient has not lost (has not done harm). May he enjoy in peace the joy of the Sabbath thereafter. The good deed that he has done will atone for him, if his intention was for the sake of Heaven and of peace.

Thus sayeth Moses, the son of my father and teacher, Israel of blessed memory, the one called

Moses Isserles of Cracow

✡

21

TEFILLIN AND THE CABALA

Solomon (ben Yehiel) Luria (born in Brest-Litovsk, 1510; died in Lublin, 1573) was at one time rabbi in Brest-Litovsk. He later conducted a yeshiva in Ostrog and, still later, another in Lublin. He was a kinsman of Moses Isserles, with whom he carried on a voluminous correspondence, as can be seen from Isserles' responsa. Luria was opposed to Isserles' study of philosophy; but he was equally opposed to the Cabala, as the responsum to be cited will indicate. His best known works are *The Wisdom of Solomon* (critical notes on the Talmud), *The Sea of Solomon,* oft-quoted legal material following the various tractates, and his well-known responsa.

The responsum to be cited marks the beginning of a chapter in Jewish religious life. In the days of Isserles and Solomon Luria, the new cabalistic enthusiasm in the Palestinian city of Safed was beginning to spread over the Jewish world. The reputation of the leading cabalists of Safed, Ari (Isaac Luria) and Hayyim Vital, was changing the mood of Jewish life, first in the east, and now was beginning to penetrate into Poland, which was the greatest center of talmudic study.

The cabalists emphasized primarily the cosmic significance of every ritual act, seeking mysterious meanings for almost every prayer and ceremony. The question which came to Solomon Luria was from a friend who had heard and who apparently favored a new cabalistic idea that there is a secret significance to the *tefillin* which requires that the *tefillin* of the arm be put on while the worshiper is seated, and the *tefillin* of the head be put on while the worshiper is standing. Luria was not a stranger to cabalistic studies. In fact, both he and Isserles believed that the cabalistic classic, *Zohar* (The Book of Splendor), was actually what it claimed to be, a sacred book written by Simon ben Yohai, fourteen hundred years before. Nevertheless, though he believed that this cabalistic classic was sacred, he did not grant that it had any bearing on religious observance (on Halakhah), which must be based on the Talmud alone.

For all his learning and forthright rejection of the Cabala as a source for ritual observances, Solomon Luria did not succeed in stopping the flood of cabalistic influence. Within a century after his time, cabalistic prayers and cabalistic procedures penetrated deeply into the life of European Jewry. But the forthrightness of Luria's protest reveals the clear mind of the talmudist and his resistance to any claim of authority by any work other than the Talmud, even though he might grant that the new claimants represented a sanctified tradition. The responsum cited is no. 98.

TEXT

A response to my dear friend, the learned Mordecai son of Tanhun:

Question:

You asked me about my own custom: whether I put on the *tefillin* of the arm sitting or standing. You ask this because you saw many of those who are scrupulous with a trivial scrupulousness (a talmudic phrase, Er. 41b) putting on the *tefillin* of the arm only in a sitting position. Know, dear friend, that new people come and desire to be cabalists and interpreters of hidden things. But from the weakness of their vision, they cannot look at the radiance (of the sun) and do not know its rising and its setting. The reason (offered by) such a cabalist is that thus he found it stated in the books of Simon ben Yohai (the supposed 3rd-century author of the 12th-century cabalistic work, *The Book of Splendor*).

Answer:

Know thou, dear friend, that all my teachers and my sacred ancestors served (were disciples to) the great eminent teachers of the world. I have seen that they did not so conduct themselves (with regard to the *tefillin*), but that they followed the words of the Talmud and the *posekim* (the deciding scholars). Indeed, if Simon ben Yohai himself were to stand before us and ask us to change our ancient customs, we would pay no attention to him. For, in most of his opinions, the law is not according to him, as Joseph Caro wrote. The proof of it is that he (Simon ben Yohai) wrote great secrets and mystic injunctions that one should not recite two (different) blessings over the *tefillin* of the head and the hand. Yet we pay no attention to that, and we do recite two blessings. Furthermore, he wrote that he who puts on *tefillin* on half-holidays (*hol ha-moed*) deserves death; yet we do put them on and recite blessings over them. Although the people of Palestine do not put on *tefillin* at all on *hol ha-moed*, it was because Solomon ben Adret came and abolished the custom, in accordance with his opinion in which he follows the *tosafot*. So you see, it (the Palestinian custom) was not based upon the *Zohar*.

(Then Luria discusses the fact that the *Zohar* was known in past generations and yet no law was based upon it. He continues:)

Therefore open thine eyes and see. If there were anything real in this suggestion (to be seated when putting the *tefillin* on the arm, as the cabalist suggests), how is it possible that no author of the past has mentioned it, or that there is no hint of it in the Talmud? You have observed quite correctly that Joseph Caro, who cites many things from the *Zohar*, does not cite this matter (of the *tefillin*) at all.

(He then says that Simon ben Yohai meant to make a sharp distinction between the significance of the *tefillin* of the arm and the *tefillin* of the head. He continues:)

But we pay no attention to this. For both of them have a single meaning and constitute a single binding, except that one is in relation to the head and the other to the heart (he refers to the verse in Deuteronomy 6.8, that the *tefillin* shall be bound as a sign between a man's eyes and upon his arms. In other words, there is nothing mystical about it).

He who wants to preach (mystical) sermons about it, let him do so. But the truth points its own way. He who does not know how to find the true meaning will easily come to heretical action (literally, "to cut down the plants," a phrase used of the heretic, Elisha ben Abuya, Hag. 14b). Furthermore, I actually found in a collection of laws (i.e., the *Kol Bo*) that it is necessary to put on the *tefillin* standing up, for there is hardly a ceremonial action more sacred than this. Furthermore, the worshiper is like a servant standing before his master: he receives upon himself the seal of his service. There is no distinction made between the *tefillin* of the arm and the *tefillin* of the head; but it means clearly that he should stand up and receive (from his Master) the seal of His service. For the essential seal of the *tefillin* is upon the hand, as it is said, *As a seal upon thine arms* (Song of Songs 8.6).

Therefore, dear friend, go not on the road with them. Have no dealings with secret things and with those who boast of new notions as if they know and understand the secrets of the Torah and its hidden truth. I wish they knew the clear truths of the Torah. How noble was Samson of Chinon, who, after he learned the secrets of the Cabala, said that he still used to pray (as simply) as a newborn child. That is enough to understand the matter. Furthermore, I will tell you, I have received as a tradition from my great father-in-law, Rabbi Kalonymos of blessed memory, who received the tradition from Rabbi Daniel, who was the chief pupil of and who served Israel Isserlein, the author of *Terumat haDeshen,* and he saw that he (Israel Isserlein, the great 14th century German authority) conducted himself just as we do. Therefore, conduct yourself in your normal way. Let them do things in their way; but remember that whoever makes changes, his hand is below and our hand is above (a talmudic phrase from M. B. M. VI.2, used generally to mean that the burden of proof is upon the one who wants to make innovations).

22

MARRIAGE WITH FALASHAS

David ibn Zimri (Radbaz: born in Spain, 1479; died in Safed, 1589, at the great age of 110) was thirteen when his family was expelled from Spain. He studied first in Safed, in Palestine. Then he became a rabbinical judge in Cairo, Egypt, where he finally rose to be chief rabbi. He held this office for forty years, during which time he conducted a noted yeshiva at his own expense and, because of his vast learning and personal generosity, attracted a large group of students, many of them distinguished scholars. At the age of ninety, he retired from the rabbinate, distributed much of his fortune to the poor of Cairo, and moved to Jerusalem. There the Turkish governor imposed so heavy a tax on him that he moved to Safed, his boyhood home. He became one of the honored members of the *Bet Din,* the rabbinical court of Joseph Caro. His name is found signed first on some decisions found in Caro's collection, *Avkat Rokhel.* He wrote a number of works commenting on and defending the Code of Maimonides. He also wrote some cabalistic commentaries. His greatest work was his large collection of responsa, of which to date seven volumes have been published.

The responsum which we cite is of special interest because of the knowledge which it reveals about the Falashas. These black Jews of Abyssinia, according to their own tradition, came there with the Queen of Sheba in the time of King Solomon. Whatever the value of this tradition, the Falashas certainly are an ancient community. But little was heard of them until recent times. Among the few older references to the Falashas is this one in the responsa of David ibn Zimri. If anybody in the 16th century should have known about the Falashas, it would have been he, who was chief rabbi in Cairo for a lifetime and whose sources of information must have been excellent. Reports of travelers from far up the Nile must surely have reached him during his long stay in Egypt.

The social attitude of the responsum is worthy of note. It discusses the eligibility of a Falasha woman to marry a Jew. The question of her black skin (she is clearly called an "Ethiopian") does not enter into the discussion at all. The chief question revolves around her claim that she had been married and that her husband was killed. Is she to be believed and is she, therefore, now free to remarry? After that question is settled (in the negative, but purely on the merits of the case), David ibn Zimri discusses her status as a Falasha. He says that the Falashas are of the same status as the Karaites. Thereupon he discusses whether we may marry Karaites, a question that was vitally important in those day, especially in Egypt where the Karaites were numerous and influential.

The responsum is found twice in his published responsa—in vol. IV, no. 219, and almost identically in vol. VIII, no. 9.

TEXT

Question:

It happened that an Ethiopian woman from the land of Ethiopia, which is called Abyssinia (Al Habash), was captured with her two sons (and sold as a slave). Reuben bought her. We asked her what her status was (i.e., her marital status), and she said that she had been married and that these were her sons from her husband, whose name was X, "and this son of mine" (she said) "is named Y." Enemies attacked them (she said) and killed all the men that were in the house, but they took the women and the children as spoil. Now it is clear (the question continues) that they are of the seed of Israel, of the tribe of Dan, who dwell in the mountains of Abyssinia (and therefore Israelites). From that time on, we considered her an *agunah* (i.e., a "chained" Jewish woman who cannot prove that her husband is dead and therefore may not remarry). In the meantime her master, Reuben, had relations with her and begot a son from her. The son has grown up. He desires to marry a woman from the Jewish community and to be part of the community. Teach us, our teacher, whether or not he is eligible to come into the community (and, if he is not eligible), how he can be made so.

Answer:

We learn in the Mishna (Yeb. XV.1) that, if a woman has been overseas (or in foreign parts) and there is peace between her and her husband, but there is war in the world, and she comes back and says, "My husband died," she is not believed (see the more correct text in IV, no. 219). Maimonides, of blessed memory, says (she is not believed) even if she says, "I have buried him," because she is making that statement by guesswork (since so many people were killed in the war, she assumes that her husband, who has disappeared, has likewise been killed). They ask the question in the Talmud (Yeb. 114b): "Should we not believe her when she says that there was a war? For what would she gain by telling a lie on that score? She could easily have said there was peace in the world and he died on his deathbed, and she would be believed (and therefore, believing her, we should declare her free to remarry). Or should we say that she is guessing (about his death, and therefore not free her)?" This question is not clearly settled (i.e., whether to free her or not). Maimonides says about her, she should not marry; but that, if she does, she may remain married, and any child of hers from the new marriage is kosher (i.e., he is not illegitimate and may marry a Jew). Thus it would seem (in the case of this Falasha) that her child (from Reuben) is kosher and that we were erroneous when we considered her still married (to her Falasha husband, on the assumption that his death was not proved).

But after looking more deeply into the matter, I find that this

is not the case. There is a dispute (among the authorities) on
the state of the law (in such a case). For Asher ben Yehiel said
(in his compendium to the Talmud, *ad loc.*) that, since the question of the rabbis in the Talmud was not settled, we must be strict
in the matter (and assume that she is still married to her husband whose death is not proved). Hence if she *does* marry a second man, she must give up this marriage and the child is under
doubt of illegitimacy. And thus, too, writes Rabbi Jacob, his son
(i.e., Jacob ben Asher, in the *Tur,* "Eben haEzer" 17), namely,
"Since we do not know that there was actually a war except
through her statement and she says her husband died in that
(supposed) war, she is not believed. The Rambam, indeed, says
that such a woman, if married remains married; but my father,
Asher ben Yehiel, of blessed memory, did not say so."

(David ibn Zimri continues and describes the races and people
of Abyssinia in the following words:) And I say that even from
her own words she must be deemed to be still married (to her
Falasha husband), for it is well known that there is always war
going on between the various kings of Abyssinia, since there are
three kingdoms in it. Some of them are Mohammedans, some of
them Christians, and some Israelites of the tribe of Dan. It seems
that (these Israelites, the Falashas) belong to the sect of Zadok
and Boethus, the sect who are called Karaites. (Zadok and
Boethus are mentioned in Abot de-Rabbi Nathan V as the found-
ers of the Sadducees, who were taken to be the forerunners of
the Karaites.) For they only know a few of the commandments.
They do not know the Oral Law at all; and they do not kindle
lights on the Sabbath. War goes on continually among them
(among the three groups in Abyssinia) and they are always
taking captives from each other. . . .

> (Since he has said that the Falashas are equivalent to the
> Karaites, he discusses now whether the Karaites may be
> permitted to marry Israelites.)

Furthermore, there is a general reason for the rule that the
Karaites are to be deemed Israelites insofar as their marriages

are valid marriages. But their bills of divorcement are not according to the rules laid down by our rabbis because their witnesses are by the law of the Torah unfit for testimony.

(If their marriages are valid but their divorces are invalid, it can happen that women validly married may be invalidly divorced and then invalidly married to other men. In such cases, their children would be illegitimate; and illegitimate children may not marry into the Jewish community.)

But (he continues) there is great danger in this investigation because many of their families have already intermarried in our community. So I do not wish to speak lengthily on this matter; better that people should act innocently (rather than wilfully). At all events, I admit that if they (the Karaites) all agreed to enter into the community, making a promise of obedience to it (*haverut*) and to accept the tradition of our rabbis to be like us, I, with the agreement of the scholars, would permit them to enter our community.

(He gives a sequence of reasons why, in spite of the questionable status of their bills of divorce, there is only a very slight likelihood of much illegitimacy among them. He concludes this part of the responsum by saying:)

The sum of the matter is that, since the prohibition (to admit them) is not clear, if all of them would agree to return to us and accept *haverut* (i.e., comradeship, the willingness to obey Jewish Law), I would, with the agreement of my colleagues, permit them to enter our community. This would be like carrying "a chip from a large beam." (The phrase is from the Talmud, Hor. 3b, in which Rab Huna said that he always judged together with a group of colleagues, so that if a mistake were made, he would only bear a small portion of the guilt—a chip from a large beam.) And this is the language of *Kaftor vaFerah* (a work by a Spanish explorer of Palestine, Estori Farhi, 1282–1357) as follows: "It is clear that we must give credence to the validity of a marriage, if one of them (the Karaites) married a daughter of Israel. As is said of an Ethiopian who married and they considered the marriage valid enough to require a bill of divorcement, so with all such cases. Therefore, the leniency is its serious-ness (i.e., if we are lenient enough to admit them, we must take their marriage seriously). The Sadducees (the Karaites) are not increasing in our time, but many of them are becoming Jews, as happened at the end of the cycle of 267, when a great com-munity of them became Jews on one day in Egypt through the Nagid (the head of the Egyptian community) Rabbenu Abra-ham; and therefore, he who is strict (and considers these mar-riages valid) will be blessed."

(Then David ibn Zimri concludes:) This Nagid (Rabbenu Abraham) seems to me to have been the son of Maimonides; and he did not object, but received them into the community.

What seemeth right in my humble opinion, I have said.

David ibn Zimri

David ibn Zimri, therefore, classes the Falashas with the Karaites. They are of Jewish descent and may be accepted into the Jewish community. However, in this particular case with which he deals, the woman's Falasha husband was not proved to have been killed. Therefore she is still an *agunah,* chained to him. Her marriage to Reuben is, therefore, not valid and her son from this marriage is not legitimate.

23

THE LOST RESPONSUM

Elijah Mizrahi (1455–1525) mathematician and talmudist, was the leading rabbi of Constantinople at the end of the 15th century. His responsa were published in two volumes. In the first volume (Constantinople, 1546) a responsum (no. 66) was removed from almost all of the copies after the book had been printed. That something was left out was evident from the confusion in the pagination of the book. In the year 1897, Abraham Berliner found in the Hamburg Library a copy of Volume One which, by some chance, still contained the responsum which had been removed from the rest of the copies. He published it among the minor publications of the Mekitze Nirdamim Society (*Sammelband,* VII, 189).

The responsum deals with an accusation made in Candia (Crete) by Joseph Algazi, a refugee from Spain and a leader in one of the communities, to the effect that Elijah Mizrahi's son, Gershon, had been converted to Mohammedanism and had remained a convert for four years. Elijah Mizrahi denounces this charge as a libel against his son. This responsum evidently was omitted by the printers because they did not like to preserve even the record of such a suspicion against the son of one of the greatest rabbis of the time.

The responsum, however, is important as social history even if it is not a strictly legalistic one (although it does discuss the laws of slander). It offers a vivid picture of the exiles from Spain and Portugal streaming eastward to Turkey and Palestine, and of the efforts made by the older settlers in the Levant to organize means for their rescue and their support.

The responsum begins with a denunciation of Joseph Algazi, who made the accusation of apostasy against Gershon Mizrahi. Then it tells of the earlier relationship between Mizrahi and Algazi, namely, that Elijah Mizrahi had received a letter from Algazi asking for a recommendation which would authorize him to serve as leader or rabbi of his community. This, Elijah Mizrahi says he gave; but now Algazi has turned and slandered his (Mizrahi's) son.

TEXT

The decision which our teacher, Elijah Mizrahi, sent to Candia in behalf of his son, our teacher, Gershon.

The sound of *tumult stamping in thunder* (Isa. 9.4), *the sound of war in the camp of the Hebrews, the sound of answering* (Ex. 32.18), I hear from a man, an empty one, the son of an empty one, a penny in a bushelbasket making a great noise (a phrase from the Talmud, B. M. 85b), who has not studied Scripture nor Mishna. There came into his mind, with the little bit of medical practice he had, "to stride over the head of the holy people" (a phrase from Meg. 37b meaning, to become the leader of the community) and to rule over them. He sought to wear the *tallit* of scholars. All who know him testify that he never saw the lights (of the Torah) in his life and does not even know the appearance of the talmudic teaching, etc.

(Then follows a description of the ban that had been declared against Algazi by the scholars of Crete and by Elijah Capsali, the old rabbi of Constantinople. Having begun with this denunciation of Algazi, Elijah Mizrahi tells of a letter that he had once received from him, in which he said that some local people had slandered him, and he asked Mizrahi's help. Mizrahi then says:)

And I, in my simplicity, pitied him; for I said in my heart, how can it be that a stranger from a distant land, exile and fugitive (i.e., from Spain or Portugal), who comes for protection, should act as violently (as was alleged) against the local population? This accusation against Algazi evidently comes from the evil hearts of the inhabitants, for they are all laborers and have no knowledge of the Torah. Perhaps it is because he had rebuked them about keeping the Law. They did not accept his words, so that they mean now to shame him. At least, so I was told by Moses Kosro; but I did not know then that he was Algazi's father-in-law. I therefore accepted all his words and I wrote to the community that they must not treat him disrespectfully, but should accept his rebukes, since I thought that his rebukes were for the purpose of guiding them to fulfill the commandments . . .

When he received this writing (this letter of defense) from me, his heart grew lofty and he thought that now he dwelt on the high places of the earth and that there was no longer a God to judge, neither to punish the wicked nor to reward the righteous. He did whatever seemed right in his own eyes, and he did not remember all the kindnesses which I did him, namely, to rebuke a holy congregation in behalf of a stranger whom I did not know. He forgot all the vows which he vowed to me in the letter quoted above.

So it happened that when he noticed that the community gave honor to my first-born son, may God preserve him, he, in his pride, spoke contemptuously of this pious, modest man, this saint from the womb and conception, Rabbi Gershon Mizrahi, my first-born son, who has the birthright of Torah and good deeds, as is known to all the congregations of Constantina. Thus slander was brought against him, saying that this man (my son) had been converted (to Mohammedanism) and remained in his apostasy for four years in Puli (Apulia). Thus they made his face white in public with false slander, until ruddiness went and pallor came (a talmudic phrase from B. M. 58b, meaning extreme embarrassment over an insult). This must be counted as equal to bloodshed, as is found in the Talmud: "It was taught in the presence of Nahman bar Yitzhak; whoever makes the face of his comrade white with shame in public, it is as if he shed this blood, for behold we see that the redness flees and the pallor comes."

Thus they heaped words against him which are not true, meaning to debase the exalted and to ascribe blemishes to the sacred. By these deeds, therefore, they (i.e., Algazi and his friends) verify the accusations which the sages of Candia had written against them.

(Mizrahi enters into a more detailed description of the sin of slander, and he continues:)

And he (Algazi) did not remember all the honor that I had done him. It is not enough that he did not honor my first-born son, who deserved greater honor than the entire community, than all the rest of the community of whom he himself said they were ignoramuses. He should have remembered that I had done him more honor than his father or his teacher could have done to him. But on the contrary, he arose and slandered and mocked and shamed his (my son's) face in public. Nor did he have regard for my personal honor; whereas all the men of the Expulsion (from Spain and Portugal) received honor at my hand and I did them many favors, as they themselves will testify, both through my efforts—in that I took the trouble for a whole year to gather money, hundreds of florins, to redeem them; and I even got into great quarrels with congregations; and I gathered for them three or four times more than 3,000 florins, and I even put under the ban many rich men who did not wish to give what we asked of them—and through my own money which, as God knows, I expended in their behalf; or at the risk of my own life which I endangered from grief and anguish day and night; or at the expense of my intellectual work in that I neglected my studies for nearly a whole year in their behalf. If he (Algazi) did not care about all these things, why did he not worry about himself, since he knows the law of the sin of slander and its punishment? And if these things did not matter to him, why did he not consider the statement: "Thine own blemish do not ascribe to thy neighbor" (a phrase from the Talmud, B. M. 59b), for even if he was not the victim of the general conversion which overtook many of the exiles of Spain and Portugal, at all events he ought

to have remembered Moses Algazi (evidently his kinsman) who
was a provoking apostate, who violated the Sabbath in public
before the eyes of all Israel, even in the days when the congregations of Spain were still at peace, and was caught many times in
immorality and was rescued from the stake through the money
of his relatives. Yet now he wants to declare unworthy a sacred,
saintly man, imputing to him the same sort of unfitness as they
(his own family) possessed.

Why did he not show sensitiveness for the honor of his relatives and neighbors and friends over whom swept the great
apostasy of idolatry, of which sin it is said, "Let a man be slain
rather than violate" (Sanh. 74a), or the communities of Portugal
which were forced into idolatry? Yet in spite of all this, he stands
up now and mocks the saintly one (my son Gershon) in the
midst of the congregation; and he ignores the unfitness (im-
purity) by which they and their relatives and their neighbors and
their chiefs and their judges were touched. He imagines that because he lives far away, there is no one to speak of the imperfec-
tion of their families.

> (Mizrahi resumes the discussion of the sin of slander. Then
> he describes how shaky was the basis of the slander against
> his son.)

It is known that, in this case (of my son), there was never any
apostasy nor breath of apostasy. There was no deed or word
at all of that sort, but only some testimony to that effect by certain Mohammedans who lived in his house when he was sick.
They testified to the government that, when he was dangerously
sick, they asked him who would bury him, for there was no other
Jew at that time in the town except three merchants who had recently departed. The Mohammedans testified that he answered
them, *"You* attend to my funeral." They reported that they
answered him: "You are a Jew and we are Mohammedans, and
this is improper." Then they declared that he had said: "I am like
you." This is the text of the testimony which they gave against
him.

When he arose from the sickness which kept him in bed for
forty days (and was told what the Mohammedans had reported

that he had said), he cried out and wept before the princes and the king and said, "God forbid that I should say such a thing." But they did not hearken to him, for they said the testimony had already been recorded and they could not change it. Then this righteous man cried out and said, "Even if you claim that I had said, 'I am like you,' as they testified, at most these are just words of a man in dangerous sickness and they neither 'go up nor down' (i.e., are not to be taken seriously)." Then, in order to appease the king, that he might agree to wait until decisions on the matter came from their famous (Mohammedan) scholars in Constantinople, which was fifteen days' journey away, he expended more than 400 florins. Then they got the decision from their own scholars to the effect that they all agreed to free him (not to compel him to be a Mohammedan); for they said, "The words of a man so dangerously sick, who is asked about who will bury him, especially when they admit that he was out of his mind with his sickness, are of no worth." When the king saw these decrees, he was angry with his officers and servants who had agreed to wait for these decisions. He did not want to accept the decision (to free my son). As soon as my son saw that they were going to accept the testimony (of the Mohammedans against him), he asked permission to go to Angora, which was five days away from the city; but the king, fearing that he might flee, assigned one of his servants to go . . .

Here, in the middle of the story, the responsum ends. Evidently Gershon Mizrahi had succeeded in escaping, for when the responsum of his father was written, he was already safe in the Jewish community of Crete.

24

✡

POLYGAMY IN TURKEY

Samuel (ben Moses) di Medina (Rashdam: born in 1505; died in Salonika, 1589) was the head of the talmudical school in Salonika and there received numerous legal inquiries from many lands. In his time, the trickle of marranos eastward had become a flood. Because of the new immigrants, the whole nature of Jewish life in the Turkish empire was changing. The various inherited customs (*minhagim*), often differing considerably, came into head-on collision. He gave the various Turkish communities the firm guidance which they needed during this painful and quarrelsome period and thus led them to achieve a united Turkish Jewry. His responsa (which number 956 and were published in four parts) are therefore a remarkable reflection of the changing life in the Levant during the process of the gradual amalgamation of differing Jewish synagogues.

A full account of this changing historical scene, based completely on the responsa of Samuel di Medina, was made by Morris S. Goodblatt, in his book *Jewish Life in Turkey in the 16th Century* (Jewish Theological Seminary, New York, 1952). Since then another complete study has been made on the same theme, by Michael Molcho, in *Sinai*, vol. XL1, page 36, on the basis of the same collection of responsa.

The responsum to be cited here is of interest against this general background because it involves the clash between the religious customs of a German-Jewish settler in Turkey and those of the Sephardi settlers. The difference concerned a crucial matter, namely, whether the ban against polygamy issued by Rabbenu Gershom of Mainz (about the year 1000) applied to non-German Jews; also, whether it applied to German Jews wherever they lived; and whether the ban was still in force after all these centuries; and finally, whether, if the ban of Rabbenu Gershom against polygamy does not apply to non-German Jews, do his other bans apply to non-German Jews—for example, the one forbidding a man to divorce his wife against her will. More specifically, the question as it is presented in this responsum deals with the question of betrothal. Is betrothal deemed to be legal marriage; and does it therefore involve Rabbenu Gershom's ban against polygamy if a man is betrothed to one woman and then marries another?

While the Spanish-Portuguese Jews did not consider Gershom's ban against polygamy as applying to them, in actual practice polygamy was not frequent among the non-German Turkish Jew. It was, of course, always theoretically possible; but efforts were made to avoid it, chiefly by putting a clause in the marriage contract to the effect that the husband should not take a second wife without the consent of the present wife. The responsum is in *Eben haEzer* no. 78 (and is also given in Goodblatt, p. 169).

TEXT

Question:

It happened in the city of Sofia that a certain German Jew delegated Reuben to go to the city of Adrianople and there marry for him a certain woman suitable to him (Jewish Law permits marriage or betrothal by agents). This Reuben did. But when he returned to Sofia, he could not find the man who had sent him. When the man (namely, the German Jew) returned to Sofia, he expressed himself discontented with the woman (whom Reuben had betrothed for him in Adrianople). He then married another woman, the sister of his (deceased) wife. The people murmured

against him on the ground that he violated the decree of Rabbenu Gershom; for the relatives of the woman (from Adrianople) who had been first betrothed to him threatened to inform
against him to the government. They say that this action (of in-
forming) is permitted (normally a Jew may not be an informer
against another to the government) because he has violated the
decree of Rabbenu Gershom (and therefore is a sinner and may
be informed against).

Answer:

God knows that it is difficult for me to answer the questioner
in this matter, as I have said on a previous occasion. (I find it
difficult) for the reason expressed by Rabbenu Nissim in one of
his responsa as follows: "On this subject I would rather leave the
matter to the French (i.e., the Ashkenazi) scholars. They know
best how far the decree of Rabbenu Gershom has spread in their
lands and how they conducted themselves with regard to it and
how therefore it is proper (nowadays) to make decisions on the
basis of it." Now if Rabbenu Nissim, of blessed memory, uttered
these words, how can I, a fledgling whose eyes have not yet been
opened, pass judgment on this case? Nevertheless, in order to
satisfy the questioner who wishes to know my opinion, I have
decided to voice it and say what appears to me (right) on this
subject.

(Di Medina begins by proving that the woman who was
betrothed by the agent Reuben in Adrianople, although only
betrothed, is to be deemed a wife in the full sense of the
law.)

Clearly it appears that we should make no distinction between
betrothal (i.e., espousal) and marriage. Since people have taken
upon themselves (accepted) the decree of Rabbenu Gershom
against taking another wife in addition to the present one, and
follow the decree even nowadays (i.e., since people do not consider that it has lapsed as some authorities say it has), what
difference then is there (in this regard) between espousal and
marriage? The fact is that an espoused woman is called a wife,
which is the meaning of the verse in Scriptures, *If a man take a*

wife (Deut. 24.1). Also, Solomon ben Adret wrote in a responsum that, if a man in a bill of divorce written for the woman he has betrothed calls her his wife, it is a valid divorce. So also wrote Rabbi Israel (Isserlein, the great German authority) in his work *Terumat haDeshen*. Even though he ought to be careful in such a divorce (given to an espoused woman) to describe her as "my espoused one," nevertheless if he did describe her as "my wife," the bill of divorce is legal.

This being the case, since the decree of Rabbenu Gershom was that a man should not take a second wife while his first is alive, therefore, a man violates the decree if he marries a woman in addition to his espoused one. If so, it is clear that this man should be punished. Quite apart from the matter of the decree of Rabbenu Gershom, why should he make a mockery of the daughters of Israel? If he did not wish to marry her, he should have given her a divorce. Even so, she would then be, of course, ineligible to marry a kohen (a kohen may not marry a divorced woman). Why should this situation have arisen? If he says she does not please him, did he not bring this situation upon himself because he violated the words of the rabbis who said that it is preferable that a man arrange his own espousal and not do it through an agent? If so, he has sinned and he should suffer. As for this poor, unfortunate girl (in Adrianople), what was her sin?

Nevertheless, if you look more closely into the matter, you will see that that teacher made the right decision who said that he should not be punished because of the degree of Rabbenu Gershom. (Evidently another rabbi had already passed on this matter and now it was being brought to Di Medina on a sort of appeal.) The reason for this is that this decree is subject to a number of doubts. One doubt derives from the point of view of time, since there are many great scholars who say that Gershom meant his decree to last only to the end of the fifth millennium (i.e., 1240). Another doubt is due to the fact that perhaps he meant the decree to apply only in those lands (the Franco-German lands). Now, there is a possible answer to these doubts, namely, first, that the German Jews continue to hold on to that prohibition even today (i.e., as long as a decree is generally accepted, it remains valid) and also in all places (of their residence). Yet, in spite of these possible objections, the status of the decree is still not free of doubt, for it is possible to say that the Germans obey it now merely out of custom and not as a decree. Also, we must keep in mind what a certain scholar said, namely, that Rabbenu Gershom meant his decree to apply only to actual marriages (not to betrothals). Joseph Colon said (in section 101 near the end) that the decree applies only if he takes a wife in addition to a wife already married to him, but where he was not married (to the first one) and desires to change his mind, who can compel him to write her a marriage document (a *ketubah*)? So it is clear that we do not compel him to marry the betrothed.

Therefore (continues Di Medina) it is clear to me that, even though according to the law an espoused woman is called "a wife," this does not apply in our case because the decree of Rabbenu Gershom is not concerned with whether he has already an espoused woman (but only whether he has a wife). For we know as a general principle, in the case of oaths and vows, that we take into consideration the phraseology commonly used by people; and in the usual speech of people, marriage is different from espousal.

Now it seems to me from all of this that, as far as the law is concerned, we cannot compel him to divorce the second woman whom he had married, nor to marry the first whom he had espoused through the agent, for the decree of Rabbenu Gershom is still under double doubt: first, the doubt as to whether he had decreed it only up to the end of the fifth millennium, and second, the doubt as to whether he decreed it to apply to all places. Even if you say that he decreed it for all places and all time, it is nevertheless almost certain that he meant it to apply to actual marriage and not to espousal.

(He then concludes as follows:) Therefore it is clear that those who threaten to report him to the government are wicked slanderers.

However, I impose upon him (the German Jew) that he appease her (the betrothed) in every way until she accepts a divorce of her own free will. For thus wrote Rabbenu Nissim in his responsum. There is (either) a decree of the separate congregations or a decree of Rabbenu Gershom accepted in all Israel, namely, that it is forbidden to divorce a woman against her will. This (clause of Gershom's decree) certainly applies to all women, whether betrothed or married, since this prohibition is widespread in all of Israel. This is not true of Rabbenu Gershom's first decree against plural marriages. Therefore it is now necessary for him to win her consent (to the divorce).

What appears to my humble opinion, I have said. I, the young one,

Samuel di Medina

25

✡

NATIONALITY OF SYNAGOGUES

Moses di Trani (Hamabit) was born in Salonika in 1505. His father had fled from Apulia. He studied first in Adrianople and then, at the age of sixteen, moved to Safed where he studied under Jacob Berab. Later, in the year 1525, he was appointed rabbi in Safed. He was one of the four whom Jacob Berab ordained during the revival of ordination. Later in life he left Safed and lived in Jerusalem. His responsa are collected in three volumes, totaling 841 items.

The responsum which we will cite gives a clear picture of the wanderings of the Spanish Jews after the Expulsion and also of the Italian Jews, who likewise began to feel the heavy hand of persecution in those days. It was an age of refugees, and therefore an age of immigrant communities in which there were separate congregations for the various nationalities. As time went on, the separate nationality congregations tried to attain some measure of cooperation. In this case an agreement was made as to which congregations newer immigrants might be allowed to join. Many Spanish Jews had fled first to Italy, lived there for a generation or two; and then, when life in Italy became difficult, they fled across the Adriatic. Were these new immigrants into Turkey to be considered Spaniards or Italians? Which synagogue might they join?

These first attempts at mutual accommodation, or mutual protection between the various nationality congregations, must have occurred all over the Levant. It is interesting to note that almost precisely the same question was asked of Rabbi David Cohen of Corfu, who lived about the same time. The question addressed to him involved various subdivisions of Italian Jews and concerned the right of the separate members to move from one Italian congregation to another. The question sent to David Cohen of Corfu begins as follows (it is responsum no. 11):

"In the city of Arta (on the Turkish side of the Adriatic) there settled four congregations, Corfuans, Sicilians, Calabrese, and Fuosans. Every congregation had its own synagogue following its local customs which the people had observed in their original homes. Now the congregation of the Calabrese agreed, in the presence of their community heads, that no one of their members should be permitted to leave the congregation and go and pray in another."

The question here asked of Moses di Trani concerned chiefly Spanish Jews who had become Italianized. The responsum is in vol. I, no. 307. The congregation is not identified, but judging by the fact that most of the immigrants were Italians, it must be one of the congregations on the Turkish side of the Adriatic.

TEXT

Question:

The congregations of a certain city agreed among themselves that anyone who shall immigrate to that city, if he and his father were born in Italy, even though his grandfather had come from Portugal or Castile or Aragon or any other kingdom, must join the congregation of the Italians; but if his father was born in any one of the abovementioned Spanish kingdoms, then even though he himself was born in Italy, he can only go to the congregation which speaks the language of his kingdom (i.e., of his father's nativity). And so with regard to the other languages.

Now, at the time when they made this new agreement, the

members of the congregation of Aragon protested, saying, "It is not just that one who is known to be an Aragonese, or from any other Spanish kingdom, should go to worship with the Italians, just because he and his father were born in Italy." (Evidently two generations in Italy were not enough to make the proud Spaniards give up their Spanish consciousness.) Furthermore, they argued that one of the congregations made a (private) compromise with the Italian congregation before the general agreement, namely, that if there do come from Italy men (of Spanish origin) who themselves and their fathers were born in Italy, the Italian congregation should not force these immigrants to join it. Because this compromise was allowed them, namely, not to be subjected to the general agreement, they publicly accepted the general agreement because, had they publicly protested, it was obvious that no such agreement among the leaders of the various congregations could be made at all. Teach us, our master, whether the members of the Aragon congregation must now abide by this agreement or not (since they protested against it).

Answer:

All that passage in the Talmud (B. B. 8b) to the effect that the members of the city can impose penalties to enforce their decisions, is quoted by Mordecai in the first chapter of Baba Batra, where he cites the opinion of Rabbenu Tam and others to the effect that it is only when originally the members of the community had agreed, that the community can enforce its rules upon one who holds back from obeying them. But if they did not all agree from the very beginning, then the community cannot coerce anyone who refuses to do what they wish. Especially is this true when there is profit for one and loss to the other (i.e., if the agreement is not of mutual and fairly equal advantage) and if they do not all agree at the time when the agreement is made. Joseph Colon discusses this matter at length in his responsa nos. 141 and 148. This applies (that all must agree initially) even when it involves the doing of a *mitzvah,* and all the more (does it need unanimous consent) in the case of a separate congregation, which is a community and a court by itself. No other congregations can force it to fulfill the agreement, since they did not feel satisfied with it from the very beginning. So David Cohen of Corfu says in section no. 14.

Here in our case the Aragonese are a congregation and a court of their own and, besides, they could suffer a loss in this matter, for if one of their tongue who was born in Italy, and his father too had (come to the city), and because of this agreement would have to go to the Italian congregation, then consider that they (the Aragonese) stand to lose what he would contribute to charity for the poor of their congregation and money to support the school, and similar *mitzvot* which are maintained by the congregation in which a man prays. No other congregations have the right to a portion of these gifts. The Italian congregation would thus have (an unfair) profit because of this agreement. Now, do not say that now (if the Aragonese are not compelled to agree) it would be a loss to the Italian congregation, for this immigrant would now join their congregation; for consider that, if it were not for this agreement, he would never think of joining their congregation since he speaks another language, even though he and his father were born in Italy. Hence, if this agreement were to stand, it would result in benefit to the Italian congregation and loss to the Aragonese congregation. Hence, since the Aragonese congregation was not satisfied with this agreement from the beginning—on the contrary, they protested against it—they cannot be compelled to maintain it.

Now, you cannot say that the Italian congregation may sometimes also lose from the agreement. If, for example, some Italian were to come, whose father and he were born, too, in another land, and under the agreement he had to go to that other congregation, I must say that this theoretical loss is not comparable to the loss to the Aragonese congregation. For, if, for example, this Italian, he and his father, were born in Germany, the Aragonese congregation would have no loss and no benefit. The loss and the benefit would be between the Italian and the German congregations. But as for such balanced losses and gains between the Italian congregation and the Aragonese congregation, it is well known that there would never come to this city any Italian family who moved to Aragon, and a man and his father were born there. For there have been no Jews in Aragon for seventy years now and we are confident that no Jew will ever live there any more. For God, blessed be He, will soon gather the scattered ones of His people Israel into the Land of Israel.

> (So Trani continues and shows that the agreement is one-sided. It benefits the Italians more than anyone else. Besides, it was not agreed to in the first place; and so it is void. He ends as follows:)

If so, this agreement is void as far as the congregation of Aragon is concerned and there is no power in the hands of the other congregations to force them to fulfill it. Therefore, whoever shall come from Italy, even though he and his father were born there, nevertheless, if his family came from Aragon, he is called Aragonese by his language and he shall join the Aragonese congregation—as is the custom, that each immigrant goes to the congregation of the people that speak his language, and not to another.

Sayeth

Hamabit

26

✡

KADDISH FOR A CHRISTIAN
FATHER

David (ben Hayyim) haKohen (Radak) was rabbi in Corfu
and then in Patras, Greece, at the beginning of the 16th century.
He was a pupil of Judah Minz of Padua and a contemporary of
Elijah Mizrahi of Constantinople. His final rabbinate was in
Adrianople. His many responsa were lost in a fire, only thirty-
three being left. These have been published and republished a
number of times. The responsum cited reveals the state of mind
of many of the early marranos, the repeated attempts that many
of them made to get safely away from Spain to lands where they
could resume the Jewish faith. This responsum deals with the
following question: A marrano tried a number of times to escape.
On his final attempt he was murdered. His son, who was suc-
cessful in escaping, asks Rabbi David haKohen whether he may
say *kaddish* for his father who was still an apostate when he died.
This is, of course, far different from the responsum of Maharil of
Mainz, cited on page 84. There the question was whether
kaddish need be said for Jewish martyrs: are they not too holy to
need such efforts at their redemption? Here the question is, do
apostates deserve the honor and the benefit of the *kaddish?* The
responsum cited is no. 30.

TEXT

Question:

The question concerns one of the apostates who left the religion of Israel for idolatry (literally, for the worship of Baal) because of the decree of the government of those days which decreed that the Jews change from the religion of Israel to the religion of Baal. This apostate was murdered on the road by robbers, who *gave his flesh to the birds of the heaven and the beasts of the field*. Now the son of this apostate is a Jew. He desires to say *kaddish* for the repose of the soul of his father. There are other mourners (present in the synagogue) whose fathers died as Jews. Do they have precedence in saying the *kaddish* (i.e., the privilege of saying the *kaddish* at the reading-desk)? Or shall we say that, although this mourner's father was slain while an apostate, he has to say *kaddish* on the same basis as these others?

Answer:

I dislike to make decisions (literally, I am one of those who fear decision, a frequent phrase of self-deprecation in the responsa). Nevertheless, in my humble opinion, at a quick glance, it would seem that this matter does not require a scholar to decide it (a phrase from B. M. 101a). Certainly this mourner, too, whose father was slain while an apostate, must say *kaddish* like one of the other mourners, on the basis of the talmudic principle (Sanh. 44a) that, even though he has sinned, a Jew is still a Jew and, as people say in a popular proverb (still quoting the Talmud): "A myrtle among the brambles is a myrtle and is called a myrtle"; and remember that Akhan (Josh. 7) transgressed against the entire Torah, and even so they called him an Israelite. Although I can expatiate on this principle, there is not time. Therefore I will deal with the matter briefly and say that a son may earn merit for his father as is mentioned in the Talmud (Sanh. 104a).

Even though the father is an apostate to idolatry and even though in the Talmud (Sanh. 112b) we are told, with regard to a city that must be destroyed because it has gone astray to idolatry, that if there are sacrificial animals in it dedicated to the altar, they too must die, we do not (in the case of such a city) say, "Let these animals graze until they get too old (for sacrifice) and then let them be sold and the money be used for charity." We do not say that (but we destroy the sacrificial animals) because *the sacrifice of the wicked is an abomination to the Lord* (Prov. 21.27), even though now they have been changed (by growing overaged). Then, even if one would say (on the basis of the above) that the son must not earn merit for his apostate father and say *kaddish* for him because *the sacrifice of the wicked is an abomination to the Lord,* therefore the *kaddish* will do him no good. Such arguing is not sound; for we learn in the Tosefta, and it is cited in the Talmud in many places (e.g., Pes. 56a) that Hezekiah, King of Judah, dragged the bones of (Ahaz) his father (who was wicked) and the rabbis praised him, for it is said (Sanh. 47a) that the reason that Hezekiah dragged the bones of his father (to the grave) was in order that his (wicked) father should have atonement.

Clearly, then, a son should do all he can to earn merit for his father, even though the father was a provocative apostate. For Ahaz (father of Hezekiah) was provocatively an idolator and did all the evil things which God hates. Nevertheless, his son Hezekiah dragged his bones (to the grave) in order that he should have atonement, and for this the rabbis praised him. If this would not have done Ahaz any good, Hezekiah would not have done so and the rabbis would not have praised him.

(David haKohen now mentions other possible grounds of objection to saying *kaddish* for an apostate. One is that *kaddish* is more than earning merit for the deceased. It is also doing him *honor,* and such a man should not be honored. Then he discusses the fact that the Talmud denounces especially those apostates who eat forbidden foods, and the apostates in Spain and Portugal certainly did eat such foods. He refutes all these possible objections. As for the last objection, the eating of forbidden food, which of course could not be denied, he makes a distinction between sins that are done provocatively [*l'hakh'is*] and sins which are done merely for one's benefit [*l'teavon*]. The latter motivation is, of course, less blameworthy.)

As for the fact that they remained there (in Spain and Portugal) and did not flee, it is for their benefit that they stay there (it is not done provocatively against Judaism). If they appear to serve Baal, it is under compulsion, that they be not slain. Thus, of course, they transgress against the commandment, *I shall be sanctified amidst the children of Israel* (Lev. 22.32) which requires that they should choose rather to be slain or else escape. So they are apostates in this matter for their benefit (not provocatively), just as that old woman and her two daughters that were captured and left their land and goods and all of Israel and were married to idolators (B. M. 39b). It was asked of Asher ben Yehiel of blessed memory, whether we judge such people as apostates who eat forbidden things provocatively; and he answered that these are to be looked upon as those who have been forcibly captured by the idolators and all that they do is for their benefit (for survival, and not for wilful provocation).

All the more is this so with regard to this apostate who, as I have heard, was slain. He had come as far as Arta (on the Adriatic coast of Turkey) to return to Judaism and was robbed on the road and lost all his money and therefore returned for a while to the kingdom (of Portugal) and earned some more money. Then he was on the way back here, to come to Arta, and on this journey robbers seized him, took all that he had to return there. So there is reason for our belief that this poor man did not stay there (in Portugal, to provoke), but for his benefit. But his intention was to return to Arta to become a Jew. Clearly he is no worse than those Jewish apostates from whom we accept sacrifices, as the Talmud says (Hul. 5a). Furthermore, when he was slain he achieved atonement. So it is proper that his son should say *kaddish* for him as one of the other mourners. May God remove from us the stench of the locust (based on Joel 2.20) and send our Messiah and deliver us from error. Amen.

Sayeth he who is burdened with the burdens of these confused times,

David, the son of Hayyim the Kohen of blessed memory

27

✡

HELPING A NEIGHBORING
COMMUNITY

Meir ben Gedaliah Lublin (Maharam: born in Lublin, 1558; died there, 1616) was rabbi in Cracow at the age of thirty. He left Cracow for Lemberg and finally became rabbi in Lublin. Wherever he settled, he established yeshivot. He wrote novellae on the Talmud which are printed in all standard Talmud editions. He received questions from Italy and from Turkey, as well as from northern Europe. The responsum which we cite gives a picture of disturbances in eastern Europe in his time. The Jews of Silesia were threatened with expulsion. They had to promise vast sums of money to stave off the threat. The city of Sülz in Silesia managed, with the help of the Jewry of Poland and Bohemia, to be allowed to remain. The problem was whether the city of Hotzenplotz was in duty bound to help pay the money which the community of Sülz had promised. This is precisely the question which had occurred 200 years earlier when the towns around Regensburg asked whether they were in duty bound to help Regensburg in a similar way. Joseph Colon of Italy said it was their duty to do so, and his opinion is quoted here by Meir Lublin. The responsum is no. 40.

TEXT

Question:

I was asked by the two households of Israel, the brothers of our Covenant, the inhabitants of the sacred congregation of Hotzenplotz and the sacred congregation of Sülz, whose noble spirit impelled them to agree and come before our court with regard to the matter that happened to them some time ago. The decree of the emperor was issued and sealed as an irrevocable imperial decree, that all the Jews who dwelt in all the provinces of Silesia should be expelled from the country (decree of Rudolph II, 1582). When this decree was carried out and many congregations were exiled, there were left only the inhabitants of the congregation of Sülz. Because of their great efforts and much expenditure, with which they appeased their enemy with "appeasements of silver," they postponed the expulsion from day to day.

Then the Lord awakened the spirits of the leaders of the congregation of Prague who, with great effort, had the decree withdrawn from the inhabitants of the community of Sülz. They appeased the enemy with the sum of 2,000 gold pieces. To gather this sum, various provinces volunteered to help their brothers of the community of Sülz; namely, the three lands of Poland volunteered to give one-fifth of the 2,000 gold pieces, and so the provinces of Bohemia and the provinces of Moravia volunteered each to give one-fifth of the total. The remaining two-fifths of the sum were imposed upon the community of Sülz together with the community of Hotzenplotz.

Now each of these two communities has chosen delegates who have come before us for me to study the case and to decide whether the community of Hotzenplotz is in duty bound to share the yoke of the expenses incurred by the community of Sülz in the matter of this expulsion. If they are in duty bound by law, they ask us then to apportion, according to our judgment, how much money they should give for this purpose. Long arguments have been made on the question of whether they really belong with Silesia or not.

Answer:

We have discovered a foundation upon which to build our decision. It is in the responsa of Joseph Colon (no. 4). This sage had already decided on a matter similar to this with regard to the congregation of Regensburg, and all the nearby communities. It is fairly certain that the same *cup of confusion* (Isa. 51.22) will be passed to them if the matter is not settled in some way. The law is that they have to share the yoke, even though for the present they have not yet been subject to the same accusations as the other places have been. He (Joseph Colon) brings his proof from the discussion in the Talmud (B. M. 108a, where it is made clear that those who live at the lower reaches of the river are in duty bound to help those who live at its headwaters to clean up the river-sources).

On the basis of all the above, we find that each of the two abovementioned congregations has relationship with the other and is in duty bound to help and to bear the yoke if such a thing were to occur again, God forbid. On the basis of this, we decide that the congregation of Hotzenplotz is in duty bound to help defray the expenses of this threatened expulsion of its brothers, the community of Sülz, with 200 gold pieces, one-half of the fifth which the three Polish lands are giving. When they have paid this sum, they will be free of all further responsibilities of sharing in the payments which have already been made by the congregation of Sülz. They only have responsibility to share in paying these last 2,000 of which they must give one-half of one-fifth.

As for the future, we decide that if there should occur similar happenings (God forbid) to the community of Hotzenplotz, the community of Sülz must bear the burden with their brothers and must help them in all efforts as much as they can afford at that time and as much as shall be decided by the judges (i.e., the rabbinical judges) who shall be in those days. Thus do we speak on behalf of truth and peace and justice.

Sayeth

Meir, the young one . . .

28

DOÑA GRACIA'S INHERITANCE

Joseph ibn Lev (born in Monastir; died *ca.* 1600) was rabbi in Salonika in 1540. Because of the outbreak of the plague, he left there and settled in Constantinople for the rest of his life. He was one of the many beneficiaries of the greatest philanthropist of that age, Doña Gracia Mendes. Doña Gracia, whose husband, Francisco Mendes, had died in Portugal, escaped with her brother-in-law and her niece to Antwerp. Then she went to Ferrara in Italy and thence to Venice. Finally she came to Constantinople. She had saved much of the vast banking fortune which her husband had acquired, and in the Turkish empire she and her nephew, Joseph Nasi (later Duke of Naxos) became merchant-princes. She supported the yeshiva and many scholars. She led in the great boycott against the port of Ancona. She rescued innumerable fellow-marranos and helped them to come to new homes where they could resume the faith of their fathers.

The Mendes family was torn by a dispute over the estate left by Doña Gracia's husband, Francisco, who died childless. Doña Gracia's sister said that Francisco had willed half of his estate to her husband, his brother Diogo, and it was this half that the sister and her daughter now demanded. Doña Gracia claimed, however, that she and her husband had been married as Christians under Portuguese law, under which the widow gets half of the estate, two-thirds of the remaining half going to the orphans, and the rest being divided among other legatees. The question for the rabbis of Constantinople to decide was this: Did Jewish Law recognize the validity of a marriage contract made by marranos under Portuguese law? If it did not, then Francisco's gift of half his estate to his brother Diogo was valid. But if the Portuguese marriage contract and inheritance were recognized by Jewish Law in this case, then Doña Gracia was entitled to keep the entire estate which she now controlled.

The rabbis who dealt with the case all decided in favor of Doña Gracia and so did Joseph ibn Lev in his famous responsum on the subject. No names are mentioned in the responsum, as was generally the case in responsa, but there is no question as to the identity of the parties. The responsum is in vol. II, no. 23.

TEXT

Question:

Teach us, our teacher (what the law is in the following case). In the Kingdom of Portugal there is a law and a custom that the widow has the right to half of the estate which the husband leaves, whether or not she brought in much or little with her dowry. There is ground to doubt that Jewish Law supports this because the estate was something that did not exist (at the time of the marriage contract; Jewish Law denies in most cases the right to make a contract over something that does not yet exist, literally, "that which has not yet come into the world"). Also there was no formal symbolic ceremony of taking possession (in Jewish contracts, some object is exchanged as symbolic of binding the contract; this is called "receiving possession"). Even though letters were written affirming this contract in the Gentile courts (in Portugal); besides, (this sort of marriage contract) is the general rule among them. Now these Jews (i.e., the husbands) died in that kingdom and their widows and heirs came to Turkey to seek shelter under the wings of the Divine Presence (the *Shekhina,* i.e., to become Jews again). Teach us, O righteous teacher, if these widows are entitled to half of the estate according to the custom of the place in which they were married.

Or should we only give them the amount of the dowry that they brought to their husband.

Answer:

It seems to me that everything points in one direction (literally, "all faces are equal") and there is no doubt at all that the widow has the right to half the estate. There is no question, of course, if she already has possession of it, that we do not take it away from her; but even if the estate were now in the hands of other heirs, we would take it from their hands to give half of the estate to the widow, as is the custom of that kingdom. Such cases come up in Salonika frequently and we have never seen anybody who objected to this at all, namely, that the widow should have half the estate.

Of course, it is clear that if there were between them (the widow and the husband in the marriage contract) only a private agreement, when they married, to divide the estate (half and half) between the widow and the other heirs, then this would certainly involve a dispute among the great scholars. For Maimonides wrote in chapter IV (no. 2) of the "Laws of Partnership" that, if partners or workingmen join together in an enterprise, even though there is the formality of acquisition (the symbolic transfer) they are not true partners. (Because partnership means actual investment of money before the partnership begins, only the actual existence of material or finished goods before the partnership between workingmen can be considered a true partnership. The mere verbal agreement without actual investment is no true partnership.) And Nahmanides agrees with him, as Jacob ben Asher states.

(Joseph ibn Lev mentions all the great scholars who disagree with Maimonides and say that it *is* legal for two men to make a condition with each other for the disposal of material or profits that are not yet in existence; just as a servant can contract to produce that which is not yet in existence, because he transfers control of his *person* which will work and create. Thus those who disagree with Maimonides say that two workingmen can contract control of each other's person and therefore of their productivity, and thus their agreement can be valid even though it calls for division of things that have not yet come into existence. After describing this disagreement between Maimonides, and those who follow him, and Abraham ben David and the *tosafot* and Asher ben Yehiel, and all who follow them, he proves from Joseph Colon of Pavia that the disagreement is not absolute. The disagreement concerns partnerships between two individuals; but if *all* the workmen of a city agreed to a sort of partnership, Maimonides would likewise say that such an agreement, even though without investment, was valid. He continues:)

Joseph Colon said: "It seems to me that the Rambam would agree that, if all the workmen of the city were to agree to work in partnership, their agreement would stand without any symbolic acquisition, and not one of them could withdraw from this agreement, because the power of the majority is strong. For Maimonides does not disagree with the other scholars except with regard to two individual would-be partners, but where the workmen of the city agree to join hands, he admits that they may do so and that the conditions that they make are valid."

Since this is so (that a widespread agreement is possible, then a widespread custom is equivalent to a widespread agreement), therefore whoever marries a woman without specifying (i.e., the exact division of the property), then because of the widespread custom which exists, she must divide the property with the heirs according to the custom (i.e., half and half).

(Then Joseph ibn Lev shows that Maimonides himself agrees that the general custom determines all such contracts. He now quotes Maimonides:)

Thus wrote Maimonides in chapter XXIII of the "Laws of Marriage": "There are many customs with regard to dowry. There are places where they write in the marriage contract more than the exact amount of the dowry by a third or a fifth or a half, etc. Whoever marries without specifying (the amount) writes the contract according to the custom of the country. Similarly what she agrees to bring into the marriage, she brings according to the custom of the country. Then when she comes to collect, she collects what is in her *ketubah* according to the custom of her country. In all these marriage contracts and their like, the custom of the country is a great principle by which we judge, provided of course it is a widespread custom in the entire country." Thus far the words of Maimonides.

(And Joseph ibn Lev quotes Isaac bar Sheshet to the same effect, that the custom, even if not widespread, is determinative in all these matters. He concludes as follows:)

From all these opinions, the matter now is clear. If this custom (of the wife getting half) were prevalent only in one part of our land, it would still override the general law (the Halakhah). All the more so, then, when in that kingdom they all follow this custom (of the wife getting half) is it a widespread and firm custom in all the province. Now, the husband died in that kingdom where this custom prevails and after that his widow and his heirs came to Turkey to shelter under the wings of the Divine Presence. So it is obvious. We do not even need to question the fact that, if the widow is already in possession of half of the property, we do not take it from her hands. But even if *all* the property were in possession (of the other heirs) we would take it from them and give the widow her portion according to the law and the custom of those kingdoms. Such cases have already come to my hand many times in Salonika. Thus I have judged and I never heard and I never saw any one disagree. That is all (that needs be said).

Sayeth the young one,

Joseph ibn Lev

29

✡

CHURCH MELODIES IN THE SYNAGOGUE

Joel Sirkes (born in Lublin, Poland, 1561; died in Cracow, 1640) served as rabbi in a number of different cities and was finally rabbi in Cracow. He was one of the foremost Polish authorities of the 16th century, and as such was asked to discuss a question arising from the influence of the Renaissance on European Jews: the matter of Church music in the Synagogue.

The Jews of Italy were greatly influenced by the Renaissance, and even their Jewish religious life was affected by that influence. They spoke Italian; they wrote Italian; they were in constant contact with Christians, and even their public worship was somewhat affected by the artistic mood of their environment. Hence the various discussions in the Italian responsa about modern choirs and modern forms of music in the Synagogue.

The Polish Jews, however, would seem to have been far from these cultural influences. First of all, the Renaissance did not spread into Christian Poland, and therefore into the lives of the Jews. It is, therefore, surprising to learn that non-Jewish melodies, some of them actually Church melodies, did find their way into the synagogues of Poland. This can be seen from the fact that Joel Sirkes, in his discussion, comes to an interesting conclusion as to which Christian melodies may be permitted in the synagogue.

Sirkes' greatest work was his commentary on the *Tur,* the Code of Jacob ben Asher. This he called *The New House.* Possibly because the great Sephardi commentary by Joseph Caro was called *The House of Joseph.* Because of the initials of its title "*B*ait *H*adash" (The New House), Joel Sirkes is hardly ever referred to by his own name, but as the "BaH," the *h* being hard. He also wrote two volumes of responsa. This responsum on Christian music in the Synagogue comes from vol. I, no. 127, and is the last part of the responsum.

TEXT

As for the fact that they sing in the synagogues the melodies that are sung in the churches, it seems to me that one can only prohibit such melodies as are specifically part of the worship (i.e., traditionally or characteristically part of the Christian ritual), since such melodies have become regularly part of the ritual. This case is just like that of the *matzeva* (the stone pillar) which was prohibited everywhere because the Canaanites made it a part of their idolatry.

(This is a reference to the fact that, although the patriarchs are described as putting up stone pillars [*matzevot*], nevertheless the book of Deuteronomy, 16.22, says: *Thou shalt not set up a Matzeva, which the Lord your God hateth.* This commandment needed explanation. How could the patriarchs [Gen. 28.18,22] have put up *matzevot* when such are hateful to God? This is explained in Sifre to Deuteronomy no. 146, and elaborated on by Rashi in his commentary to this verse—namely, that originally these *matzevot* were beloved by the patriarchs; but once the idolators had adopted them as a part of their worship, they became hateful. Thus, Sirkes says, whatever is actually a part of Christian worship should not be part of the Synagogue worship. Then, because it was possible to argue that, in spite of the fact that these melodies are Christian, they were, or might well have been, originally Jewish, and may therefore be used, he continues as follows:)

Now no proof can be adduced (to permit use of such melodies as are part of their worship) from the statement in the Mishna, Sanhedrin 7.3, which discusses the four modes of execution followed by the court. The Mishna says that beheading was done with a sword "just as the (Roman) government does." In the Talmud, Rabbi Judah explains that, because of the law against following the statutes of the Gentiles, we should not execute criminals the way the Roman government does. To which the rabbis say, since the Bible itself speaks of this method, we are not imitating the Romans whenever we use the sword, for "not from them have we learned it." On the same basis (continues Sirkes), one might argue that the principle applies also to those melodies (which have become a regular and characteristic part of Christian worship), namely, "that we did not learn it from them," but from the art of music; and (the arguer would continue) that we cannot be as strict as Rabbi Judah who would prohibit anything that is Gentile custom, for the law is according to the *rabbis;* and therefore he (the arguer) would say that even those melodies which have become a characteristic part of the worship are usable because, as the rabbis said with regard to the use of the sword in execution: "We did not learn it from them." This argument (says Sirkes) is no real proof, as we see from the *tosafot,* whose comment to that place in the Talmud, namely, Sanhedrin 52b, takes up exactly this question. It says that if it has become a custom among the pagans, then even if it is written in the Torah, that fact no longer matters and we cannot follow the biblical custom. So (concludes Sirkes) it is with these melodies. But, if they are not characteristic (of Christian worship), it appears that there is no prohibition against using them, for in this case we can surely say, "Not from them did we learn them."

See also the next chapter, the responsum on music in the Synagogue by the Italian rabbi, Judah Leon of Modena.

30

JEWS AND MUSIC

Judah Leon of Modena (born in Venice, 1571; died there, 1648) was a descendant of a distinguished French-Jewish family. His grandfather, Mordecai, a physician, was awarded the knighthood of the Golden Fleece by Charles V. Judah Leon was given a typical Renaissance education by his wealthy father; his studies included singing and dancing. At the age of twelve, he translated the first canto of Oriosto's *Orlando Furioso* from Italian into Hebrew verse. At the age of fourteen, he wrote a booklet denouncing gambling. The booklet was translated into a number of languages.

Judah Leon's life was dogged by misfortunes. His father lost his wealth and Judah was compelled to become a teacher. His own family life was tragic: two sons and one daughter died young; his wife became insane. He himself was plagued by the besetting sin of gambling, which he had denounced so eloquently in his youthful book. In spite of all his difficulties, he wrote many works. He became one of the rabbinical board of Venice and was so famous a preacher that priests and noblemen flocked to hear him.

He was not outstanding as a legal authority. In fact, the collection of his responsa remained in manuscript until published in the year 1957 by Solomon Simonson. However, at least two of his responsa were well known. One was directed against the *herem* (anathema) issued by the rabbinate of Venice against all forms of gambling. This responsum demonstrated that the decree was not in accordance with Jewish Law; it is published in the famous talmudic encyclopedia, *Pahad Yitzhak,* written in the 18th century by Isaac Lampronti of Ferrara. Another famous responsum dealt with the question of music, as to whether or not it is wrong for Jews to sing and to play musical instruments. Some scholars had insisted, on the basis of certain talmudic statements, that from the time of the destruction of the Temple, Jews had no right to indulge themselves in any music at all. Modena's responsum refuting this somber point of view was published as an introduction to the book of synagogue songs by the noted Jewish pioneer of Italian music, Solomon dei Rossi. It is this responsum, now found of course in the new edition of his responsa (*Zikne Yehudah,* no. 6), which we cite here.

TEXT

Question:

We have among us some who know the art of music. Six or seven knowledgeable young men of our congregation lift up their voices in the synagogue on holidays and festivals and chant the songs and praises "Ein Kelohenu," "Alenu," "Yigdal," "Adon Olam," and the like, to honor the Lord by orderly arrangement of the voices in accordance with the musical art (i.e., in harmony). There arose a man to drive them out with the speech of his lips. He said that it is not proper to do so, for, since the Temple was destroyed, rejoicing is forbidden, songs are forbidden, and even praise of God through singing is forbidden. (They are forbidden) because of the verse: *Rejoice not, O Israel, among the nations* (Hos. 9.1). He made of these singers a mockery in the eyes of the multitude who heard their voice, even though most of them were learned in the Torah. Now let the "royal" word come forth from the teachers of the Torah as to whether there is any prohibition in the matter, whether the voice of the objector is right, or the voice that is *pleasant to praise the Lord.*

Answer:

This matter is discussed in the Talmud (Git. 7a). We read there as follows: "They sent (this question) to Mar Ukba: Is music forbidden? He drew a line (on paper) and wrote to them: *Rejoice not, O Israel, among the nations* (Hos. 9.1). Why did he not send them the verse: *Drink not wine with singing* (i.e., and instrumental accompaniment, as is implied in Isa. 24.9)?" (The answer is) if he had sent them the latter verse, I might suppose that only instrumental music is forbidden but vocal music is permitted (therefore he sent them the first verse to indicate that *both* are prohibited). From the fact that he did not send them the second verse mentioned, we learn then that the oral music is also forbidden. Therefore the man who (here in Venice) prohibited the choir, did so because it is vocal music. Also he saw what is written in the *Tur,* "Orah Hayyim" 560: "They forbade all kinds of singing, both by instrument and by mouth." And also Maimonides explains in a responsum (no. 370, ed. Freimann): "that even by mouth it is forbidden and even at a banquet, and it makes no difference whether the song is in Hebrew or in Arabic." Perhaps also he has not seen the opinion of the other scholars.

> (Modena cites all the objections to music in the Talmud and among the later scholars, in order that the negative case be fully stated. Then he analyzes the legal status of music among the Jews as follows:)

Now, consider: he who examines carefully, in their respective places, all that has here been cited, will find that there are six distinctions to be made in this matter. Two of them have to do with the production of the music and four with its intention and its occasion. One is music by instrument; two, music by mouth; three, music at a wine banquet; four, to pamper oneself as kings do (who rise and retire to music); five, to rejoice bride and groom, or for any other *mitzvah.* I add here still another (i.e., the sixth), namely, learning the art or engaging in it so as to remember it when the time comes to perform a *mitzvah.*

The first classification, instrumental music, is as all agree the most serious. With regard to that, Mar Ukba, cited above, knew that no one would disagree, and therefore he did not feel it necessary to quote a verse to prove it. Instead, he quoted that which would be proof of the prohibition of vocal music. So, too, Maimonides wrote (*Yad,* "Laws of Fasting," V.14): "They decreed that we are not to play on instruments; all singing for the sake of enjoyment is forbidden; and it is forbidden to hear it, because of the destruction of the Temple."

Now we must understand the intention and the occasion of music. It is now clear that vocal music, which is not at a wine festival, is permitted. We see this from what Rashi wrote, when commenting on the statement of Mar Ukba, that it is forbidden to sing at wine festivals; from which we derive (says Judah Leon) that we must not assume that singing is prohibited everywhere and under all circumstances.

(He analyzes all these opinions to show that they do not mean a general prohibition, but only music under special circumstances, namely, at wine festivals, to pamper oneself as kings do, etc. Then he continues:)

Vocal music, not at a festival nor for self-pampering as kings do, but to rejoice in the Law or to learn the art, or at the command of princes and rulers and the like, and of course for a *mitzvah*—all of the authorities will grant that it is permitted.

(The reference in the phrase "at the command of princes and rulers" is to Solomon dei Rossi, to whose book this responsum was a preface. Solomon dei Rossi was official singer and musician at the ducal court of Tuscany.)

(Our decision) depends upon the reason for the music. The prohibition was due to the destruction of the Temple and to the exile in which we find ourselves. How can we rejoice when out Temple is desolate and we are in exile? It is with this in mind that they said in the Talmud (Sanh. 101a): "The ear that hears song will be uprooted, and song in the house means destruction in the end, etc." But if the music is for a *mitzvah,* such as bringing joy to bride and groom, and the like, "even a lad can write" (a reference to the verse in Isa. 10.19 that it is completely permitted). In fact, even instrumental music and music at a banquet of wine, which are the two gravest subdivisions of the law, are permitted for the sake of bride and groom. Thus the *Tur*, "Orah Hayyim" 338, says in the name of Abi haEzri (Eliezer ben Joel haLevi, 13th century) that it is permitted on the Sabbath to tell a Gentile to play, on instruments, songs at wedding parties; for if a *mitzvah* is involved, asking a Gentile is permitted. So, you see (says Judah Leon) he actually calls it a *mitzvah* to play on instruments at a wine banquet.

In fact, Maimonides, in the "Laws of Fasting," V.14, also concludes: "Already it is an established custom among all of Israel to sing praises to God at banquets of wine." The *Tur, ibid.,* says that it is permitted to utter songs and praises over wine at a banquet; and Caro quotes the *Semag* there, namely, that to rejoice bride and groom is song of *mitzvah* and permitted. So does Joseph Caro say in his short book (*Shulhan Arukh*, "Orah Hayyim" 560.3) and Moses Isserles adds there: "Thus for the needs of a *mitzvah,* as in the house of bride and groom, it is all permitted." Isaac Alfasi (Ber., beginning of ch. 5) said that the statement of Mar Ukba about vocal music being prohibited applies only to human love songs, rejoicing in human beauty, what the Arabs call *Ashar;* but no Israelite need refrain from words of song and praise and recollection of the kindness of God.

(Modena continues citing the authorities which indicate that music is permitted for a worthy purpose. He continues more specifically:)

Of course, it is a duty incumbent upon the cantor to make his voice beautiful in prayer. If he can make his voice as impressive as these ten singers (well and good). But if he cannot, then it is good that, by his side, to help him, should stand those whom God has graced with a pleasant voice. This need not be organized but can be in the nature of an aria, as is customary all the time among the Ashkenazi congregations. They sing with him. It happens sometimes that they organize their voices (into a choir). Can this be counted against them as sinful? For it is written, *Honor the Lord with thy riches* (Prov. 3.9), which the rabbis interpret to mean: if God has enriched you with a beautiful voice . . . (*Pesikta d'Rav Kahana,* Buber, p. 97a). Should we then say that, because God has graciously given these people the knowledge of organizing music and they come to honor the Lord with it, they have committed a mortal sin? God forbid! For if it were a sin, then we should decree that the cantors should bray like donkeys and sing in unpleasant voices, and then one could apply to them the verse: *They raise their voice against Me* (Jer. 12.8). If you are going to say that music is forbidden, then you will have to say that it is forbidden also for an individual to sing, as the Talmud says: "The voice of a sheepherder is forbidden" (Sota 48a), and he is an individual. Then those of us who know music and use it in our prayers and praises would be a mockery among the nations who would say that we no longer have any wisdom, but make noises at God like dogs and ravens.

(After this sarcasm, he continues to mention the dancing performed by great scholars, as recorded in the Talmud. Then he explains the verse in Psalm 137: *How can we sing the songs of the Lord in a strange land?* as referring specifically to the special songs sung by the levites in the Temple in Jerusalem. It was only these Temple songs which were referred to in the psalm. He concludes as follows:)

There is no place for complaint, except possibly against those who learn this art, not for singing in the synagogue or for a *mitzvah,* but for its own sake. Yet even this is surely permitted, for we have indeed proved above that Rashi and the *tosafot* and Maimonides and all the great ones of the world forbade vocal singing only for self-indulgence, as with wine or as kings do; but that in every other way it is permitted. All the more is it permitted to learn it, for it is a right and proper thing to do, in order to rejoice bride and groom, and in order to praise God in the synagogue, and for every other such *mitzvah.* How can people do these (worthy) things if they do not first learn the skill? If they know a little of the art and want to perfect it and fix it in their minds so that it should not be forgotten, all this is permitted.

This is how the matter is seen by the humblest of the pupils; and he has taken it to heart. Now his eye turns to the "rivers of honey and wisdom" (i.e., to the rabbis) to confirm or to annul what he has set down. The lion speaketh and seeketh good (a double pun on the verse in Prov. 28.15, which in the original has an entirely different meaning; he uses the verse to refer to himself because his name is "Aryeh" which means "a lion").

Signed, the young one,

Judah Aryeh of Modena

Following this responsum there are four paragraphs, each one an endorsement of Modena's decision by one of the rabbis of Venice.

31

✡

THE RIGHT TO LEAVE PALESTINE

Yom-Tov Zahalon, rabbi of Safed (born in 1557; died *ca.* 1638) was a man of independent mind who frequently disagreed with other scholars and even with his teachers. The responsum which we cite deals with a theme that occupies an important place in Jewish Law—the obligation to live in Palestine. The Talmud speaks of the superiority of Palestine over all other lands from the religious point of view, of the commandments which can be observed only in Palestine, and of the greater wisdom that comes to a scholar of the Torah in Palestine. It therefore speaks of the sin of leaving Palestine if one is a resident there, and the duty of settling in Palestine if one lives elsewhere. While many of these laws are discussed in many places of the Talmud and are referred to in later legal works, they aroused special discussion during the time when the Spanish exiles settled in the Holy Land and hoped for the early ingathering of all the exiles. Earlier opinions, from the time of the tosafists, sometimes called attention to the dangers of travel from western Europe or from northern Africa, and therefore did not consider the duty to emigrate to be an urgent one. But in the 16th century the subject becomes a favorite one in the responsa, especially in the responsa of Sephardim who had settled anywhere in the Near East—in Egypt, in Turkey, as well as in Palestine. But the Sephardi sages in Palestine were always their greatest authorities, and many a great rabbi from the other lands ended his career in the Holy Land.

Yom-Tov Zahalon, a Sephardi who was rabbi in Safed, then holiest of the Palestinian cities, was very firm on the duty of moving to Palestine and staying there. Nevertheless, in the independence of his mind, he decided to the contrary in the case of a young German-Jewish immigrant, and granted that he had every right to return to his native land. The responsum is no. 85.

TEXT

Question:

This concerns the intelligent young man, Reb Mordecai, the Ashkenazi who came from Germany, having left his father and mother and his birthplace, to settle in the Holy Land, the glory of Israel, in Safed, may it be forever established. Amen. Now life hems him in (literally, "the place is narrow for him") and he cannot get settled (the phrase is from Kid. 50a), for he does not find peace alone, and he cannot find a wife. Therefore his health is impaired. He asks us whether he is permitted (by Jewish Law) to leave Palestine; for he fears he might fall into sin (remain unmarried). Now, with the mercy of God, I will answer according to the subject that I find merit for him, and would permit him to emigrate.

Answer:

(Zahalon begins with an analysis of the relevant sources, beginning with the Talmud and continuing with Maimonides and others, which discuss the reasons why a man might be permitted to leave Palestine, namely, to marry, to study Torah, and to avoid famine in the land. But the journey must be only temporary. When the permitted purposes are achieved or their realization attempted to the utmost of one's ability, the traveler must return to Palestine. He continues, p. 78d:)

Thus we have concluded that it is permissible to go outside of Palestine to marry a wife. Now this Mordecai, since he is going to marry, is of course permitted to go. Yet so far it seems (from the above sources) that this is conditional, namely, he must return after he marries unless, to be sure, his wife's parents make the premarriage condition with him that he shall not take her out (of her native land). Then he is naturally free (of the obligation to return) because he could not find a wife unless he accepted the condition of remaining there.

In fact, after going more deeply into the matter, it seems justified to say that the opinion of the *tosafot* and Maimonides, that an emigrant must return, applies only to one whose dwelling-place and that of his fathers has been in Palestine. Such a person is forbidden to leave, excepting only to marry; and he must then return. But this man (Mordecai), who came from a distant land to the Holy Land, had intended to find here a wife and a home. Now, since he could not get settled here, then his very coming to Palestine was based upon a condition that was not fulfilled. You can learn (about such conditional immigration) from the statement in Kiddushin 50a which speaks of a man who sells his property, intending to go to Palestine, but could not get settled; and Rashi there says that this means he could not find a means of livelihood there or a dwelling-place. Thus we see that these two conditions can prevent the consummation of the sale of the property (i.e., the sale which the man mentioned in the Talmud made on condition of going to Palestine), even though he did not make this condition explicit. Thus it was in his (Mordecai's) mind to go to Palestine to marry a woman, but he did not find her. Also he could not find a livelihood here. I, who speak, can tell you that from the day he came here, I brought him here to my house, with God's help, and he ate at my table. He served me and I found no evil in him. On the contrary, I saw him eager to study the Torah and to serve scholars. Yet he did not find the repose of a wife. Therefore he must now leave Palestine. Hence he is permitted to go; in fact, even if he settles there permanently (this is permitted), since from the very beginning he came here with the intention of marrying and did not find a wife (his immigration was conditional).

(Zahalon goes into a further analysis of the permission to leave Palestine for the abovementioned special purposes, and he continues with an analysis of a passage in Maimonides which, it seems to him, was made for the purpose of defending those who live outside of Palestine. He interprets it as follows:)

Indeed, the intention of Maimonides was to defend those who dwell outside of Palestine. Our teacher did not think it right to say that whoever dwells outside of Palestine was as if he has no God (as the Talmud says). That is why he wrote that the meaning of the Talmud, which says that a man should always live in Palestine and not outside of it, does not refer to those whose ancestors for generations dwelt outside, after being exiled from the Holy Land at God's decree. What can such persons do? We do not say with regard to such a person that he must not dwell outside of Palestine, for then what would become of the people of Israel and their rabbis who dwell outside of Palestine? Evidently, then (says Maimonides), when the Talmud says that no one shall dwell outside of Palestine, it means that no one shall leave Palestine to dwell outside. That is why the Talmud specifically says "whoever leaves Palestine, it is as if he worships idols."

(Then he completes in more detail this interpretation of the meaning of Maimonides' statement, and concludes as follows:)

My general conclusion is that this Reb Mordecai is permitted to go outside of Palestine to marry. I have found support for my words in a decision which a famous German rabbi wrote. His name was Rabbi Naftali Hertz, of blessed memory. He made this decision with regard to a young man who came from Germany to Palestine, but had to leave in order to marry. He permitted him to leave and even to settle permanently outside of Palestine. He even decreed a *herem* (anathema) against any one who mocked this young man by saying that he violated the law by leaving Palestine. For this young man acted according to the law, etc. (So far the decree of the German Rabbi; and Zahalon concludes:) This is correct. May the Rock of Israel deliver us from error and show us wondrous things in His Law.

Thus is the prayer of the young

Yom-Tov Zahalon

32

✡

EXILES LOYAL TO DISPERSED CONGREGATION

Jair Hayyim Bachrach (born in Leipnik, Moravia, 1639; died in Worms, 1702) moved at the age of twelve to Worms with his father, who had been elected rabbi of this ancient community. When he received his rabbinical diploma, he served as rabbi first in Mainz, then for three years in Coblenz, and then returned to Worms. There he taught and lectured for many years.

His father hoped that his learned son would succeed him as rabbi in Worms. But the community in Worms had a rule that no member of a family living in Worms should be elected rabbi. Therefore another man was elected to succeed his father. In the year 1689, the French armies of Louis XIV captured and burned the city of Worms and the ancient community was completely dispersed. Bachrach was compelled to lead an unsettled, wandering life, residing in various cities in the Rhineland. But ten years after the burning of the city, scattered members of the Worms community returned to the ruins and re-established the community. Bachrach, now deaf, old and sick, was elected to be its rabbi. This was in 1699; he lived three more years and died in 1702.

He was an independent systematic thinker; and his responsa (in the well-known collection *Havot Ya'ir*) show great inde-

pendence of mind. The problem dealt with in the responsum
which we will cite is one that throws light on at least one reason
for the remarkable continuity of Jewish tradition. Many of the
customs which differentiate the Ashkenazim from the Sephardim,
and which Moses Isserles recorded in his glosses to the *Shulhan
Arukh*, were developed in the various Rhineland cities. Yet these
cities were constantly being disrupted, especially their Jewish
communities. Their homes were constantly attacked and the
people frequently expelled. How was it possible to re-establish
these communities and through the centuries maintain in each of
them a sense of unbroken continuity? How could these various
ritual and ceremonial customs have been kept functioning in this
constantly interrupted historical experience and endure to become permanent customs in Jewish life?

Bachrach explains the unique religious attitude which gave
continuity to all these local customs. The question is asked of him
whether a son is in duty bound to continue the special practices
of additional piety, beyond the requirements of the Law, which
his father had adopted. Bachrach explains that it is the duty of
the son to continue the special pieties of his father. Then he extends that obligation to the community, declaring that it is in
duty bound to maintain through all the generations the special
religious practices adopted as special acts of piety by the community in past generations. He illustrates it by his own experience
during the destruction of Worms, and shows how these pious old
customs were resumed ten years later when the city was re-established. The responsum cited is no. 126.

TEXT

I have been asked by a learned and God-fearing man whether he
is in duty bound to observe the pieties and the fasts on Monday
and Thursday which his father had observed, having vowed to
do so all his life, especially on the 10th of Adar, on which day his
father was accustomed to fast, and also to distribute charity all
year because of a miracle that had happened to him, as is im-

plied in the account of the piety of the people of Bet-Shean in the Talmud (Pes. 50b). I answered him at length. The essence, in brief, of what I said is this: It appears, from the episode of the citizens of Bet-Shean, that it is obligatory on sons to conduct themselves according to all the pieties which their fathers had adopted.

(The citizens of Bet-Shean came to Rabbi Yohanan and wanted permission to abandon a pious custom of their ancestors. Their ancestors had refused to go on the journey from Tyre to Sidon, where a fair was held on Fridays, because they did not wish to neglect the preparation for the Sabbath for the sake of business profits. The sons said that their fathers were rich and could afford to make that sacrifice; but they, their sons, could no longer afford to do so. Rabbi Yohanan said that nevertheless they must not abandon the pious practice of their fathers.)

This holds not only if the fathers took these pieties upon themselves by explicit public statement. Even if it were merely a custom that they followed, even so the custom must be looked upon as equivalent to a vow. Thus the people (the previous generations) of Bet-Shean had never formally decided to follow this pious practice (of avoiding business opportunities on Friday), but this was merely their custom. Thus did Isaac bar Sheshet explain the situation in his responsum no. 399. Joseph Caro cites it and declares it to be a law in the *Shulhan Arukh;* "Yoreh Deah" (214.2) gives the law as follows: The pious practices which are accepted by the majority are incumbent upon them and upon their children. Even such pious customs which were not adopted formally by the citizens of the city by a public agreement, but are merely followed by them of their own accord . . . (are incumbent upon the coming generations).

(Bachrach turns the discussion from his answer to this individual inquirer to give an illustration from the experience of the community of Worms and shows how customs are incumbent upon the succeeding generations in a community. He continues:)

So far my answer. Incidentally, I shall now write about a matter which will illustrate this. After our community was destroyed (for our great sins) and our city was made desolate, in Sivan 449 (1689), the men of our community, who were scattered as corn is scattered by the winnow, asked me whether they were in duty bound to observe those extra fasts which were the special custom of the congregation, and other such acts of piety as were customary there, inasmuch as the city was now desolate and made into an eternal ruin by the kingdom of France. (The questioners continued:) All the Jews and Christians had abandoned hope that the city would ever be rebuilt in our time since the war continued to rage. Furthermore, should peace come and the inhabitants of the land find rest, who knew when the city would be rebuilt and re-established and when the sacred flock would return there? Therefore it came into the mind of some of them to say that all the special fast days and customs were now void (since the community which had observed them was no longer in existence). And (the questioners continued) even if settlers did come, after this hopeless situation, in another generation, or even in this same generation, it was no longer obligatory to confirm and establish the ancient customs because this would now be an entirely new community.

I answered them that this opinion of theirs was incorrect. Even if some few individuals had given up hope, they must follow the feeling of the entire congregation (who must be assumed not to have despaired). The mercies of God have not ended and our rabbis said, "Persecutions always cease" (Ket. 3b). Though wars and the provocations of kings are always present, yet in the end there is always peace. How much the more was this true of this mother-city in Israel, this most ancient congregation. Behold, the scrolls of the Law and the holy articles and all the records of the congregation had been safely removed and locked up. Furthermore, how many other proofs were there from the Torah (that we should not give up hope for restoration). But good sense requires that I should abbreviate here, for I have already written elsewhere about the matter of community taxes and imposts (to what extent they were still obligatory).

The summary of the matter is that this destruction was only

like an expulsion, or a flight before an earthquake, or before an oppressor. Even if all of the people left, nevertheless we hoped every day for the salvation of the Lord in a natural way. Hence, it was certainly their intention to return and therefore it was incumbent upon them to maintain all the strict observances of the earlier community.

Thus it is, according to my humble opinion.

Jair Hayyim Bachrach

Evidently this question was asked him before 1699, when the congregation was restored. He must have met many former members of the community during the years of his wandering after the destruction of Worms. He told them to keep up their hope, to maintain the old customs, for the community would surely be restored. So, indeed, it was.

33

✡

DAVID NIETO AND PANTHEISM

Zvi Hirsch Ashkenazi (*"Hakham* Zvi": born in Moravia, 1658; died in Lemberg, 1718) studied in Salonika and there saw the disturbances in the community in the aftermath of the career of the false messiah, Sabbetai Zvi. This early experience led him to a lifelong effort to suppress the followers of that notorious impostor. It may be that many of the difficulties which he experienced later in his varied career were due to the tension between him and those who still had a lurking sympathy for the false messiah.

He stayed for a while in Constantinople. He moved to Alt Ofen in Hungary where, during the siege of the city, he saw his wife and daughter killed by cannon shot. He went to Sarajevo, where he was rabbi until 1689. Although he was a German, he was greatly honored by the Sephardim and they gave him the title *hakham,* which they usually gave their rabbis. Thereafter he always called himself *Hakham* Zvi.

He married the daughter of the rabbi of the triple community, Altona, Hamburg, Wandsbeck. His father-in-law founded a *klaus* in Altona (a word similar to the word "cloister," and usually an endowed school for the study of the Talmud), where the *hakham* stayed and taught and attracted many distinguished pupils. Later he was elected alternate rabbi of the three communities. The great German community of Amsterdam then invited him to be rabbi. He stayed there for three years, found trouble in the community, and went to London, on the invitation of the Sephardi community. He returned to live in Altona, and ended his career as rabbi in Lemberg.

The responsum which we cite has considerable interest for the history of Jewish religious thought. Generally in the past it had been the Sephardim, especially in Spain, who cultivated philosophic and scientific studies, while the Ashkenazim in northern France and Germany had scorned these disciplines and confined themselves to the study of the Talmud. But here an Ashkenazi rabbi settles a philosophic dispute in a Sephardi congregation.

In 1703, David Nieto, the Sephardi rabbi of the London congregation, preached a philosophic sermon which certain opponents considered heretical. The Sephardi authorities of Amsterdam were asked to pass judgment as to whether the sermon constituted heresy or not, but they refused to answer. Finally the question came to *Hakham* Zvi who was an Ashkenazi. The Sephardim were willing to listen to his opinions, for since he had studied in Salonika and had been rabbi in Sarajevo, they considered him half Sephardi. They accepted his answer vindicating David Nieto.

David Nieto, the storm center of the controversy (born in Venice, 1654; died in London, 1728) was educated at the University of Padua, where he took a degree in medicine. He was invited to the English Sephardi congregation in 1701. There, in 1703, he preached a sermon in which he declared that God and Nature were one. This was a dangerous-sounding doctrine in those days. First, it sounded suspiciously like the teaching of Spinoza, who had used the terms "God" and "Nature" as synonyms. Moreover, it was much like the Deist philosophy of the time, which taught that God was essentially unknowable and had nothing to do with the management of the world, that the world was managed by the forces of nature. Nieto explained that he meant that "nature" is merely a term for the working-out of God's governance of the world. (For a full discussion of the subject, see *The Theology of Haham David Nieto,* by Jakob J. Petuchowski, especially pp. 15–16, 118 ff.)

Hakham Zvi's defense, which apparently ended the dispute, is no. 18 in his collection.

TEXT

From the officers and leaders in the London congregation in England, the exalted and upright magnates, officers of the sacred congregation Gates of Heaven, in the great city of London. May God bless them with life and peace forever.

Your treasured letter seeking the word of the Lord for guidance has strengthened me and led me to speak on matters beyond my competence. You ask me regarding a dispute in a subject that I cannot search out. But we are commanded, Seek peace and pursue it. *The following is the essence of your question.*

Question:

The exalted sage, David Nieto, rabbi in the sacred congregation "Gates of Heaven," preached a sermon in the congregation. This is its essence translated from English into our sacred tongue:

"People say (these are the words of Nieto) that I said that God and Nature, and Nature and God, blessed be He, are both the same thing. I did say that, and I will defend and prove it, since David defends the same idea in Psalm 147, as follows: *He who covereth the heaven with clouds, who prepareth the rain for the earth, who causeth the mountains to sprout froth grass, etc.* But incline your ears to this, O children of Israel, for it is the first principle of our faith: the name 'nature' is only an invention of the later scholars of the last four or five hundred years. It is not found in the words of our older sages. But God causes the wind to blow and the rain to fall, so it is clear that God performs all these actions that the later scholars call 'nature.' There really is no such thing as 'nature.' That thing that they call 'nature' is really God's providence. That is what I mean when I say God and Nature are one. This opinion is right and pious and sacred, and those who do not believe it should be called heretics." (The rest of the question develops Nieto's ideas in his own words.)

Answer:

I note that the words of the exalted sage (i.e., Nieto) are the same as the words of the *Kuzari* (i.e., Judah Halevi) in the first section no. 76 and no. 77. His commentator, Judah Moscato (16–17th century, Italian preacher and scholar, whose commentary on the *Kuzari* is in all the usual editions), writes after many premises, as follows: "He, blessed be He, is called 'nature' truly; as is mentioned there, He puts His seal on all created things." This, too, is the opinion of those who give exact attributes to God when they say that God sits and feeds all animals from beasts to insects (a phrase from the Talmud, Shab. 106b).

So we (says Ashkenazi) congratulate this sage who preached the sermon, since he knows the opinion of the philosophers who speak of nature. *He despised the evil* (of their opinion) *and chose the good* with intelligence (a phrase based upon Isa. 7.15), the sacred words of the holy ones of our people who say that everything comes from God's providence.

I have heard but I do not understand the complaints of those who murmur against him. Is it because he said that there is really no such thing as nature, which should include all existence outside of God? Do they consider this a diminution of God, that He works without intermediary? Let them know that those who seek the intermediation of nature for the general management of the world are close to falling over many stumbling blocks. But this is not so with those who believe in God's providence in everything, for wherever they go, they walk securely. Of course if they (the complainers) think that the words of the preacher referred to the detailed facts of nature—as the heat of fire and the wetness of water—and they wish to accuse the preacher that he meant to say that the heating or moisture is in itself God, as far as that is concerned there is not a single fool or boor among all the skeptics of the world who would believe that—let alone a sage among the people of God, who believes in God and His holy Law? All the more then are the words of the preacher clear and definite (when he says) that they (the objects of nature) revolve around the axis of God's general providence, when he says that God alone causes the wind to blow and He causes the rain and dew to fall. From this it is proved that God makes all these things.

Let not the stubborn mocker object, thinking that it is not proper to describe the working of God by the name of nature, and think this is a diminution of His glory. What would they gain by shouting complaints against this preacher? Behold, the great sage, Isaiah Levi (Hurwitz), known for his wisdom and piety, in his famous book, *Two Tablets of the Covenant,* which is received with love throughout the scattered homes of Israel, wrote at the beginning of his book, in the name of the author of *Abodat haKodesh* (Meir Gabbai, 15th century), who was a great and famous Sephardi rabbi and whose books were scattered all through the world, that the reward for those who do God's commandments and the punishment for those who violate them, are all natural rewards and punishments. To this all who have eyes and knowledge in the wisdom of truth agree.

(He continues with this argument:)

So we must congratulate the great sage, David Nieto, for the sermon which he preached, whose purpose it was to warn the whole people not to let their hearts go astray after those philosophers who speak of nature (i.e., as a separate force, as do the Deists), for many stumblings can come from that. He illumined their eyes with his true faith by saying that everything exists through God's providence. So I say to him, may his strength increase. Whoever murmureth against him after seeing my words, I suspect him of sinfulness. Now, although all these things are clear and plain, and do not need further support to refute every complainer, nevertheless, I invited two of the most educated scholars of our city to join me. After discussing the matter, all three of us agreed on the words mentioned above, that they are true and just.

Written here in Altona on the 6th day of the month of Ab, of the year 1705.

Signed,

Zvi Ashkenazi, S.T.

(The initials S.T. are generally used by the Sephardi scholars in signing their name. They are taken by some to mean *Siman Tov,* an omen of happiness; others take them to mean *Sephardi Tahor,* a pure Sephardi, which certainly Ashkenazi could not have used in his own name.)

34

✡

BARING HEAD IN SYNAGOGUE
TO HONOR A KING

Jacob Reischer (born in Prague; died in Metz, 1733) was a rabbinical judge (*dayyan*) at Prague. Later, he was rabbi at Reische (Rzeschow), Galicia; hence his name, Reischer. He was rabbi in Anspach, Worms, and finally at Metz. He wrote a number of commentaries on earlier legal works and one on the popular anthology of non-legal passages of the Talmud, *Ain Yaacob*. His commentary was called *Iyyun Yaacob*. His chief fame rests on his collection of responsa, *Shebut Yaacob*.

The question with which he deals in the responsum cited here is still a matter of discussion among Jews, namely, whether bareheadedness is forbidden by religious law. He deals with a special form of the question, which obviously was of practical concern in his day, namely, whether the worshipers are permitted to take off their hats as a mark of respect if some high dignitary of the state, a duke or a king, visits a synagogue. In discussing this specific question, he gives a complete and balanced summary of the whole question of bareheadedness in Jewish worship. The responsum is vol. III, no. 5.

TEXT

Question:

If a great ruler or a duke comes into the synagogue, is it permitted to remove the hat from the head in order to honor him, even though one remains standing with bared head?

Answer:

The essence of the law and the prohibition of uncovering the head has no essential root or clear source in the Talmud. For the prohibition of leaving the head in disarray (*peruei rosh*), which is forbidden in the sanctuary itself, does not mean the uncovering of the head, but rather letting the hair grow long, as is explained in the Talmud (Sanh. 22b) and in Maimonides in the "Laws of Entering the Sanctuary," ch. I.

But Maimonides, in the "Laws of Prayer," V.5, writes: "A man shall not stand at prayer with uncovered head." Joseph Caro, in his *House of Joseph,* to the *Tur,* "Orah Hayyim," no. 91, says that the *Kol Bo* (a 14th-century legal work of undetermined authorship) quotes Rabbi Meir of Rothenburg as saying that there is no prohibition against walking with uncovered head; for the statement in the Talmud (Shab. 118b) that Rab Huna said, "Count it to my credit that I have never walked four cubits with uncovered head" simply means that (keeping the head covered) is an act of special piety (i.e., not a requirement). But Alfasi said that we must prevent people from entering the synagogue with uncovered head. (So far is the statement of Joseph Caro. Then Reischer continues.)

From this, Joseph Caro came to the conclusion which he recorded in his *Shulhan Arukh* that "*some say* that we should keep people from entering the synagogue with uncovered head." Now since there is no clear prohibition against bareheadedness, but covering is only special piety, and we know that there are many cases when things are forbidden (out of special piety) that the rabbis permitted in order to maintain peace with the government, we must surely permit this (to uncover the head in the presence of a duke, etc.,) in order to maintain peace with the government.

Furthermore, one should notice that Alfasi was careful to say that one should not enter the synagogue (with uncovered head). He means specifically to be careful about covering the head at the time of entering. This is in accordance with what the *Zohar* writes, that one must enter the synagogue in the morning wearing *tallit* and *tefillin* in order to fulfill the verse: *I will enter and bow down to Thy holy sanctuary in awe of Thee* (Psalms 5.8). So it is written also in the responsa of David ibn Zimri, VI, no. 36 (should be IV, 36) and the responsa of Meir of Lublin, no. 34. If, therefore, one has already bowed down in the synagogue, then it is not so serious a matter, especially when peace with the government is concerned.

In fact, more than this. Solomon Luria decided, in his responsum no. 72, that it is absolutely permitted to pray and to read the *Shema* with uncovered head. Although the proof which he cites there is not conclusive. (Reischer proves that Luria's proof is subject to question. And he concludes as follows:)

At all events, did not the rabbis permit the hair to be cut in the *Kumi* style (this was a special style of fringe haircut favored by the pagans) because of keeping peace with the government, as we find in the Talmud (B. K. 83a) even though that involves "the ways of the Amorites" (a phrase referring to forbidden superstitious practices)? If so, such permission applies here too. Even more than this, we find in the *Shulhan Arukh,* in "Yoreh Deah" 150.3, in the note of Isserles (speaking of the permission to doff one's hat when priests go by clad in canonicals) as follows: "Even if there is upon the garments (of the priests) a cross, there are some who are lenient in permitting the removal of our hat before them." All the more is it permitted (in this case of a visiting ruler) where we are not concerned with this matter (that we might be saluting a cross). No one certainly disagrees with it. So it seems to me.

Of course, if it is possible to explain to the ruler that we are prohibited to appear in the synagogue with an uncovered head, perhaps he might be satisfied, just as was the case with that pious man mentioned in the Talmud (Ber. 32b to 33a, who was at prayer, and did not answer the greeting of a ruler who had greeted him. The pious man explained the reason and the ruler was appeased). Certainly if we could do that, it would be praiseworthy.

Thus it seems to me, the humble one,

Jacob

35

✡

KIDDUSH AND THE GOUT

Isaac Lampronti (born in Ferrara, 1679; died there, 1756) was a physician and rabbi. He studied medicine at Padua, and completed his rabbinical studies in Mantua. In Ferrara he first became head of the Italian yeshiva; then the Spanish yeshiva joined his. In 1718, he was a full member of the rabbinate and finally became president of the Jewish schools of the city. His greatest literary achievement was the remarkable rabbinic encyclopedia, *Pahad Yitzhak,* an immense work arranged alphabetically, dealing with all the themes of Jewish Law, beginning systematically with the earliest sources down to the sources of his day. Illustrating certain subjects as they came up, Lampronti included many responsa by his Italian colleagues and many which he himself wrote. While he was teacher of the community and rabbi, and while working on his great encyclopedia, he actively practiced medicine and visited his patients every morning. A half year before he died, the Church ordered all tombstones in the Jewish cemetery destroyed. Therefore, when he died, no tombstone was erected on his grave. However, in the year 1872, the city of Ferrara placed a plaque of honor on the house in which he had lived.

The responsum which we cite is on page 150 of the volume *Kaf,* and deals with a question which must have interested him both as rabbi and as physician. The question involved a man who had the gout. In an earlier responsum on the same subject, on page 147b, he used the scientific word *podagra*. How can such a man recite *kiddush* on Friday night and celebrate the Seder at Passover? Is wine mandatory? If it is, cannot he recite a blessing and have someone else taste it? Lampronti discusses the entire question rabbinically. Perhaps the only evidence of his medical knowledge appears when he says towards the end that the man can taste a little wine and it will not hurt him.

TEXT

Question:

A man has been warned by doctors not to drink wine because it will harm him; he is therefore told to keep away from it completely. He does not taste even the wine of a *mitzvah* (i.e., *kiddush, habdalah,* etc.). He recites the *kiddush* blessing over the cup; then others taste it. Does he do right by following this procedure to begin with?

(The phrase "to begin with" is a phrase used in Jewish Law as the opposite of "after it has been done"; *l'khat'hilla,* as opposed to *b'di'avad,* which are close to our English terms "before the fact" and "after the fact." That is to say, certain actions are forbidden before they are done, but having been done, they are often valid. The questioner, therefore, believes that not to taste the wine, having blessed it, may be a valid performance of the *mitzvah* after the fact; but he wants to know whether this would be permitted if the man had inquired before he said the blessing.)

Answer:

From two places in the Talmud, in tractate Nazir (3b and 44a), the proof is clear that the drinking of the wine at *kiddush* and *habdalah* are an essential part of the commandment. According to the words of the commentator there, the drinking is a commandment based upon the Torah; but according to the opinion of the decisors (*posekim*) there and in tractate Pesahim 105b, it is merely an additional rabbinical requirement. Since this is so, it is clear that the man has not followed correct procedure (by letting someone else taste the wine). It goes without saying that this is the opinion of the gaonim and the *Halakhot Gedolot* (a gaonic legal work), who believe that the man who recites the *kiddush* is required to taste it himself, and so also says the *Tur*, "Orah Hayyim" 271. This goes without saying. But even according to the opinion of Rashi in the Talmud (R. H. 29b) and the *tosafot*, and Asher ben Yehiel on Pesahim 105b, who believe that it is quite sufficient if one of the people at the table tastes the wine, even this opinion (of Rashi and the *tosafot*) applies after the fulfilment of the duty involved. But, to begin with (*l'khat'hilla*, that is, if they were asked first), they would all admit that we require that the man who recites the *kiddush* should taste the wine.

(He then goes into a fuller discussion of the variety of opinion on this matter, and continues as follows:)

At all events, we come to this conclusion: that all the decisors agree that all the people at the table must taste the wine; but that first of all the man who recites the *kiddush* must taste it. It is clear from this that the one who abstains from wine because it harms him has not the right to free himself from tasting the wine of the *mitzvah*, namely, by reciting *kiddush* over the wine and letting someone else taste it. . . . Now if you said, "Let us rather follow the decision of Moses Isserles which is the reverse of this; for note that he wrote in "Orah Hayyim" 272.9 that one who does not drink wine because he made a vow (not to drink wine) may recite the *kiddush* and let others drink who are at the table with him." Such a reliance upon Isserles here will not do; for his opinion itself is difficult and we are in doubt as to whence he derived his decision. For if it came from *The House of Joseph* (Joseph Caro), as seems to be indicated from what he (Isserles) said in his *Ways of Moses* (to the *Tur*), as quoted by *Magen Avraham*, I searched there in *The House of Joseph* and did not find that he says that clearly at all.

(He continues with this analysis of what Joseph Caro really said in *The House of Joseph* to the *Tur*. And he continues as follows:)

We return to the decision, namely, what is impossible (for example, if no wine were available) is considered to have been done (*b'di'avad*) and must be accepted as legal. But in our case, it is (*not* impossible, but) easily possible for him to taste a little bit of wine. That much will neither benefit nor hurt him at all. He who observes the commandment will not come to harm. It is the proper thing for him to force himself a little and taste. We have a responsum of Solomon ben Adret, no. 238, cited by Caro in *The House of Joseph*. Ibn Adret was asked whether one who does not drink wine all year, because it harms him or because he dislikes it, may conduct the entire Seder on Passover over *matzot*. His answer is: "Every one who has wine must force himelf to drink. Even though it is the law that he who does not have wine may perform the Seder over *matzot* alone, nevertheless, we do not conclude what is possible (if he *has* wine) from a situation that is impossible (if he has no wine)." These are the words of Ibn Adret. Now one can go more deeply into the matter and ask, why did not the questioner ask about tasting the *kiddush* of the whole year (and not only about the Seder)? Apparently, either the man tasted the wine all year and did not mind it (but four cups would be too much for him at the Seder); or, perhaps, he recited *kiddush* over bread all year, preferring it to wine. At all events, it is enough for our subject to take the alternatives, namely, that if this man keeps away from wine entirely, he can rely on those scholars who believe that if one does not like wine, he may recite *kiddush* over bread. Then let this man recite *kiddush* over bread. But if he is concerned with the opinion of Rabbenu Tam, that a man must make sure to have wine, then he has to look for wine; and his case is identical with the one decided by Solomon ben Adret with regard to the four cups of wine on Passover, namely, let him force himself a little and drink. It is really an argument *a fortiori*. If, with regard to the drinking of the larger quantity of wine (at the Seder) Ibn Adret says that he should force himself a little, then all the more would he say so (that a man should force himself) about the small quantity of the Sabbath *kiddush*. This is what has "come up in my net" now (i.e., what I have drawn from the sea of learning). The eye which is as clear as a day that is all sunlight will clarify these words as if they had been given on Mount Sinai.

36

COMPELLED TO RAISE A BEARD

Samson Morpurgo (born in Gradisca, Austria, 1681; died in Ancona, 1740), a rabbi and physician, studied medicine in Padua and spent most of his rabbinical career in Ancona, where he also practiced medicine. So great was his service to the city during the influenza epidemic of 1730 that he was given a testimonial by Benedict XIV, who was then archbishop of Ancona.

The question discussed by Morpurgo throws light upon the social customs of the Jews of Italy. It is clear from many Italian responsa that a large number (perhaps the majority) of the Italian Jews did not wear beards. In Isaac Lampronti's *Pahad Yitzhak* there are responsa about men who removed their beards with a razor, which is forbidden by Jewish Law. Azulai also discusses the habit of many Italian Jews of shaving with a razor, a habit which he strongly deplores. However, in another responsum, Azulai defends the right to remove the beard with scissors or with clippers.

Morpurgo deals with an interesting form of the question, which reveals a clash of custom between the beardless Jews of Italy and the bearded Jews of Turkey. Some Italian Jews lived in Salonika, Turkey, and the rabbis of Turkey threatened them with expulsion from the community if they did not raise beards. Morpurgo comes to the defense of the Italian Jews in Salonika. The responsum is vol. I, *Yoreh Deah,* no. 61.

TEXT

Question:

I was approached by the men of the Italian provinces in
Greece, who dwell in the city of Salonika, that city great in
morals and knowledge. They asked whether the rabbis there have
the right to browbeat and to threaten them against removing
their beards with scissors as is their old custom, saying that if
they do not let their beard grow, as is customary among the
Jews of Salonika, they will pursue them and drive them from
the land or separate them from the community. The question is
this: If the sages of Salonika carry out their threat and decree
anathema against these Italian Jews, what will be their status
under Jewish Law?

Answer:

Now, I will not answer my questioners as to the details of that
event, for I may be suspected of the sin of contentiousness. But
I will turn to those great scholars and speak words to reach the
hearts of the shepherds of Israel, who have been taught to lead
the flock of Jacob with gentleness and kindness, and to guide the
sheep of his pasture in this our Exile, scattered to the four corners
of the earth, which has left our people no greater virtue than to
observe the laws of God. After that appeal, I will speak in the
bitterness of my spirit on the question of whether any rabbinical
court in our day has the authority to compel the multitude to be
strict with regard to certain leniencies of the law, and to compel them to follow the path of special piety in such matters as
the Torah does not forbid, neither the Written nor the Oral Law,
since the days of Moses until the last Moses among the scholars
of our time (i.e., Maimonides) who is above them all in worth.
Thirdly, if a man does not know the secret studies of the Cabala
but obeys all the commandments according to our accepted tradition, will such a man be admitted to Paradise, or will that soul
suffer extermination (in other words, must a man obey the
cabalistic elaborations in order to be a worthy Jew)?

(The first part of his responsum is a rather remarkable cata-
logue of the many laws which are no longer observed by the

people and which the rabbis, in their wisdom, have not forced them to obey, lest the people openly rebel and add thereby the sin of rebellion to the sin of neglect. He speaks as follows:)

I speak of the first matter first. Every intelligent man knows well that a large proportion of the commandments are neglected by us since we are sunk among the nations. Our sacred predecessors, the masters of the Law, hid their face in the ground and turned their eyes downward (a talmudic phrase, Sanh. 19b) as if they could not see these plagues and their consequences. This was after they had debated the matter and saw by their broad wisdom that, just as it is commanded to say something that will be listened to, so it is a commandment not to say something that will not be listened to (a phrase from the Talmud, Yeb. 65b, meaning that, if the teacher knows beforehand he will be disobeyed, he should not give that particular command and thus lead the people into open rebellion). In the case of many matters, they derived "the possible from the possible," and they did not derive "the possible from the impossible," especially with regard to the people scattered among the nations.

(In other words, they did not insist upon that which was impossible to observe. He now gives a number of such examples of things difficult or almost impossible to observe.)

Thus it was with the wearing of sandals on the 9th of Ab and on Yom Kippur on the street, and covering the *tzitzit* (fringes) on the corners of the garments and having fringes on the outside garments that have four corners. They were lenient in this matter; except for chosen spirits of great piety among them, (for example) the glory of our country, the prince among our people, Samuel Aboab, of blessed memory, who commanded his sons and his household after them to make one corner of their garments round to avoid doubt (on the need for fringes on the outer garments). As for the commandment of *tefillin* itself, the wearing of which is deemed to be equal in value to the whole Torah, we children of the exile do not wear them all day as Rabbenu Yeruham said, quoted by Joseph Caro in *The House of Joseph* to "Orah Hayyim" 37, because of deceivers and Jews living outside of the land. So, too, they allow us to do business with Gentiles before their holidays, on their holidays and after their holidays (which the Talmud forbids); and to send on those days gifts to the rulers, and we bow down and remove our hats before priests.

(After discussing all of these leniencies which are now customary, he ends with the significant leniency of allowing the people to bring cases to the non-Jewish courts. He concludes this section as follows:)

Who does not know all these things? If we came to smite and to punish for all these laws that the majority of the people are lenient with, to such an extent that over the years they consider them permitted, we would make life unlivable for everyone and we would lead people into open sin and rebellion. Therefore, the shepherds and leaders of Israel, in their fear of God, whenever they found a commandment neglected, would weigh in their broad intelligence the loss incurred by stern rebuke against whatever reward it would bring; and the reward of silence against its possible loss. They would weigh the seriousness of open rebellion against the lesser sin of error, and therefore would be very careful not to add to the sin of the community. . . .

(He turns to the second question, as to whether it is right to compel the people to obey the extra refinements of observance developed through cabalistic interpretations of the ceremonies and the laws. He shows that these cabalists, in all their additions to the law, disagree among themselves and that many of the great scholars objected to their elaboration of the ritual observances. Then he goes into the question of the right to remove the beard, p. 102, bottom of col. c.)

After we have covered all these parts of our argument, I will now come to the actual subject which is before us, namely, the shaving of the beard. I say that we possess a faithful tradition from our fathers, man from man back to Moses, that the term "destruction" (of the beard) applies only to destruction with a razor (i.e., any other removal of the beard other than with a razor is permitted. See M. Mak. III.5, and Talmud, *idem* 21a). Whoever argues against this principle is arguing against the truth and says, in effect, that the Torah is not God-given.

Indeed, from the language of the *Tur* ("Yoreh Deah" 181) it would seem at first blush that, while a man is not actually guilty of a sin unless he destroys his beard with a razor, still there is some prohibition against destroying it (by other means). But Joseph Caro in his *House of Joseph* removes this error from our eyes and says clearly that such a man is not guilty (if he removes a beard by means other than with a razor). It is not only that he is not guilty but, even to begin with (*l'khat'hilla*), he is also *permitted* to shave the beard with scissors and even with scissors like a razor ("scissors" like a razor is explained by Joshua Falk in his commentary *Perisha* to the *Tur* [ad loc.], as: to cut with scissors so closely that they leave the face as smooth as if it were shaved with a razor). He (Joseph Caro) returns to these words three times.

Now one cannot bring proof to refute this (permission) from the *Terumat haDeshen* (Israel Isserlein, no. 295) who wrote that there is some scintilla of prohibition of shaving with scissors, and there would therefore be some ground for strictness; but the people are not careful in this matter. Now (continues Morpurgo) Isserlein did not actually doubt that the talmudic definition of "destruction" (of the beard) meant only by using a razor, but he was concerned about using "clippers like a razor." You see how the latter part of his statement reveals the meaning of the beginning (i.e., that he knew that scissors are permitted). He wrote later: "We must be careful not to cut the beard with scissors that are very sharp. For then we might be cutting it with only the lower part and not the upper part (which would be like a razor) if the scissors are very sharp." But if it is not too sharp, then the lower part cannot cut without the aid of the upper part (then it is really a scissors and not a razor). Joel Sirkes follows him by saying that a very pious man should not shave even with "scissors like a razor," though it is permitted even to begin with. If a man leaves a little hair and does not cut too close to the flesh itself, there is no objection to it. Sabbatai Cohen agrees with Rabbi Sirkes that this is the essence of it, namely, that since all the scholars agree that cutting with scissors is permitted, then the statement of Israel Isserlein (that scissors might possibly be prohibited) is merely an additional severity.

(Morpurgo ends his responsum with an appeal to the rabbis of Salonika to be gentle with the Italians who live in their midst. And he concludes as follows:)

Therefore comes my plea in all the ten languages of prayer before that prince of his people, the "golden head" in the city of Salonika. I plead to his heart which is as broad as the entrance to the Temple. I say to him that the Torah is compared both to fire and to water, to heat and to cold, to drive away and to bring near, according to the need of the hour . . . and may the King of Peace establish between us blessing and peace and gather our scattered ones among the nations that redeemers may go up to Zion.

These are the words of him who is burdened with troubles, who lets his small voice come from the walls of his humble school where there is no originality, etc., etc., here in Ancona, in the year 1723, *the hyssop in the wall* (I Kings 5.13), who honoreth and loveth the rabbis.

Samson Morpurgo

37

✡

IRON SMELTING AND THE
SABBATH

Meir ben Isaac Eisenstadt (born in 1670; died in Eisenstadt, 1744) was twice rabbi in Szydlowiec and came under the patronage of the famous financier Samson Wertheimer, who brought him to Worms where he was for two years teacher of Talmud in the *klaus*. (The *klaus* was a small college of scholars maintained by wealthy men. The rabbis studied all day and recited the *kaddish* in memory of the family of the donor. *Klaus* is, of course, related to the word "cloister," and is similar in function to the chantries maintained in England for an analogous purpose among Christians.)

After his two years in the *klaus*, where he became a friend of the famous scholar and later rabbi of Worms, Jair Hayyim Bachrach, Meir Eisenstadt left Worms when the French conquered the city (1701). For a short time he was rabbi in Prossnitz, in Moravia, where he was the teacher of the young Jonathan Eibeschuetz, destined to be one of the greatest rabbis of the next generation. Then he returned to Szydlowiec to be a rabbi there a second time. From there he went to Eisenstadt and remained there as rabbi until his death. He was one of the most honored rabbinical authorities of his time, known especially for his collection of responsa, *Panim Me'irot*, "Radiant Countenance" (the adjective *me'irot* "radiant," being, as was customary, a reference to his first name, Meir).

The responsa literature, while primarily concerned with the application of legal principles, reveals a great deal of the daily life of the Jews in the past. In the responsum by Meir Eisenstadt cited below there is offhand reference to some of the large business ventures undertaken by the Jews of Poland. Reference is made to contracts for the collection of taxes for the government, and contracts for the minting of coinage. These types of contract are mentioned incidentally in this responsum in connection with the main subject of discussion, a contract for the digging and the smelting of iron ore.

The problem came before the rabbi in relation to the question of work on the Sabbath. The smelting in the furnaces had to be a continuous process, since the furnaces could not economically be put out one day a week and then reheated. Therefore the work had to be done also on the Sabbath. This immediately brings up, in the complicated area of legal enactments the question of what sort of work a Jew may ask a Gentile to do for him on the Sabbath. Of course, the prohibition against work on the Sabbath is incumbent upon Jews alone. It is not considered one of the seven commandments which, according to Jewish Law, Gentiles are to obey. Gentiles may, without sin, work on the Sabbath. Nevertheless, it is not permitted for a Jew to benefit directly from the work done for him by a Gentile on the day of rest. This is based upon the interpretation of the verse in Exodus 12.16 where, speaking of the holiday (the law is the same in this regard for holiday and Sabbath), *no work shall be done in them*. That is taken to mean that no work shall be done even in your behalf by a Gentile.

The law is codified in the *Shulhan Arukh,* "Orah Hayyim," sections 244, 245, 246. The simple principle, that a Jew may not benefit from work done for him by a Gentile on holidays and Sabbaths, required an elaboration and closer definition, especially in cases where the work could not be interrupted, or where the financial loss would be great if it were interrupted. Hence the law goes into matters of partnership with Gentiles, or lending tools to Gentiles, or contracts with Gentiles to do a certain job.

In general it was forbidden for a Jew to benefit from whatever his partner or contractor did at his (the Jew's) behest on the Sabbath. But if the work were such that it was actually immaterial to the Jew whether the Gentile worked on the Sabbath or not, and the Gentile therefore worked at his own wish, the Jew could benefit from that work. Or if the contract involved payment for the entire job and the Jew left it to the Gentile's own decision what days he should work, it was legal for the Jew to make the contract. But if he hired Gentile workmen by the day, not by the total job, it was illegal according to Jewish Law for a Jew to benefit by their work.

There are further refinements to the law. Even if it is a job contract and the Gentile himself determines whether he will work Saturday or Sunday or whenever he chooses, and even though the Jew may therefore legally make such a contract, nevertheless we must be concerned for the appearance of things. If, for example, such a contract were made in the city where it would look as if the Gentile was hired to work on the Sabbath, even though this was not so, yet for "the look of things" (*mar'it 'ayin*), such a contract is not to be made. But if this contract is for work at some distant place, where it will not appear to the Jewish community as if the Jew has hired someone to work for him on the Sabbath, then the job contract is permissible.

The responsum from vol. I, no. 38 of *Panim Me'irot,* deals directly with the problem of partnership and contracts with Gentiles in the case of an iron-smelting contract held by a Jew.

TEXT

Question:

When I came to Szydlowiec, I was asked concerning those Jews who held the smelting contract which they had made with the prince, giving them permission to dig in the mountains and to bring out the dust (ore). They make iron from the dust, burning and refining the dust in fire day and night. And they do not interrupt the work (i.e., it is continuous). Thus also do the glassmakers. The question is how they should conduct their business in view of the Sabbath laws.

Answer:

At first blush it would seem that job contracts made for work within the confines of the (Jewish) district are prohibited only because of "the appearance of things," since those who see the work will say that the Gentile is hired by the day (and therefore there would be a prohibition for the Jew to benefit from the work which the Gentile does on the Sabbath. But this smelting contract is actually forbidden by *law*), for it differs from a *building* contract, which is not actually prohibited, since the Jew gets no benefit from the fact that a man hurries to build on the Sabbath (because he could finish the job without Sabbath work in ten weeks, but now finishes it in nine) . . . With the smelting of the ore, however, which goes on day and night for the making of iron, if they do not work on the Sabbath day the Jew stands to lose (if the work were interrupted).

(Eisenstadt now refers to the fact that Maimonides permits the hiring of a Gentile by the year to write a book, i.e., as a scribe, or to weave a garment; and if that Gentile works on the Sabbath, it is permitted, which would imply that the Jew who has the smelting concession could hire Gentiles by the year, and it would be permitted if they work on the Sabbath. He proceeds to explain that the situation is not quite analogous. Maimonides' permission of Sabbath work by Gentiles hired by the year applies specifically if the writing of the book or the weaving of the garment could easily be done within the year, and the Jew does not care whether the Gentile works on the Sabbath or not, since the work will be done in any case; but if the work required the Gentile to work on the Sabbath, the contract would be illegal for the Jew to make. Then follows a long analysis of various authorities which seem to refute his conclusion—that a Jew may not make any contract in which he is concerned whether or not the Gentile works on the Sabbath—and he shows that none of these opinions basically disagrees with his conclusions, and that therefore the contract for the ore-smelting is basically prohibited since the Jew *is* concerned with the work going on on the Sabbath. He ends the responsum with an analogy:)

A Jew who intends to set forth on a journey immediately after the Sabbath is forbidden to give his laundry, right before the Sabbath, to a Gentile laundress to wash his shirt and to return it to him immediately after the Sabbath; for in this case it is impossible for her to do this work unless she does it on the Sabbath, even though actually he does not pay her for the day, but for the job.

(He finally comes to this conclusion:)

In the case before us, I have gone over the whole matter and cannot find any clear permission, except with regard to the digging out of the ore from the ground (not the smelting). Since at times the workmen (the miners) rest from their labors (therefore they work and rest according to their own decision), it is permitted him to hire the workmen by job-contract: that is to say, "For ten wagonloads of ore, I will give you thus and so," and the Jew therefore does not benefit by the work that the miner does on the Sabbath, because the miner, if he wished, could finish the job at night; and he thus labors by his own decision. But with regard to the smelting, in which the burning and the refining goes on day and night without cessation, in this case (since, unlike the digging of the ore, the workman has not a choice of his own when to work and when not to work), there is no way of permitting it, unless he sells to the Gentile before the Sabbath all the large ingots of iron and for so and so much money. The Gentile then works for his own profit and turns the ore into smaller ingots while working for himself.

In this case there would be no concern about what "things appear to be" to the public because he merely sells, to the Gentile, part of the concession or privilege which he has gotten from the duke. Then, in payment of the debt (i.e., for the sale of the concession on the Sabbath), the Jew can then take the small ingots and sell them. Thus it is with the melting of glass. He may sell the whole concession to the Gentile before the Sabbath, and the Jew may take in payment the pieces of glass which were made, the Gentile having worked in his own behalf.

What appears to my humble judgment, that have I written.

38

✡

A GIFT FROM HAYM SOLOMON

Aryeh Loew ben Hayyim Breslau (born in Breslau, 1741) was rabbi of Rotterdam at the end of the 18th century, at about the time of the American Revolution. He had served as rabbi in a *Bet haMidrash* in Berlin, and then was rabbi in Emden. But for most of his career, down to his death, he was rabbi in Rotterdam. He was of high standing as an authority on Jewish Law, and also had considerable general learning, counting many Christian scholars among his friends. The responsum cited is from his book *Penei Aryeh*, no. 41, and deals with a rather interesting set of circumstances.

Haym Solomon, who is best known in the United States for his financial help to the Continental Congress at the time of the War for American Independence, must have achieved a wide reputation among the Jews of Europe as a generous philanthropist. It is evident from the following responsum that he was frequently asked to help worthy people in Europe, and that he responded generously.

The responsum states that a wealthy man, Gumpel of Wolfenbuettel, had asked Haym Solomon of Philadelphia to give a sum of money to a certain worthy man who needed help. Haym Solomon agreed to send the money, and did so; but by the time the money arrived in Europe from Philadelphia, the poor man, in whose behalf Reb Gumpel had solicited the alms, had become rich.

Now Gumpel wanted to know what, according to Jewish Law, was the proper thing to do with the money. Should he, for example, return it to Philadelphia? Or could the man for whom it was solicited accept the money, now that he was no longer poor? This is the question with which Aryeh Loew Breslau deals in this responsum.

TEXT

To the honored magnate and scholar, Gumpel Wolfenbuettel, may the Lord protect him:

Question:

With regard to the matter about which you have informed me, that the philanthropist (*ha-nadib*) Reb Haym of Philadephia, had inclined his ear to your words in behalf of X, and gave him a certain sum (ten *hagrim*) to be received through you. I rejoice greatly at the generous-heartedness of this man and his noble nature, whose ears are attuned to hear upright words. But you are now in doubt as to what to do, since God has "given enlargement" to X, and he no longer needs to receive charity. Perhaps (you suggest) the proper thing is to return the money to the philanthropist, Reb Haym, so that he can do with it what he wishes; and you would thus not discourage further charity. I know that your intentions are noble and that it is my duty to let you know what seems the right thing to do in this matter.

Answer:

According to the law, if the generous Reb Haym, may God preserve him, has already entrusted the money into your hands, and you have had possession of it even for one moment in behalf of the ultimate recipient while he was yet poor, then Reb Haym can no longer recall the gift under any circumstances. He has already moved the money from his domain and you have fully acquired it in behalf of the recipient. For it is a general rule of the law that we can acquire things in behalf of a man in his absence (or without his consent). This is expounded in the *Shulhan Arukh* ("Hoshen Mishpat," no. 125). Since you have acquired the money for the recipient, it is as if it already has come into his hand and he does not need to return it later when he becomes rich. Even if he, Haym Solomon, had not yet sent the money, but had merely written to your honor asking you to give this sum in his behalf to X, and therefore has not removed his money from his own domain, even so Reb Haym must fulfill the vow, i.e., the promise which he has made. This is explained in the *Shulhan Arukh* ("Yoreh Deah," no. 258.12), namely, that "he who promises to give a gift to his neighbor who is poor, (the promise) is to be considered a (formal) vow made to charity, and it is forbidden to retract it." Now, although after that, the poor man has become rich, nevertheless at the time the vow was made he was poor; therefore there is here no error in the essential element of the vow and it must be fulfilled.

(Breslau discusses the possibility of Reb Haym asking to be relieved of the vow, since the recipient does not need it. Vows may be thus cancelled by the permission of a rabbi or a scholar. Therefore, Breslau marshals various opinions as to the permissibility of asking the release of a vow made to charity. He continues as follows:)

. . . although it seems to me far-fetched that the philanthropist, Reb Haym, would ever ask to have his vow rescinded, since Maimonides wrote at the end of his "Law of Vows" that all vows to the sanctuary must be fulfilled and that one should not ask to have them released except in great emergency.

(Breslau discusses a further complication that may possibly apply to this situation. It is possible that the law may hold that, even if Haym Solomon has merely pledged the gift and had not yet sent it, that the very making of the pledge proclaims the gift as the actual possession of the ultimate recipient. This is based upon a principle of the law involved in making promises to give a gift to the Temple. Such a promise to the Temple is basically different in its status from a promise to give or transfer property to a secular person in a business transaction. In a business transaction, the ultimate recipient does not take legal possession until the object is actually moved into his possession [*mesirah*], that is to say, only when an actual transfer occurs does the recipient get legal possession. But the Temple acquires possession the moment the promise is uttered. The principle is stated as follows: Promising [*amirah*] to the Temple is equivalent to a transfer [*mesirah*] to a secular person. Now Isaac Alfasi and other scholars believe that a promise to charity is equivalent to a promise to the Temple and therefore the mere making of the promise gives the donee legal possession. Whereas the *HaMa'or* ["Book of Illumination," by Zerachiah haLevi, 12th century] and Solomon ben Adret [rabbi in Barcelona, 1235–1310] believe that a promise to charity is not equivalent to a promise to the Temple and therefore a mere promise to give charity does not give the poor man legal possession. He must actually receive it. Since this matter, therefore, is moot, he merely mentions it and proceeds to his conclusion:)

Therefore, it seems to me, as far as the law is concerned, that if the one who has made the vow, namely, Haym Solomon, does not ask to have the vow rescinded, he must give the money into the hands of the original recipient (i.e., the formerly poor man). He is not even permitted to delay, as is explained in the first chapter of Rosh Hashanah 6a. Commenting on the verse (in Deut. 23.24): *What thou sayest with thy mouth fulfill,* the Talmud says, this refers to the immediate fulfilment of a charity promise. But the recipient should bear in mind the opinions of *HaMa'or* and Rashba (who say that mere promising with regard to charity does not give the intended recipient legal possession). Then the recipient, in order not to be in the class of those who take charity when they have no need, must give the money to another poor man. It seems that the recipient can give it to any poor man he wishes, or even to one of his relatives, for we hold that the satisfaction of doing a favor is not to be counted as money, as Maimonides says. Even according to those who say that the satisfaction of doing a favor is a financial asset, it is not likely that, for the sake of such benefit, one would take charity (that he does not need).

What appears to my humble opinion, this have I written.

39

TO PROHIBIT DANCING

Joseph Steinhardt (1720–1776) was rabbi of Upper Alsace and then of Nieder-Ehenheim in Lower Alsace. Finally he was rabbi in Fürth until his death. He was one of the best known German talmudists of his time, receiving questions from Hungary, Italy, the Netherlands and Switzerland.

The responsum which we cite reveals the fun and pleasure that the Jews of the time managed to find in life, in spite of the endless restrictions and persecutions. The very fact that a number of responsa voice stormy objections to the habit of people of dancing, even men and women together, is an evidence of the fact that the rabbis were fighting against an irrepressible impulse. One of the most puritanical of these denunciations of the dance is this one from the beginning of the 18th century. That it hardly availed against the playful spirit of the people is obvious from the fact that Steinhardt could mention only two communities which were able to suppress popular dancing. The responsum which we cite is from his collection of responsa *Zikhron Joseph*, "Orah Hayyim," no. 17, and is written to the community of Plass.

TEXT

From the Lord of Peace, much peace and great kindness, to Jacob, the perfect man dwelling in tents, *the tents of the Torah, etc., Rabbi Jacob with his colleague, and to the head of the community, David Lev, and to the other leaders of the community.*

Question:

Your letter reached me last Friday before the entrance of the Sabbath, Bride and Queen. After I had read two or three pages of it, I stood shaken and desolate. I share all your sorrow at the great breach (of the Law) which the unbridled children of our people made in your city in contemptuously violating our sacred Torah and proper Jewish demeanor, in profaning the holiday by dancing, against which the rabbis have decreed, even when men and women dance separately. This we learn from the Talmud (Betza 36b): We do not clap the hands and we do not dance, etc. So it is stated furthermore in the *Shulhan Arukh*, "Orah Hayyim" 339 (as to the Sabbath) and 524 (as to the holidays). Now it is known to every intelligent person that clapping of the hands and dancing, even without instruments, is forbidden because of the concern lest one desire to utilize (and repair) a musical instrument. All the more is it forbidden with musical instruments. In his responsum, *The Gate of Ephraim* no. 36, Ephraim haKohen forbids dancing even on the half-holidays. But these people here made circles and danced, boys and maidens together. There mingled with them men and their wives, *Yea, jackals danced there* (phrased after Isa. 13.26). . . . Behold, your honors have asked me if you did well when you prohibited them and decreed an anathema that they should not continue to sin on the second day of the holiday. But these sinners rebelled against the anathema and rose against the leaders of the community. After they were reminded of the prohibition, they (the rebels) informed against them (the rabbi and the leaders) to the government. So the *hazzan* was forced to retract his prohibition. Now they have become more riotous; and they put your honor to shame with abuse and one of the fathers of these corrupt sons led in this trespass.

Answer:

Certainly you did well to protest with all your strength against these men who sin against their souls. It was right to do so.

Every rabbi in his city should protest with all his strength and abolish the dancing on the holiday, especially of girls and boys together, and certainly against this rabble, and to forbid the mixture of men and women. It is mentioned above and explained in the "Orah Hayyim," no. 529 (4), that men and women shall not mingle. No distinction must be made in this regard between the married and the unmarried men and women; for there is no step more likely than this to arouse the evil desires and lead towards adultery. For they gaze into the faces of women and maidens at the time of the dancing. (Here he goes into a very frank description of the moral danger of mixed dancing.)

The rule of the matter is that there is no greater protective fence against lewdness than to abolish the dancing of men and women together, whether married or unmarried. There is no step closer than this to lewdness or to adultery or to accustoming people to sin. So we, who received God's Law on Mount Sinai, are in duty bound to build fences and hedges that Israel should not do that any more. In my humble opinion you did not do well in that, because of your fear of punishment from the government, you and the officers withdrew and annulled your prohibition against these young men who are void of the commandments. We are in duty bound to expose ourselves to danger, at least to the danger of the loss of money, in order to maintain an enactment which we make to fence up a breach in Israel, etc.

> (He says that the same thing that happened in the city which writes to him now, happened to him when he was in Alsace. He tells how he persuaded the government to be on his side and prohibit dancing among the Jews.)

Now, behold everything that happened to Jacob (the rabbi of Plass) had happened to Joseph (namely, himself). When I first came to Nieder-Ehenheim in Alsace, where I was rabbi of the two provinces, somebody told me quite inadvertently that it was the custom of the young people there to rejoice on the festivals by arranging dances with the maidens. Thereupon, immediately, on the eve of the holiday, my order was sent around by the sexton of the court that they must not do so or there would be a penalty of 10 gulden, half of which would go to the government and half to charity. Then they sent and told me that they had already received permission from the government to have this dance and I could not undo his words (the governor's), for through the dance much wine is sold in the inn, and the government gets a certain amount from every measure of wine that is sold. Then I sent to them and said that not all the winds of the world would budge me from my position and cause me to annul my decree. The government is not permitted to make us give up our religious customs; for, thank God, the Kaiser and the other lords of the land by whose shadows we are protected, give us, in all the places where we dwell, the right to fulfill the commandments of our Law and to punish those who would wish to violate even the slightest commandment.

Finally they went to the government and informed against me. The governor sent word to me, with great respect, to come to him; and so I did. He asked me why I had done what I had done. I said it was because it is a great sin against our religious customs, as is explained in many places in the Talmud and the legal works and the book of ethics. But, because he knew the Bible, I said to him as follows, "It is written in the book of Judges, chapter 21.21, *Behold* (it is a festival) *if the daughters of Shiloh go forth to dance.* Since Scripture does not say 'to dance with the boys,' evidently Scripture means that the maidens danced alone." (Then he mentions other verses which he interpreted for the governor.) For this reason, I said to him, the community in Fürth and the community of Metz passed a decree that boys should not dance with girls at all, even at weddings, and imposed a great fine on any one who violated this. Such is the custom there to this day that the girls dance in one place and the boys in another place, and God forbid that the boys should mingle with the girls. Would that they did this in all the other places of Israel. . . . Then the governor said to me, "Good! Your words seem acceptable and right. At all events, I wish to write to the authorities of Metz." So he did. After he received the answer, he sent for me and told me that the government of Metz wrote him that my words were right. Then he praised our laws and our customs.

So you see that you did well to forbid this folly and hilarity, to decree a ban against them if they violate it. Those who transgress your words and support these rebellious youths are without doubt under the ban of Heaven and deserve great punishment because they profaned the honor of our sacred Torah and despised your honor and that of the leaders in your community.

May God send us our Messiah soon. Amen.

These are the words of him who seeks peace for thee with full heart, the young one,

Joseph Steinhardt

40

✡

ON CHILD ADOPTION

Jacob Emden (born in Altona, 1697; died there, 1776) was the son of Zvi Ashkenazi (see page 176, above). He studied first under his father, and later in his father-in-law's yeshiva in Ungarish-Brod, Moravia. For years he refused to accept a rabbinical post and traveled about selling jewelry; but in 1728, he finally accepted the rabbinate of Emden. He served for five years as rabbi and then moved back to his native city, Altona, where he remained for the rest of his life. He obtained permission from the government to open a printing establishment and printed a number of Hebrew books.

A brilliant but quarrelsome man, he fell into dispute with the occupants of the rabbinate of Altona-Hamburg-Wandsbeck, seeming to resent anyone who occupied a rabbinical office once held by his father. His most famous controversy, one that shook the Jewish world for a generation, was with Jonathan Eibeschuetz. He accused Eibeschuetz, who became rabbi of Altona-Hamburg-Wandsbeck, of giving amulets in which the name of the false messiah, Sabbetai Zvi, was used. He was a critical and brilliant talmudist and a prolific writer. His most famous books are his responsa, *She'elat Yabetz* ("Yabetz" being an abbreviation of Jacob ben Zvi) and a prayer book with a long commentary which is still widely used.

The responsum which we cite deals with a question which

nowadays has assumed great importance, but which was discussed very little in the extensive Jewish legal literature of the
past, namely, the question of child adoption. There is no section
of Jewish Law which deals with the subject directly. While kindly
Jewish families often raised orphans in their house, there was no
legal machinery for formal adoption of the orphan as the legal
child of the people who raised it. The Mishna was written when
Palestine was part of the Roman Empire. The Romans had a
widespread custom of legally adopting children. Yet there is no
law of adoption in the Mishna and later in the Talmud.

Child adoption, which has become so frequent in modern
times, is certain to give rise to many questions in Orthodox Law.
In recent years, in Palestine and in America, a number of responsa on some of the questions involved in adoption have been
written. Whatever is written will undoubtedly go back to the
opinions expressed by Jacob Emden in this responsum which
deals with the question in a thorough yet rather roundabout way.
The basic question involved is whether an adopted child is in
every legal sense the child of the adopting parents. The general
implication of Jacob Emden's answer is that the adopted child is
fully the child of the adopting parents. But, unfortunately, his
answer is not as clear as we might prefer it to be. The occasional
uncertainties in his answer are due to the form in which the
question happened to come to him. It will be remembered that
the responsa do not discuss theoretical themes, but answer specific cases as they are presented. It so happens that the status
of adopted children has become involved here with the question
of a vow. A man made a vow to debar himself from accepting
any benefit from his children. Is he then barred by this vow from
accepting any benefit from the child who was raised in his house
(i.e., adopted)?

Now with regard to vows, the tendency of the Law is always to
restrict their effect as much as possible. Men in excitement or in
desperation make certain drastic vows. The invariable tendency
of the Law was to limit those hasty vows. Therefore here, in the
question presented to him, desiring to delimit the scope of this

man's vow, Jacob Emden says that the vow does not debar him from receiving benefit from the adopted child. But generally, beyond the question of the vow, the adopted child is deemed to be fully his child. The responsum is I, no. 165.

TEXT

Question:

A man raises an orphan in his house, but has other children. He makes a vow to accept no benefit from his children. Is the orphan included in this vow?

Answer:

Since your question includes the statement that he has children (of his own), this means that you are sure that, if he had no other children, it would make a difference and he would be forbidden (to receive any benefit from the orphan he raised, on the ground that the orphan would unmistakably be the one referred to in his vow). But what is obvious to you is still dubious to me. Of course, with regard to the merit of performing a worthy deed, the Talmud says (Meg. 13a) that he who raises an orphan in his home is to be considered as if he had begotten him. Nevertheless, this does not apply to vows. For after all, such a child has no higher status than a man's own grandchildren who are often called "children" in many places in Scripture. Yet, when it comes to vows or to gifts (if a man says, "I give this to my children"), grandchildren are not included under the term "children." In the case of vows, we follow the (intent of the) usual speech of people (that is to say, when determining what the man meant by his vow, we decide it on the basis of the common usage of words). The formal language of the Law is different (from common parlance). Nevertheless, the matter is not free from doubt (i.e., it is possible that the vow does apply to this orphan). For certainly one might say that the child's status is better if the man has raised him for a worthy purpose. For, behold, in that case "it is truly as if he begat him." This is true if he raises such a child, not only an orphan child but even a child who has parents. If any child is raised by another man for the sake of *mitzvah* (that is to say, for example, to make a scholar of him), he is considered his child. If this "parent" has no children of his own and he raises this one to be his son and his heir, the child calls him "father" and he calls him "my son."

In this case, I would perhaps have some doubt, yet I would come close to saying that they are forbidden to each other when a vow is made (not to have benefit from each other; even in the case of vows, the adopted child, when the man has no children of his own, could be considered his son). For such a child is considered as if the man really created him. For this is the way people speak (and in vows we follow the daily language). Sometimes we do follow the technical language of the Torah, even when it is not identical with the language of daily speech, as in that case in the Talmud (B. B. 143b; where a man promises some gifts to his children, the Hebrew word for "child" is generally translated "son." Does it here mean "daughter" too? In other words, the language is ambiguous). So in such case of ambiguity the language of Scripture comes and helps decide the matter. But here, certainly the language of daily speech supports the language of the Torah (and an only adopted child raised for a noble purpose would certainly be the man's son).

But, if a man has other children of his own and also raises another person's son, it seems to me that then the vow means (to keep him from benefiting from) his actual sons.

(Emden goes into a rather full discussion of what is meant by "son" in the case of gifts and inheritance. He continues as follows, referring to a famous responsum of Meir of Rothenburg found in the *Hagahot Maimuniyot:*)

I found in a responsum in the *Hagahot Maimuniyot* to Maimonides' "Laws of Judgments," with regard to a gift, as follows: If a man makes a deed of gift to the son of his wife (i.e., by her previous marriage) and he uses this language: "Give it to our son," this is correct language and is often used. (In other words, a man may call his wife's son his son in a deed of gift, and the document is legal because it employs the common verbal usage.) If so (continues Emden) one might conclude that this would apply also to vows (as in the case discussed). Yet it is not quite a proof (in other words, it is not a complete analogy). It may be that in the case of the gift (to his wife's son whom he calls "our son") the situation is different, because she might also have signed separately and that would make it necessary to say "our son." Also in this case cited, it is not clear whether he had any other sons of his own.

(So Emden continues to analyze this case and concludes that it is not quite analogous with the case with which he deals, namely, that of a vow. He decides as follows:)

Therefore from this case we can derive no conclusions about the vow which the man made, since it is not clearly differentiated whether there are other children or not.

What appears to my humble opinion, I have written.

Signed,

Yabetz, S.T.

(He uses the initials "S.T.," customary in the signature of Sephardi rabbis, a custom which his father before him also followed occasionally.)

It is evident that Jacob Emden here was troubled by a number of uncertainties. The question was not clear. He did not know whether the man had any other children besides the adopted one. If he had, then it would be possible to restrict the scope of the vow (as the Law always tries to do) by saying that the man meant in the original speech only his own natural children. But, of course, if there are no other children but the adopted one, then the vow holds. In other words, even in the case of vows, which the Law always tried to delimit, an adopted child is a child in the full legal sense.

41

✡

JEWS AND HUNTING

Ezekiel Landau (born in Opatow, Poland, 1713; died in Prague, 1793) served as rabbi in Jampol, but most of his career and his fame came as rabbi of Prague where he served till his death. He was perhaps the greatest legalist of his time and, although he loved modern learning, he greatly feared the influence of modernism upon Jewish life. In the year 1773, a fire destroyed most of his manuscripts and that misfortune led him to record and print his writings.

The late Walter Rathenau, who associated frequently with the German aristocracy, never enjoyed hunting with them. He found it cruel and repulsive to his Jewish sense of mercy. He once said that any Jew who says that he enjoys killing animals in a hunt is not telling the truth. It is, indeed, difficult to imagine that Jews, trained as they were to be sensitive to the suffering of all living things, have ever indulged in hunting. Nevertheless there are at last two responsa, which indicate that at certain periods Jews did participate in that sport, and that some hunted for a livelihood.

One responsum is by the famous rabbi Isaac Lampronti, who lived in Ferrara, Italy, in the early 18th century. His responsum deals chiefly with the legal aspects of the situation. Since the shooting of an animal makes it unfit for food for Jews, for an animal must be properly slaughtered according to the laws of

Shehita, he discusses whether it is permitted deliberately to make an animal *trefa,* unfit for food.

The second responsum (which we here cite) is by Ezekiel Landau, the famous rabbi of Prague who was virtually a contemporary of Isaac Lampronti. He discusses the matter only incidentally from the legal point of view, but predominantly from the ethical and emotional point of view. The responsum is in volume II of his responsa collection *Noda b'Yehudah* ("Yoreh Deah," no. 10). It was in answer to an inquiry in behalf of a Jewish magnate who had acquired a large country estate and wanted to know whether, from the point of view of Jewish Law, it was permissible for him to hunt the wild animals on his estate. He did not ask the question himself, but asked it through a friend, Gomprecht Oppenheim, himself a scholar.

TEXT

The answer of peace to that scholar who is engaged in the Laws of Horeb (Sinai), the honored scholar of the Torah, Rabbi Gomprecht Oppenheim, may God preserve him.

Question:

I have received your letter. I do not know you personally. But (I note that) you have put your question in the language of wisdom. I answer all such who ask in this manner.

The essence of the question concerns a man whom God has rewarded with broad possessions. He has villages and also forests in which there stalk all the wild animals of the woods. He asks whether it is permitted for him to go in person to shoot with the blazing rod (i.e., a gun), to hunt; namely, whether it is permitted to a Jew to do this thing in view of the law against cruelty to animals or the law against general destructiveness.

Answer:

(Landau begins his response with a technical discussion as to which of the two prohibitions is the stricter, cruelty to animals or destructiveness. He concludes that there is no need to be too lengthy on this technical question, since it is permitted in any case to slay animals for the benefit of man and that this consideration cancels both the laws of cruelty and of destroying living things. Therefore, after the technical discussion, he goes into the morals of the question, as follows:)

Indeed, I wonder at the essence of the question itself. We do not find mention of hunters (in Scripture) except Nimrod and Esau. This (hunting), then, is not the way of the children of Abraham, Isaac and Jacob (of course, in order to get leather for shoes, etc., it is understandable). But how can a Jew kill a living thing without any benefit (to anyone), and to engage in hunting merely to satisfy "the enjoyable use of his time"?

It may be argued that bears and wolves and other predatory animals are always ready to do harm and that therefore whoever anticipates (the harm) by killing them has done a good deed. Yet even this is an error. For the law is not according to Rabbi Eliezer who says so (i.e., that it is praiseworthy to kill dangerous beasts). Even with regard to killing a snake, Maimonides and Abraham ben David disagree (as to its permissibility), in chapter 5 of the "Laws of Sanhedrin," section 2. Moreover, with regard to the opinion of Rabbi Eliezer (that it is right to slay predatory animals), we follow the explanation of Resh Lakish, namely, that this is (proper) only when they have already slain somebody. In such a case, we can argue that such animals as have been trained and belong to somebody may not be slain, but only such may be slain as are ownerless and wild and are dangerous, as is explained in the Talmud, Shabbat 121b.

Even this does not apply to our case here. For there, in the Talmud, it is permitted to slay them only when they invade the habitations of man; but to pursue after them, in the woods, their own dwelling-place, when they are not accustomed to come to human habitation, there is no commandment to permit that. Such pursuit simply means following the desires of one's heart. In the case of one who needs to do all this and whose livelihood is derived from it, of him we would not say that that (hunting and killing) is cruel, as we slaughter cattle and birds and fish for the need of man. In such case it makes no difference whether we slaughter kosher animals for our food or non-kosher ones for their hides, since all living things are given to man for his needs. But he who has no need to make a livelihood from it, and his hunting has nothing to do with his livelihood, this is cruelty!

So far I have spoken only from the point of view of proper ethical conduct, that a man should keep himself far from such action. But now I will add that it is even directly prohibited by law. For, consider, whoever engages in this pursuit needs to penetrate into the forests and to bring himself into great dangers where wild animals lurk. Scripture says, *Guard well your lives,* i.e., do not bring yourself into danger. That the danger is great can be seen from the words of Esau. Who was a greater expert in the hunt than Esau, of whom Scripture testifies, *And Esau was a man who knew hunting,* and he said of himself, *Behold, I am about to die.* Scripture means this literally, namely, that he actually endangered his life every day among the packs of wild animals. Thus Nahmanides interprets the verse. How, then, can a Jewish man bring himself into the places of packs of evil animals, even though, of course, the Torah permits a poor man who does it for his living to get into danger, as all merchants do who go overseas, for in matters of his livelihood he has no choice, etc. Therefore I say that, in this matter of hunting, there is actual prohibition for there is danger.

(He concludes:) Therefore he who will listen to me will dwell safely and quietly in his house and will not waste his time with such matters. Were it not for the fact that I love this magnate, who is famous for his good qualities, I would not involve myself in answering this sort of question; but I know that this magnate and all his household have a fine reputation. Therefore it is my duty to protect all his household with all my strength, so that they should not give occasion to those who hate him to hate him (more) out of envy; for they will now find reasons to murmur against him.

And may this be (the greeting of) peace from me who is burdened with many concerns.

42

✡

A PRAYER TO HASTEN DEATH

Hayyim Palaggi (born in Smyrna, 1788; died there, 1869) was
the chief rabbi (*Hakham Bashi*) in Smyrna from 1852. He was
highly respected as a legal authority among Oriental Jews. He
answered many questions and wrote on many themes. Even
though he left numerous unpublished manuscripts and lost manuscripts in a fire, he published twenty-six books.

The theme which is discussed in this responsum is one that has
become rather prominent in recent years in medical circles.
Should a doctor keep a dying patient alive, thus preventing and
delaying his imminent death? Of course, Palaggi discusses the
question, not from the point of view of medicine, but from the
point of view of prayer. Since prayer was considered to be a force
for healing, should we continue to pray in behalf of a greatly
suffering patient who is near death anyhow? Should we, by the
healing power of prayer, keep the patient, as it were, forcibly
alive? While discussing the subject from the viewpoint of using
prayer as a therapeutic agent, it cites all the relevant legal
material necessary for a more general discussion of the theme.
The responsum cited is from *Hikkeke Leb,* I, no. 50.

TEXT

Question:

A God-fearing scholar has a pious wife. For our many sins, the woman has been sick with a long, enduring sickness for more than twenty years. She is plagued and crushed with pain. Her hands and legs are shriveled up and she is therefore housebound. This woman has borne these sufferings patiently and her husband has met them without bitterness. He has not troubled her even for an instant. On the contrary, he shows her special love, so that she should not grieve because of this (i.e., that he may be resenting the burden).

This woman, because of her great pain, prays to God that He take her life so that she may find rest from her suffering. Her sons bring her physicians and many medicines and have hired a servant for her that she should have no household worries. But her pains have now greatly increased and even the doctors have despaired of her recovery from this sickness. She pleads with her husband and her sons that they should pray for her death and asks particularly that her sons ask God's mercy for her (to take her life). But her husband and her sons do not listen to her. On the contrary, they seek out scholars to study in her behalf. They continue to give charity and atonements and oil for the candelabra of the synagogue, in order to obtain healing for her.

Now, teach us, O righteous teacher, whether there is any prohibition involved if they should really pray for her to die in order that she may find rest . . .

Answer:

(The first part of his answer consists of a general discussion of obligation described in the Talmud, by which a husband is bound to love and cherish and protect his wife; of how wrong it is, according to the talmudic law, even to think of her death, if, for example, he wishes she were dead, that he might marry someone else. After discussing how sinful it is for a husband to wish his wife dead, Palaggi proceeds to show that in this case all these talmudic cautions are not applicable. He continues:)

But all this (the prohibition against wishing one's wife dead) applies only when such wishes are without her knowledge or due to hatred. But here, where she wishes it herself and can no longer endure her pain, under these circumstances, it is possible to say that it is permitted (to wish, or even to pray for her death). I come to this conclusion from what the Talmud says in Ketubot 104a. We are there told that on the day on which Rabbi Judah (the Prince) was to die, the rabbis decreed a fast and said that anyone who should say that Rabbi has died would be put to death. But the servant-maid of Rabbi Judah went up to the roof and she said, "The angels seek Rabbi Judah; the earthlings seek him too; may the earthlings conquer the angels." Since she saw how much suffering Rabbi Judah underwent, she changed and said, "May the angels conquer the earthlings." But the rabbis continued to pray for his recovery. She then threw a pitcher from the roof among them. This interrupted their prayer. And he died.

Now it is made clear in this section of the Talmud that the servant-maid of Rabbi Judah saw his great pain. Furthermore, we know from the Talmud and the later scholars that they learned laws from this servant-maid (she was a learned woman). She was full of wisdom and piety. Therefore we may learn from her this law, that it is permitted to ask mercy for a very sick person that he may die, so that his soul may come to rest. For if this action of hers were not according to the law, the Talmud would not have quoted it. Or if they had quoted it, simply because it was an incident that occurred, and they did not think that she had done well (in stopping the rabbis in their prayers) the Talmud would have said so. As for the rabbis who continued to pray that he should live, they did not know Rabbi Judah's suffering as much as the servant-maid did . . .

So the law emerges in our case that this woman who suffers all these agonies, and asks that others pray for her that she die, it is certainly completely permitted them to do so. I have also seen the words of Rabbenu Nissim to Nedarim 44a, in which he says, "It seems to me that there are times when it is necessary to pray for the sick that he die; as, for example, if the sick person suffers greatly and it is (in any case) impossible for him to continue living much longer." We learn this from the story of Rabbi Judah . . .

(Palaggi continues with the caution that there is some danger that people might think ill of the sons for praying that she die, although they have every right to. People may imagine that they are trying to get rid of the burden. Yet on the other hand, they cannot pray that she should live and continue to suffer. So he concludes with the following counsel:)

But others, who are not related and would be free of any of these suspicions, if they would pray that she should die and find rest, they may do so; for it is all for a high purpose and God searches the heart.

(He concludes with a reference to the medieval mystical work, *The Book of the Pious*.)

As it is said in *The Book of the Pious*, no. 234, that we must not cry out aloud at the time when the soul is departing, in order not to cause the soul to return (i.e., not to revive the dying person's hold on life) and bear more pain. Why did Ecclesiastes say, *There is a time to die?* It means that, when the time comes for a man's soul to go forth, people should not cry aloud so that his soul should return, for he can only live a short time and in that short time he must bear great pain. That is why Ecclesiastes said, *There is a time to live and a time to die* . . .

So here you have it explicitly (continues Palaggi) from the words of *The Book of the Pious*, that there is no justification for praying for one when he is already dying. See also what Isserles says in "Yoreh Deah" 339.

This is what, to my humble opinion, I have written hastily, for my strength is weak and may the Almighty God say, "Enough" to our troubles, deliver us from error, and show us wonders from His Law. Amen.

43

✡

BOOKS PRINTED ON THE SABBATH

Jacob Ettlinger (born in Karlsruhe, 1798; died in Altona, 1871), German leader of modern Orthodoxy, was one of the earliest German rabbis to receive a university education. He represented the merger of modern culture with talmudic learning. He was rabbi in Mannheim in the early part of his career, but most of his rabbinical career was in Altona. He was a strong opponent of the Reform movement which began in his day in Germany. He was the last rabbi in Germany to serve as a judge in civil law, because in the year 1803 the Danish government (Altona belonged to Denmark) abolished the right of rabbis to serve as civil judges. He is perhaps best known among talmudic scholars for his notes on many talmudic treatises, entitled *Arukh l'Ner,* and also for his responsa, *Binyan Zion.*

The responsum which we cite was written to the leading Orthodox rabbi of southern Germany at the time, Seligman Baer Bamberger, whose son was married to Ettlinger's daughter. The question discussed was part of the problem which was beginning to disturb European Orthodoxy, namely, the increase in the number of Jews who worked on the Sabbath. The question of their status in Jewish Law was a serious one, for, technically, a man who violated the Sabbath in public was described in the

Talmud as equivalent to an idolator. But such a complete rejection, of course, could hardly be carried out, since Sabbath violation became almost the rule in western Europe. (See responsum of Eliezer Deutsch, p. 256.)

Ettlinger discusses this question in two places: vol. II, no. 23; and vol. I, no. 15, which is here cited. The discussion of the second responsum takes a special form and involves the question of whether a pious Jew may do business with another Jew who works on the Sabbath. Specifically, the question is this: May we assign the printing of Hebrew books to a Christian printer who employs Jewish workmen who work on the Sabbath? If we do, are we not aiding these Jewish printers in their iniquity? That this problem is a vital one can be seen from the fact that at the time of the present writing, it is a subject of great agitation in New York. There the form of the question is largely this: May yeshivot and the like print notices in Jewish newspapers which are printed on the Sabbath? Ettlinger's responsum seems to be the first discussion of the subject.

TEXT

Question:

Your honor has asked me whether we should be concerned about having a book printed by a Christian printer who employs Jewish workmen, when we may well presume that they will print the book on the Sabbath. Thus we would be violating the command against placing *a stumbling block before the blind.*

> (This verse from Lev. 19.14 is used in the Law to describe the sin of leading someone else to sin when the other person may not even be aware that it is a sin. He is blind to his spiritual danger and we are putting a stumbling block in his road.)

Answer:

In a well known passage the Talmud says (Ab. Zarah 6): "Rabbi Nathan said, 'Whence do we derive that a man should not hand over a cup of wine to a Nazirite?' (i.e., to one who is under a vow not to drink wine) or a limb torn from a living animal to a son of Noah (non-idolatrous Gentiles are called "children of Noah." Among the seven commandments that they are expected to observe is to refrain from eating the limb from a living animal). The reason is (implied in the verse): *Place not a stumbling block before the blind*. . . . But this applies only when the two people stand 'on the opposite banks of the river.' " (That is to say, if the Nazirite could not reach the wine unaided, or the child of Noah could not reach the forbidden food without your handing it to him; in other words, if the occasion of sin were, as it were, "on the other side of the river," then you are guilty for making it accessible to him.) For if you did not hand it over to him, he could not sin.

Thus is it written in the *tosafot* on that page: According to this, you may not hand over any forbidden food to Jewish violators, even if it is theirs; for it is known that they would eat it, and they are forbidden to do so since they are still considered Jews. But this applies only when the Jewish violator stands in a place where he could not reach it if you did not give it to him, as the Talmud says, "when they stand on opposite sides of the river."

From this is seen (continues Ettlinger) that the *tosafot* say that, simply, when it is not "on opposite sides of the river" (i.e., if he could reach it without you), then it is permitted to give him what is forbidden, and this action does not involve violating the verse: *Put not a stumbling block* . . . Since this is the case, we need not be concerned about the possible violation of *put not a stumbling block* in the case of the question we are discussing. For clearly the printer has much work in the doing of which these Sabbath violators would work on the Sabbath, even if they did not have work given them by a Jew.

(Since Ettlinger is speaking to a fellow-expert in talmudic law, he now goes into a highly refined analysis of the limitations of the law of putting *a stumbling block before the blind,* and to what extent it may apply here in the case of the Jewish printers who violate the Sabbath. Within this discussion he speaks of another ground of prohibition against giving them work, namely, that it is forbidden in general to give help to sinners. After analyzing a host of different opinions, he concludes as follows:)

As far as law is concerned, the outcome of all this is that it is forbidden to hand over forbidden work to one who cannot get it himself. This is forbidden by the law of the Torah because of the verse: *Put not a stumbling block before the blind.* But where he can get the work himself, even though it is possible that because of the (Jewish) customer he will increase his forbidden acts, that is permitted even by rabbinic law. Of course, actually to assist him at the very time of the sin or where he demands the work specifically for a forbidden purpose is forbidden even by rabbinical prohibition, even though he could get the forbidden work himself (i.e., if he specifically asks for work to do on the Sabbath, this work must not be given to him). In all this there is no difference between a Jew and an apostate.

According to this, on the matter of our specific question, whether to print books at the establishment of a Gentile printer who employs Jewish workmen who work on the Sabbath, clearly there is no ground for concern; for they can do the work without your giving it to them. Besides, they do not ask for it specifically to do on the Sabbath, for if there were such a specific demand (to work on the Sabbath) even work by a Christian would be prohibited (for a Jew to order). Therefore there is no ground for prohibition (since the Jewish workman does not specifically ask it for Sabbath work).

Moreover, there seems to be yet one more reason why the law against putting *a stumbling block before the blind* does not apply here, namely that the customer does not give the work to a Jew at all, but to the Gentile master. If so, this is only *a stumbling block* in the second degree (i.e., he gives it to the master and the master gives it to the Jewish workman). Although the Talmud says (Ab. Zarah 14a) that with regard to a Jew suspected of violations, we must guard against the sin of *stumbling block* even in the second degree; yet where he gives the work directly to the Gentile, this sin of the second degree does not apply. . . . But at all events, for the reason which we have written, there is no ground for concern. There is neither the sin of *stumbling block before the blind,* nor the sin of helping at the time of iniquity.

Thus it seems to my humble opinion, the young one,

Jacob

44

✡

JEWISH FIRST NAMES

Elazar Fleckeles (born in Prague, 1754; died there, 1836) was a pupil of Ezekiel Landau (see p. 216, above). At the age of twenty-four he was rabbi of Kojetein, Moravia. In 1870, he was a rabbinical judge in his native city of Prague. He was greatly honored and widely respected for his scholarship. His responsa, *Teshuba Meahabah* (A Loving Answer) are published in three volumes.

The brief responsum which we cite reflects the old Jewish habit, in times of renewed contact with the outer world, of changing Jewish first names to more fashionable ones. A pupil had asked him a question about Jewish first names. He had heard that it is wrong for Jews to name a child for any biblical character earlier than Abraham. Fleckeles gives the origin of that belief and assures the questioner that the earlier names are quite proper and available, an important fact to know (he implies) when Jews are again changing their traditional first names to modern ones. The responsum is no. 35 in vol. I.

TEXT

As for your question whether there is any objection to calling (a child) by any of the names that preceded Abraham our father, of blessed memory—you have heard some people objecting to it.

I will, therefore, record for you the words of the sacred man of God, the author of *Birkhei Joseph* (Hayyim Joseph David Azulai) to "Yoreh Deah," nos. 265, 6. These are his words: "It is not proper to call (a child) by the name of Adam or Noah or Shem or Eber, for we should not take any names except from Abraham onward. Whoever is called by the name of Japhet and the like, of those biblical characters who preceded Abraham, does not belong with those who toil in the Torah and do the will of God. These are the words (says Azulai) of Joseph Trani (in his responsa I, no. 276). But the author of *Kneset haGedolah* (Hayyim Benvenisti) wonders at this statement, for, indeed, we do find the name (Rabbi) Benjamin son of Japhet (a Palestinian rabbi of the 3rd century, Ber. 33a). God forbid that the father of Rabbi Japhet broke the fence of the Law (if it had been really illegal to use the pre-Abrahamitic name). Similarly, we can call attention to the Rabbi Akavyah son of Mahalalel (Mahalalel was also a pre-Abrahamite name). The fact is, people are not particularly careful about this and call their children by the names of Adam, Noah, etc." (Thus far the quotation from Azulai, and Fleckeles continues:)

I can also mention that Reuben called his first son Enoch and yet there was an Enoch before Abraham. Now, for our many sins, people call their children with names similar to the names of the "Ishmaelites." In Egypt (our ancestors were redeemed because) they did not change their names (Bem. Rabbah 20.22).

Because of my many burdens I have shortened this.

I seek your welfare, always. The young one,

Elazar Fleckeles

45

✡

THE SWINDLING SCRIBE

Akiba (ben Moses) Eger (born in Eisenstadt, Hungary, 1761; died in Posen, 1837) was a gifted talmudist, but for a long time refused to take the post of rabbi, not wishing to profit from the study of the Torah. Eventually, due to economic necessity, his father-in-law having lost his fortune, he took the rabbinate of Markisch-Friedland in West Prussia. Later he was called to the important rabbinate of Posen. He always felt heavily burdened by the responsibilities of the rabbinate, and constantly sought some humble position as a teacher. He was a man of kindly and gentle nature and was universally beloved.

He wrote notes to various talmudic tractates, to the *Shulhan Arukh,* and frequent reference is made to his responsa. In fact, the responsum which we cite is quoted extensively in the *Pit-hei Teshuba* to "Yoreh Deah" 281, note 8. The theme of the responsum dealt with what must have been a painful experience, both to the questioner and to Akiba Eger who answered the question.

A scribe had been swindling his customers for two years. He was found to have sold *tefillin* which were worthless: the parchment scrolls which they contained, instead of having the required biblical passages written on them, were completely blank. Meantime, during these two years, the scribe had written two Sefer Torahs. Were these scrolls fit for use in the synagogue?

A scribe's profession was deemed to be especially sacred. The Talmud, Sota 20a, records that Rabbi Ishmael said to Rabbi Meir, a young scribe: "My son, be very careful, for thy work is the work of Heaven." A scribe was expected to be in a reverent mood when he wrote these documents. In fact, before writing the Sefer Torah, he was required consciously to declare that he was writing it for a sacred purpose. But if a scribe had proved to be a swindler, as this one had, could his work be deemed sacred and fit for use during religious services?

This responsum is interesting also from the negative point of view. There is not the slightest denunciation of the scribe. No word of rebuke escapes the gentle Rabbi Akiba Eger. He discusses the problem with judicial calm, carefully confining himself to an analysis of the laws involved. Incidentally, in speaking of a certain responsum by another author, he reveals the method of composition used by many of the great scholars. As they studied, they made notes in the margins of the books. These notes were often copied and published. The responsum cited is no. 69.

TEXT

To my dear friend, Rabbi Aaron, of the congregation of Silz (Sülz):

Question:

This is with regard to the scribe concerning whom it was revealed that for two years he sold *tefillin* which contained parchment without the biblical sections written on them. In the meantime this scribe had written two Sefer Torahs. What is the status of these Sefer Torahs?

Answer:

Indeed, this scribe is considered an apostate "for his own satisfaction."

(The Law makes a distinction based upon the motivations which impel a man to violate it. If a man violates the Law

for his own pleasure or satisfaction or benefit, *l'teavon,* the
sin is less grave than if he violates it in provocation,
l'hakh'is.)

This scribe's apostasy is merely for self-benefit, *l'teavon,* for
he did this to make financial profit. This being the case, since it
was not for "provocation," he is "kosher" to write a scroll. This
is in accordance with the line of decision of the scholars; as
Joseph Caro said (to "Orah Hayyim" 39), the kind of apostate
who is unfit to write scrolls and *mezuzahs* is one who is an apostate against the entire Torah, or an apostate provocatively against
one commandment. The *Magen Avraham* (Abraham Abele
Gumbiner to the same reference in the *Shulhan Arukh*) adds that
the same prohibition applies to a man who is an apostate to the
particular commandment involved, whether for benefit or for
provocation (that is, a man who does not believe in circumcision
cannot circumcise, and one who does not belive in the Torah
cannot write a Torah). Why is this so? For we hold with Asher
ben Yehiel, who said at the beginning of the tractate Hullin, that
an apostate who eats *trefa* food, neither particularly for his benefit nor to provoke, his slaughtering is unfit, for he is not to be
considered worthy of slaughtering. So here, not being a man who
puts on *tefillin* himself (if he is an apostate as to the commandment of *tefillin*), he is not considered a wearer of *tefillin* (therefore cannot write them). However, if he is an apostate only for
his personal benefit, even with regard to this particular commandment, he is fit (kosher) to write it.

But (says Rabbi Akiba Eger to the rabbi of Sülz) you lay
emphasis on the concluding words of the *Magen Avraham*
(Abraham Gumbiner) who quotes the *tosafot* as considering a
man unfit to write a Sefer Torah even if it seems clear that he is
an apostate merely for his own benefit. Therefore you say that
it is not necessary to inquire for what reason he is unfit, for in
this case we do not argue (in his defense) that he would not
lightly set aside that which is permitted and (turn to) that which
is prohibited.

If you will forgive me, that is not the way to understand the
Magen Avraham. Notice that he did not say that he is not to be

trusted to write a Sefer Torah; it merely says that he is personally unfit.

> (Akiba Eger here argues that, while in general the man may be unworthy, the *Magen Avraham* does not mean to say that he is not therefore to be trusted. He will proceed to prove by a number of analogies that a man may be unworthy in his dealing with certain commandments and yet may, as far as his personal life is concerned, be trusted. For example, a man who himself eats *trefa* food for his own pleasure or benefit, nevertheless, if one examined the slaughtering knife and found it suitable, before the man begins *shehita,* one could trust him to slaughter properly, for he would not go to the trouble of doing it wrong, when doing it right would be simpler. This is in accordance with the principle that a man would not wilfully abandon that which is permitted and go to the trouble of looking for that which is not permitted.)

But you also quoted the words of the responsa *Shebut Yaacob* (by Jacob ben Benjamin Cohen, "Yoreh Deah," no. 60) who tells about a scribe who erased the sacred names from unfit parchments of a Sefer Torah (it is forbidden to erase sacred names; that is why unfit Torahs have to be buried); and he wrote upon these parchments copies of the Megillah (Book of Esther). How can such a person (when he writes a Sefer Torah) be trusted to have written the Names of God in the Sefer Torah with the necessary sacred intention?

> (Jacob Cohen argues that a scribe who illegally erased God's Name from a worn-out Sefer Torah cannot be trusted to write a new Sefer Torah with proper dedication to the honoring of the Name of God, as he is required. Hence, the newly-written Torah is not fit for use.)

(To which Akiba Eger says:) His words are not conclusive. I will transcribe for you what I wrote on the margin of the responsa *Shebut Yaacob* (which you have just quoted). I said as follows: In my opinion this is not clearly so. As for the fact that he committed the sin of erasing the Names of God, he did this for personal benefit (not for provocation) in order to make profit; and with regard to an apostate for self-benefit, we say (in a case of *shehita*) that we examine the knife (and let him slaughter the animal), since we go on the presumption that a man will not (wilfully) abandon that which is permitted and (take the trouble to) turn to that which is prohibited. So also with regard to sanctifying the Names of God by the scribe when he writes the Torah. This is not so much trouble. There are only words that he needs to utter (then why should we not trust him to do it?).

(He concludes his responsum with a new argument:) Furthermore, I have another branch (i.e., of the tree of my argument). If this scribe wrote these Sefer Torahs for the people of the city in which he lives (this will make a difference), for we hold (*Shulhan Arukh,* "Yoreh Deah" 119b) that if a man is not suspected of eating forbidden food, but *is* suspected of *selling* it, one may be a guest at his house and eat with him. Similarly, we can say that the scribe may be suspected of causing others to stumble (by selling them worthless *tefillin*), but it was not suspected that he himself did not put on *tefillin*. If so, we can say that the Sefer Torahs which are for reading (in the worship) by all the members of the community, and he among them—how many times will they call him up to this Torah and he will utter the blessing over it? And he also needs to fulfill the duty of the reading of the Torah every Sabbath. This is just like the case of the man who sold *trefa* meat. You may be his guest and eat with him.

(Eger concludes:) We rely upon this reasoning, that since he himself will need that Sefer Torah, and is not suspect of sinning himself (as to his personal observances, his Torahs are usable). But in this matter I am not willing to rely upon my own opinion without the concurrence of great rabbis.

So it appears to my humble opinion, your friend,

Akiba the son of my teacher Rabbi Moses

46

✡

DELAYED BURIAL

Moses Sofer (or Schreiber: born in Frankfort, 1763; died in Pressburg, 1839) was the founder of modern Jewish Hungarian Orthodoxy. He became rabbi in Mattersdorf, Hungary, where he established a large yeshiva. In 1803, he became rabbi in Pressburg. The yeshiva which he established there became world-famous, and his disciples carried his strict principles to many great communities. No Orthodox rabbi in Hungary equaled his authority nor the reverence in which he was held.

In April 1772, Duke Frederick of Mecklenburg informed the Jews of the duchy that they would no longer be permitted to bury their dead on the same day that death took place, since such hasty burial might result in some being buried alive. The Jews of Schwerin (in Mecklenburg), considering the decree unjust, since it would compel them to violate Jewish religious law, wrote both to Jacob Emden in Altona and to Moses Mendelssohn in Berlin, asking for help. The problem aroused a considerable Jewish legal correspondence which is published in *Bikkurei haIttim* (1822–1823, p. 209–23b).

Mendelssohn advised them to conform to the decree. He said that even in ancient times our ancestors were concerned with this danger of burying alive. Therefore they placed the deceased in a cave-crypt and then visited the cave for three days. Nowadays, said Mendelssohn, when interment is immediate and direct, it is impossible to observe whether the buried is still alive. Therefore we should certainly wait three days before burial. The decree of the Duke of Mecklenburg is not against Jewish Law, but is actually in accordance with the more ancient custom.

Jacob Emden of Altona, in two friendly letters to Mendelssohn, refutes his arguments. He mentions that all Jews (Ashkenazim, Sephardim, and Orientals) bury their dead on the day of death. This widespread custom cannot be lightly set aside. Clearly the chances of live-burial must be remote if the rabbis took no cognizance of it.

A generation later a similar order was decreed in the Austro-Hungarian empire. Thus the question of the permissibility of delayed burial came before the greatest Hungarian rabbinical authority, Moses Sofer. His responsum is based to some extent upon the letters of Jacob Emden to Moses Mendelssohn.

The responsum cited is in Sofer's collection *Hatam Sofer* ("Yoreh Deah," no. 338). Although the name of the recipient has been omitted, it seems clear that it was the famous Galician rabbi, Zvi Hirsch Chayes of Zolkiew (cf. article by Meir Hirshowitz in *HaDarom,* V–VI, 118).

TEXT

Peace and all happiness to the rabbi, Light of the Exile, diligent and skilled, verdant olive tree of beautiful fruit (name not given), *head of the Rabbinical Court and the school of the congregation* (not given).

Question:

Your valued letter reached me and your precious spirit is in your question concerning the city *A* in which the doctor is a kohen and the laws of the country are that the dead may not be buried unless the doctor has examined and testified that there is no hope after they have fallen (i.e., that they are surely dead). The question is whether (the doctor who is) a kohen may enter even to touch and examine (the body). Your eminence wishes to permit this, and builds his foundation upon two things: 1) that the generation which preceded us permitted the keeping of bodies overnight, although this is actually a violation of both a positive and a negative commandment, and yet they permitted it because of the possibility of danger to life, therefore we should permit it now; and 2) your permission depends on the responsa *Bet Yaacob* (by Jacob ben Samuel of Zosmer), who argues the desirability of permitting a kohen to enter a room where an invalid is dying.

Answer:

When I read these words emanating from the mouth of a man of your standing, I was shaken and terrified, asking myself, who and what sort of a person was this in the generation which preceded us who had permitted the keeping of the dead overnight and, indeed, permitted it according to the opinions of the sages of Israel? I have never heard nor seen such an opinion. Behold, your eminence depends (for his argument) on the great tree (phrase from the Talmud, Pes. 112a, where it means to rely on a great authority), namely, the responsa of Jacob Emden, vol. II. But your imagination and memory misled you. For it is not found there at all, but in the *Books of the Gleaners* (in the magazine *HaMeassef,* "The Gleaner"), and in the book *Bikkurei haIttim.* There are found letters from the year 5532 (1772) in which the sage Moses of Dessau (i.e., Mendelssohn) argues to permit that which the sages of Israel had forbidden, because the doctors of our day say that the exact dividing point between life and death is not known except by the decay of the flesh. He brings his proof from the Mishna (Nid. X.3), which says that people with running discharges, etc., continue to cause uncleanliness (after death) until their flesh decays (which indicates that real death is indicated by the decay of the flesh). Thus too did Maimonides decide the law. Mendelssohn's further proof comes from the beginning of chapter VIII of the tractate Semahot, to the effect that we visit (to inspect) the graves of the dead for three days after burial; and that once they found a man alive and he lived thereafter for twenty-five years and begot children. And, continues Mendelssohn, if we are permitted (by Jewish Law) to delay burial because of the honor of the dead, in order to bring him coffins and shrouds, etc., how much the more should we delay burial because of danger to life. He added that in those days they buried them in crypts and he (if not really dead) could knock upon his crypt-wall, but nowadays when we bury them actually in the earth, there is all the more reason for us to delay burial. But (continues Moses Sofer) Jacob Emden (to whom Mendelssohn wrote) refutes him with a hundred refutations (a phrase from B. B. 85b). Also there are letters from the rabbi of Schwerin approving the opinion of Emden. Therefore I do not know who (which authoritative scholars) would dare permit the delay of burial. I imagine that since, in the kingdom of the Kaiser (i.e., Germany), they had become accustomed to this delay owing to the order of the king, the Jewish law was forgotten until people imagined that the delay was actually according to the law of the Torah (which, of course, it is not).

(Moses Sofer stresses the fact that to keep a body over-night, i.e., not to bury on the day of death, violates both a negative and a positive commandment.)

We see without doubt that, when the Torah speaks of the criminal who is put to death, and says first, negatively, *thou shalt not allow his body to lodge overnight,* and then, says positively, *thou shalt surely bury him,* that whoever allows the body to stay overnight thereby violates both the positive and the negative commandment. Thus, too, we are given the measure of what constitutes death. Perhaps (behind the command of the Torah for immediate burial) there was a tradition from the ancient students of nature, even though their old knowledge has been forgotten by the medical science of our day. Our rabbis relied on these ancient students of nature in many cases, as is explained in Talmud Shabbat 85a (where they relied on old wise people as to the layout of fields to avoid mixed species), and they based their reliance (on these old wise folk) upon the text, *Remove not the border which the ancients have set down* (Deut. 19.14). Or if, in the case of death, they did not have a tradition from these old students of nature, at least they must have received the direct test from Moses, or they relied upon the implication of the text, *all that hath the breath of life in its nostrils* (Gen. 7.22). Whether he is alive or dead, depends on whether there is breath in his nostrils, as is explained in Talmud Yoma 85a (where the question is discussed of digging a person out of a ruin which has collapsed upon him).

(Now Sofer pauses to refute the argument of his correspondent who denies that the test of breathing is sufficient proof of life or death, as in the case of a man buried under a ruin, because he considers that a special case. In this case the Talmud states that if on the Sabbath a house has fallen on a person, we may dig away the ruin until he is found; if found alive, we dig further, but if found dead we stop digging on the Sabbath. There the test of life and death is given. They dig down to his nose and if they find breath they continue to dig. Therefore the presence or absence of breath is the sign of death. The correspondent says that the case of a ruin is a special case, that with ordinary dead we should not rely merely on breath, but wait three days. This Moses Sofer refutes. Then he continues and says:)

The truth shows its own road. For many hours or days before actual death—as is known to the experts, such as the men of the burial societies who deal with the dead in our time—long before the time of actual death his senses have ceased and he lies in a coma like a stone, near death, and those who are experienced in the matter, i.e., the burial society, stand by him and watch for the instant of the final leaving of his soul, according to their traditional knowledge, that is to say, by his breath and his pulse. To the uninitiated standing around, there seems no difference in his appearance before or after the leaving of his soul until the actual decay of the flesh, which may occur a day or two days afterwards. But the experts knew to the moment when he died.

(Moses Sofer says that the Talmud reference cited by Mendelssohn describes the death according to the knowledge of the average folk, which may take days before they recognize the decay of the flesh; but the experts know exactly when the moment was. Then he discusses various other sources, such as Semahot, ch. VIII, and the law of the Rambam about visiting graves, and disposes of them, and finally concludes as follows:)

At all events, this is our conclusion. We have no other authority than the words of the Torah, and the tradition of our fathers and whoever murmurs against that murmurs against the Divine *Shekhina*. The religious prohibition of keeping the dead overnight stands firmly in its place, except, of course, for the command of the Kaiser (which, of course, we obey).

(The rest of the responsum deals with the question of prohibiting a doctor who is a kohen from examining the body to determine death according to government decree, since a kohen may not be in contact with the dead, except, of course, at the burial of his own close relatives.

Essentially, Moses Sofer makes a defense of tradition based upon the idea that its knowledge as to when a person is dead was rooted either in ancient wisdom now forgotten, or in direct tradition through Moses from Mount Sinai, or in the precise knowledge of the experienced men of the burial society. He concludes that of course we must obey the government's law, but we do not admit that the government law is in agreement with the law of the Torah.)

47

✡

A FALSE CLASSIC

Mordecai Benet (or Marcus Benedict: born in Hungary, 1731; died in Karlsbad, 1829) was chief rabbi of Moravia. He was a genius as a child. At his Bar Mitzvah his teacher proudly exhibited three manuscripts which the child had written: one, a commentary on the Bible; another, on the Haggadah of Passover; and the third, notes on certain talmudic tractates. Mordecai Benet completed his rabbinic studies in Joseph Steinhardt's yeshiva in Fürth. Then he had a position in a *klaus* in Prague. In 1789 he was made chief rabbi of Moravia. His responsa are in two volumes, one called *Har haMor* (Mountain of Spices), and the other *Perashat Mordecai* (The Interpretation of Mordecai). He was a clear and logical thinker. He did not object to modern education, but strongly opposed reforms in Jewish ritual.

The responsum which we cite is of considerable interest in Jewish literary history. It involves a volume that was published in 1793 purporting to be a hitherto unpublished collection of the work of the great 13th century scholar, Asher ben Yehiel. The book was called *Besamim Rosh* (The Best of Spices). It was published by Saul Berlin (1746–1794), who was the son of Levin Hirschel, the rabbi of Berlin. Saul Berlin was a first-class talmudic scholar who had joined the ranks of those who stood for modernizing Jewish education, although he was rabbi in Frankfort-on-the-Oder. He said that he had bought this manuscript from a

Turkish Jew in Piedmont and now published it with his own commentary.

The book created a sensation because many of the ideas supposedly expressed by Asher ben Yehiel five centuries earlier were very much like some of the ideas expressed by the religious reformers. Saul Berlin's father proclaimed the authenticity of the book and wrote in defense of it. In fact, the great Ezekiel Landau also wrote an approbation of the book.

In this responsum, Mordecai Benet denounces the book as false and spurious. It is interesting to note his arguments and to compare them with the arguments of Leopold Zunz to the same effect in his *Ritus,* pp. 226–228. Zunz, of course, approaches the problem of the authenticity of the book from the scientific point of view. He discusses style, discovers anachronisms, and the like. Yet it is remarkable that Mordecai Benet, a classical talmudist, in denouncing the book, uses virtually the same arguments that the scientific scholar, Zunz, used.

The responsum was written as a letter to the father of Saul Berlin, the honored rabbi of Berlin, who had defended the authenticity of the work. Benet reveals his early biblical studies by the brilliant use of biblical phrases in his honorific introduction addressing Rabbi Zvi Hirsch of Berlin. It is virtually impossible to convey in English the interweaving of biblical verses which continue through three paragraphs. One paragraph will perhaps give some idea of the style. The responsum is no. 5 of *Perashat Mordecai.*

TEXT

The man whom God has given rulership, faithful in all his house *(Nu. 12.7); the generation is not orphaned and* Israel is not widowed *(Jer. 51.5); with all his strength he walks with God and is* faithful to the Holy One *(Hos. 12.1); banner of the generation,* flask of heavenly manna *(Ex. 16.33); the great gaon, the central pillar, thus is his sacred name Zvi Hirsch, rabbi of Berlin: Peace to all his household.*

(Then follow two more such honorific paragraphs. The second paragraph ends as follows:)

. . . Behold, fear and great darkness is spread over all the children of Perez (meaning Israel) with regard to the book which is called *Besamim Rosh*. It is called by this name so that its waters may spread incense over all who pass on the road to the Torah, but (instead) it giveth poisoned waters and sendeth forth its arrows to the mark (Sam. 3.12); *burning instead of beauty* (Isa. 3.24) and instead of incense, corruption *melteth our heart to water*, etc.

Alas, *a Hebrew has been brought here to mock* (Gen. 39.14) at all the essentials of our religion. Jacob uproots and biteth the heel (Gen. 3.15). It is said in this book, section 251 as follows: "Therefore it is agreed among all that no man can truly understand the principles of the Torah and the commandments from what he can learn by interpreting the verses of Scripture and the words of the rabbis. Only that mind which learns and is trained in the books of the scholars of the nations (can understand the Torah)."

(To which Benet comments): Where then is our wisdom and our intelligence in the eyes of the nations? Have then our hearts been kept from wisdom until we finally satisfied them from the books of other people? Then where is the source of the wisdom and understanding which our fathers and our father's fathers had, out of whose mouth this Torah never budged, and who despised the books of these (pagan) investigators. "Away, away," they called out to such books and to their *ragged eminences* (a phrase from Ezek. 16.16). Did they, our fathers (who never studied these foreign books), not know the essence of the Torah and the commandments? Did they not understand the laws until Aristotle came, that fortress to the deceivers who walk in his heels? The philosopher Leibnitz is a copper wall (i.e., a fortress) to those who throw off the yoke because of his words. Not so, O father (speaking to Rabbi Zvi Hirsch). Asher ben Yehiel in his responsum no. 54 was very explicit that we should not draw water from their wells.

(In other words, Asher ben Yehiel was the great opponent of philosophy. Then how could he possibly have said, as this book quotes him as saying, that you cannot understand the Torah unless you understand Aristotle?)

Furthermore, he (the author of this book) speaks bitterly against Maimonides when he (Maimonides) lays down the foundations of the essentials of the faith. He (the author of this book) says: "Who permitted him (Maimonides) to add to the Torah and to set down essentials of the faith, deriving these from his own ideas? Furthermore (the author said) Maimonides found this neither in Scripture nor in tradition, etc."

(To which Benet comments:) Would that he had remained silent, and it might have been accounted to him as wisdom (Job 13.5), for his words are empty. Indeed, our rabbi, Maimonides, neither added nor subtracted. All his words are clearly based on Scripture and the Talmud, and *the righteous can walk by them* (Hos. 14.10) . . .

Also, he brings shame on all Israel and the Torah when he says as follows (as if it were Asher ben Yehiel speaking): "This degraded generation, in which the Torah is confused and the laws twisted, gropes like the blind along the wall and creates falseness, and the Torah is sealed as a sealed book, as if a kettle were upended over it."

(To which Benet comments:) The mouth that speaks these words, whoever it really be, is an unblown fire and his sickness will not cease; for he slanders the daughter of Jerusalem and brings the battlements down to the earth. He extinguishes the fiery Law of truth which Moses commanded us as an inheritance. Behold it is a falsehood that he appends to this the seal of Asher ben Yehiel. Whereas Asher ben Yehiel in his responsum no. 55 said: "Is this not so? In my day and in my place did we decide the laws from parables or analogy (i.e., from Greek sources)? While I live there is Torah in Israel, whose proofs are brought from the Mishna, the Babylonian and the Jerusalem Talmuds." His testimony is trustworthy for he was a foundation-stone of the Torah and its high fortress even in his youth. He did not refer merely to himself, for he would never imagine in his heart that he was wiser than all his generation, God forbid.

(In other words, Asher ben Yehiel, who, as we see from his responsa, proudly indicated that all laws in his time were derived by logical analogy from the Jewish classic sources, could not have said that the laws were all a confusion and that the people grope about as the blind in darkness.

So Mordecai Benet takes up all the other strange passages in the book *Besamim Rosh* and proves from the authentic responsa of Asher ben Yehiel that Asher ben Yehiel could not possibly have been the author of these statements. This brilliant literary analysis unfortunately is not complete, and the editor adds the following note at the end:)

Only this much did I find in the copy. It seems that the responsum is not complete here, but what there is testifies of what the total must have been.

Certainly Mordecai Benet proves in masterly fashion that the passages which he cites could not possibly have been written by Asher ben Yehiel, but that, of course, is still not a complete proof that the bulk of the book may not have come from a genuine ancient manuscript. Clearly, Saul Berlin, who at best was a dubious character, inserted radical opinions and ascribed them to Asher ben Yehiel. The rest may well have been genuine. Saul Berlin's own commentary appended to the book is a typically learned talmudic commentary. The book is still quoted nowadays, although it is used with caution.

48

✡

SECEDING TO FORM A NEW
CONGREGATION

Moses Schick, one of the great Hungarian leaders, was, for the
better part of his career, rabbi in Chust. The breaking up of congregations was a problem with which he dealt several times. On
the whole he was opposed to such action; but he found justification in the instance before us because, as he says, the separatists
are in this case followers of true Judaism.

The medieval Jewish congregations were coextensive with the
Jewish community. The civil and the religious life were virtually one. The Gentile authorities imposed taxes upon the entire Jewish community and the community assumed the responsibility of pro-rating the tax upon each householder. Any attempt,
therefore, to make private arrangements with the secular authorities was considered treachery to the community. The community
guarded its unity and used the weapon of excommunication
(*herem*) to prevent any breakdown of communal unity, in spite
of differences in financial status. This identity of community with
congregation served well until modern times, when differences in
religious attitude began to appear among Jews. Sometimes it was
the Reform movement which gradually conquered a community,
forcing the Orthodox members of the community to worship
contrary to their convictions. Sometimes, after the Hasidic move-

ment grew in eastern Europe, the worship of the Hasidim, modeled after that of the Sephardim, was sufficiently different from the Ashkenazi ritual of the community that the Hasidim felt they needed their own synagogues.

This growth in modern times of religious differentiations precipitated a difficult, complicated and often bitter controversy in the realm of Jewish Law. All the legislation of the past had piled up precedents against dividing the community; yet now, in spite of all precedent, some division became necessary. Division was especially difficult in cases where Orthodox groups desired to break away from a non- or semi-Orthodox community. Being Orthodox they could not break away unless their action were not only in response to their immediate spiritual needs, but justified by the decisions of Jewish Law. Before it could be so justified, great ingenuity and much discussion were required.

In Germany, when Samson Raphael Hirsch, the founder of modern neo-Orthodoxy, was called to Frankfort, he found only a handful who proclaimed themselves Orthodox. He wanted to break away from the Liberalized community and build a separate Orthodox community. In the legal discussion that followed, the other great Orthodox authority in Germany, Seligman Baer Bamberger, of Wuertzburg, disagreed with Hirsch as to the permissibility, and certainly as to the duty, of the Orthodox to break away and form a separate congregation. Finally, Hirsch founded his separate congregation in Frankfort, after the government of Prussia, in 1876, passed an enabling act, permitting secession. This was a sort of poetic justice, since in the early Middle Ages it was the pressure of the Gentile communities through the governmental burden of taxation which necessitated the unity of the Jewish community. Hirsch's congregation, which grew large and influential, was always known as the Secession congregation (*Austritts Gemeinde*).

In Hungary the problem of secession was not local but national, because the tendency to reform and modernization began on a national (and almost governmental) level. First the Hungarian government, during its period of independence, and then the Austrian government in 1867, passed a law whose purpose was to modernize Jewish life. A general Jewish congress was convened by the king at Budapest, in December 1868, for the purpose of modernizing the organization of the communities and the schools of Hungarian Jewry. This attempt at modernization aroused the Orthodox to protest and they petitioned Parliament to accept separate Orthodox communal regulations. Thus the Orthodox Jews broke away. They were not the only group thus to separate. Another group would not join the Orthodox, but still refused to modernize their old communal congregational statutes. This came to be known as the "Status Quo" group. Then the Hasidim in many communities, insistent on their own ritual, also broke away.

If whole congregations chose the same party, the dissensions were not too bitter. But it frequently happened that one group in a community chose one party and a different group chose another. What were these dissenting groups to do? If they were non-Orthodox, they would not hesitate to form their own congregation. But if they were Orthodox, they were concerned with the legal question of whether they had the right, according to Jewish Law, to break off from the main community.

This was the question answered by Rabbi Moses Schick.

The responsum is in his volume, *Orah Hayyim,* nos. 34 and 36.

TEXT

I have been asked whether, if part of a congregation has accepted the manifesto or regulations (*Constatierung*) of the Orthodox and desire to separate themselves from the rest of the congregation, they are permitted to do so according to the laws of the Torah; and, if the rabbi of the community has proclaimed a prohibitory decree, whether that prohibitory decree is legal. Now it seems to me that in "Hoshen Mishpat," no. 163, it is explained that a community is considered to be a partnership. With regard to partners, the law is ("Hoshen Mishpat," no. 176) that, if a fixed time has been set for the duration of the partnership, the partners are not permitted to separate (within that time limit). But if no fixed time is set for the duration of the partnership, they may separate. As for the "partnership" of a community, it would seem that, since no fixed time has been made for its duration, they (any group) should be permitted to separate. Nevertheless, see *Shulhan Arukh,* "Orah Hayyim," at the end of 54, where it would appear that they are not permitted to separate, even if they so desire, merely to set up separate High Holiday services, or if they wish to engage another cantor. Furthermore, the *Magen Avraham* (Abraham Abele Gumbiner, 17th century) says that a part of a community may not establish a synagogue of their own.

> (He continues for a long paragraph to marshal all the past laws against permitting part of a community to break off from the general community. Then, towards the end of the responsum, he begins to state the reasons why they may, as follows:)

Nevertheless, the *Magen Avraham* quotes Joseph Colon (Italian rabbi, 15th century) as saying that, if there is some little justification, a group may not separate from the larger group; if, however, it is clear that there is great justification to change or to separate, it is permitted to do so. This surely applies here in the subject we are discussing. The manifesto of the Orthodox was made by the agreement of the sages of Israel in order to strengthen the religion. It is a duty of all to accept such decrees, as we know from "Yoreh Deah," no. 228.33, namely, that if a man swears that he will not participate in the decrees of the congregation, his oath is a false oath. This implies that, in case of decrees whose intention is to guard against religious violation, we are by law in duty bound to follow them. This is certainly a great reason, and for a great reason we may separate.

But even with regard to the first matter of which I have written, namely, that the partnership (of the community) has an implied understanding not to separate, nevertheless—as Isserles makes clear—if one of the partners has done wrong, there is a discussion among various authorities as to whether one partner may separate from the partnership. Those who say that he may not declare, however, that the violator must pay damages for what he has done. But what if his wrongdoing is in matters that cannot be repaid? All then admit that the partnership may be dissolved. . . . So it is in our case. When one side (i.e., the Orthodox) wants to obey the commandments and the other side does not so wish, all agree that they may separate.

✡

49

MEIR BAAL HaNES.

Meir Ash (died 1861) was rabbi in Ungvar, Hungary. His responsa, *Imrei Ash,* published in two volumes, are widely used and frequently quoted.

The responsum cited deals with one of the most familiar semi-religious objects in every old-fashioned Jewish home—the little, rectangular, tin charity box bearing the name of Meir Baal haNes. Meir Baal haNes is often identified with Rabbi Meir of the Mishna, who was a pupil of Rabbi Akiba. Perhaps this identification is due to the fact that the Talmud mentions (Ab. Zarah 18b) certain miracles which he performed. Yet this must be a mistaken identification. The Talmud, although it speaks lavishly in his praise, nowhere calls him "Meir Baal haNes" (the Miracle Worker). The Meir Baal haNes now buried in Tiberias, to whose grave pilgrims come to light candles, was some other Meir (see the article, "Meir Baal haNes" in *Otzar Yisrael*). Before the 19th century the money given in honor of Meir Baal haNes was not intended for the poor of Jerusalem. Just as people lighted candles on Yom Kippur for the souls of their own relatives, so they gave money for oil or for candles all through the year for the soul of Meir Baal haNes. Then, a little more than a century ago, when Russian and Polish scholars emigrated in larger numbers to Palestine, certain leading Russian rabbis decided that the money, or some of the money, given by people for candles or oil in honor of Meir Baal haNes should be transferred to the support of the poor in Palestine. The money given in honor of Meir Baal haNes has, therefore, since the beginning of the 19th century, been collected from all Jewish households for the support of poor scholars in Palestine (see also the *Otzar Yisrael* article, "Halukkah").

This decision to change the use of the money involved a problem in Jewish Law. It is an old question, going back to the Talmud, whether money used for one charity may be diverted to some other use which the donor did not intend. The question came for decision to Meir Ash, who was the leading Hungarian authority of his time. His answer deals with the basic problem of the law, whether charitable gifts may be changed from their original purpose to another. The responsum is no. 102, vol. I.

TEXT

Question:

Some time ago, I received a letter from that Light of the Exile, Rabbi Hayyim Nathan Dembitzer, of Cracow. He asked me to endorse the decision of the worthy men in charge to turn over the money, originally collected for Meir Baal haNes, for the maintenance of the wretchedly poor who are in the Holy Land. Rabbi Dembitzer also sent me the manifesto which had previously been issued to this effect in Brisk (Brest-Litovsk) by the great rabbi there, L. Katzenellenbogen, and the other signatories.

Now, since the great men of our generation have already expressed the thoughts of their broad mind on this matter, I do not know why I need (to say anything), why *the voice of the dove* (Isa. 38.14) should be heard with the roaring of the lions. It would be better for me *to stay hidden among the baggage* (I Sam. 10.22) and be hidden in the tent and not to make my voice heard. But since the great rabbi has urged me to write my humble opinion, I am unable to refuse any longer and I say as follows:

Answer:

It is clear to my humble opinion that, even if it is true that the author of *The House of Joseph* (Caro) and Moses Alshech (his pupil) decreed long ago that all the money collected for Meir Baal haNes be given to Palestine alone, nevertheless I have no doubt that their decree applied only to such gifts as were given without qualification in honor of Meir Baal haNes. For it is known throughout all Israel that what is given to Meir Baal haNes is for the benefit of the poor of Palestine; and therefore he who gives a gift, without specifiying it, really gives it according to this prevailing custom (to be expended according to the prevailing custom), as is cited in the various legal opinions. Therefore, whoever wants to change that is (legally) at a disadvantage.

But that those two rabbis should have decreed that no man may give money in the name of Meir Baal haNes other than for the poor of Palestine (is strange, for) how could any court decree that a man should not be able to give to what his heart desires? No one can forbid the use of a man's property for himself or for others.

Therefore, without doubt, the words of Solomon Kluger (of Brody) are correct when he says that the ban (of Caro and Alshech) does not mean this (that the money can be given only to Palestine). At all events, if a scholar says something, we do not reject him (Hul. 7a), especially so great a scholar as the one who made the decree that, if one even specifically says that he gives the money for the lighting in the synagogue, the money may be sent to Palestine. In this regard there is a root for his words in what Joseph Colon said (in his responsum no. 128) and is cited in the *Bet Joseph* (of Joseph Caro) to "Yoreh Deah" 296 and 299, as follows: "If a man donates money for illumination in the synagogue, and if without that gift there is enough for adequate lighting in the synagogue, then, although through that gift the lighting would be increased, nevertheless, the officers can change the use of the gift and give it to the poor. But, if without that gift there is not enough illumination in the synagogue, then it is forbidden to divert the money into gifts for the poor."

According to this, therefore, since nowadays in most congregations of Israel there is enough illumination provided by the congregational money, in that case he who makes a gift for illumination (we may assume that) his intention is not merely to increase the illumination or that the illumination be necessarily at his expense. For, consider, even without his gift, *the children of*

Israel would have light in their dwelling-places (i.e., in their synagogue). Therefore it was quite right of the rabbi of Brisk to command that all the money that is given in the name of Meir Baal haNes for lighting in the (his) synagogue can be sent by the officers to the poor of the Holy Land. He who desires that his gift be only for the lights in the synagogue of his city, and not for the poor, should nevertheless give it without specification, and thus there shall never be any lack of money for light. But even so, if he does make the gift without specification, the officers can still give it to the poor, according to the words of Colon and Joseph Caro, and there is no ground for concern that this man has not fulfilled his vow.

> (After going further into the matter, he speaks of the special value of this charity. He then cites a statement from the Jerusalem Talmud at the end of Peah, in which there is a discussion of all the money spent in building synagogues; and one rabbi says that some of the money could well have been used to support students and the sick-poor. Then Meir Ash proves that those who now live in Palestine are both scholars and indigent sick, and the money can be taken even from synagogue needs and be used for their support. He puts it thus:)

Consider these poor inhabitants of the Holy Land who left their native countries to walk before the Lord in the land *upon which the eyes of God are always turned* (quotation from Deut. 11.12) and to dedicate their days and their nights to the study of the Torah and live lives of poverty; behold, they surely are among those who can be called "workers of the Torah" and they can also be called "poor" and "sick" as their lives are always in danger. Therefore, even if it is possible to be concerned that, if the money which was given for lighting be sent and there is not enough for that purpose (lighting), even so it would be a *mitzvah* to use it for the poor of Palestine.

(So he concludes:) There can be no objection to the decree made by the rabbi of Brisk and the other great rabbis whose words you have sent to me.

These are the words of your friend, the young

Meir Ash of Ungvar

50

✡

MODERN SABBATH VIOLATOR

Eliezer Deutsch of Bonyhad (1850–1916), famous Hungarian rabbi, is one of the rabbinic authorities to give consideration to the status of the modern Sabbath violator.

The Talmud (Er. 69a) defines an apostate as one who violates the Sabbath in public. This definition is codified as law in the *Shulhan Arukh* ("Orah Hayyim" 385.3) as follows: A Jew who violates the Sabbath in public is, in effect, an idolator. This is based upon the doctrine that the Sabbath is, in a unique sense, a covenant between God and Israel, and if a man persistently and publicly violates the Sabbath covenant, it is as if he violated all the commandments.

In the modern era this stern judgment has become difficult to maintain. The constant contact of Jew and Gentile in business relations has led many Jews to do business on the Sabbath. These public violators of the Sabbath could not be easily spurned as apostates. Many of them still considered themselves loyal and religious Jews, except for these business necessities. Then how should they be classified today in the face of the decision of the Talmud and the *Shulhan Arukh,* which plainly declare them to be apostates and idolators?

As was to be expected, the problem arose in modern times first in Germany, where Jews first came into close contact with the Gentile world. Jacob Ettlinger (1798–1871), rabbi of Altona, in his *Binyan Zion* (n.s., no. 23) discusses the problem. In his responsum he says: "As for the sinners in our time, I do not know how we are to judge them. For our sins, this plague has spread so far that to most of them this (violation of the Sabbath) seems to have become 'permissible' practice. They pray the Sabbath prayers, and then they go and violate the Sabbath."

It was indeed difficult to proclaim that a regular attendant at synagogue services was an apostate because he believed that necessity compelled him to work or do business on the Sabbath.

The discussion of the problem spread as modern life invaded more and more lands of Jewish residence.

The form of the problem as it came to Eliezer Deutsch was in itself interesting. When a scribe had completed writing a Sefer Torah, it was customary to have a "completion celebration" (*siyyum*) in the synagogue. At this *siyyum* the members and guests were asked to make contributions to defray the costs of the scroll. To encourage their generosity, they were given an opportunity to write their names symbolically into the scroll. This was done in the following manner: the scribe wrote the last few lines of the Torah in hollow letters to be blacked in at the *siyyum*. If the donor's name was Abraham, for example, the scribe picked out the hollow letters spelling "Abraham" and guided the donor's hand as he filled them in.

The responsum to be cited appears in *Tvuot haSadeh,* by Eliezer Deutsch, p. 80b (written Wednesday, New Moon of Heshvan, 5661 [1901]).

TEXT

Question:

May we permit Sabbath violators to "write in" their names in the Sefer Torah, when the law considers them to be renegades and idolators? Does not the law say specifically that a Torah written by an unbeliever must be burned, or at least is unfit for use?

Answer:

Peace and all good life and blessing to my beloved friend, the scholar outstanding in learning and fear of God, the dear and honored . . . Moses Klafter, in the city of New York.

Your valued letter has reached me. Now with regard to the question that it is the custom in your place that, when a Sefer Torah is being donated to the synagogue, certain letters are left (incomplete) at the end of the Torah and whoever gives most money is allowed to fill in these letters, thus completing the scroll.

Now there are among such people men who violate the Sabbath in public and therefore are to be considered apostates, and you are in doubt if that fact does not render the Torah one "written by apostates" and therefore unfit for public use.

I answer you in brief as to what is stated in the *Shulhan Arukh*, "Yoreh Deah," no. 281, namely, that a Sefer Torah which an apostate has written is unfit for public use. The law applies specifically only to the man who violates the law *provocatively* (*l'hakh'is*), but not to the one who violates it because of his needs or desires (*l'teavon*). The violators of the Sabbath that are found in our day are not to be classed as "provocators," for they do all that they do because of their livelihood. Although they may violate the Sabbath even in such matters which do not concern their business, that (too) is only because "one sin brings another in its wake," and, alas, it seems to them by now as if it were all permissible. At all events, there is no ground for the suspicion (which is basic to the original law declaring an apostate's Torah unfit) that this man would write the Torah for *idolatrous* purposes or with idolatrous intent, since he does not do this provocatively at all.

It is true that, according to the opinion of the *Magen Avraham* ("Orah Hayyim," no. 39, end of section 3, based upon the *tosafot* in Ab. Zarah 26b), it is quite clear that even a violator for his own *desires* (i.e., not a provocator) is ineligible to write a Sefer Torah. Yet this opinion (continues Deutsch) applies only if he writes the entire Sefer Torah, for in that case one would have to be concerned with the law (of the proper correction of scribal errors), namely, the necessity, when certain letters are by accident run together, to scrape out the whole letter, whereas he, being lazy in the matter (not being pious), might content himself with scraping out only part of the attaching line. Therefore the Torah would be unfit because of "engraving in relief" (*hak tokhot,* Git. 20a). But all of this does not apply to our case here, where he writes just a few letters and a skilled scribe is standing by his side who vouches for him and shows him how to write. Besides, the man writes no Name of God and there is, therefore, no ground for suspicion (of idolatrous intention); and obviously he writes under the authority of the scribe who guides him. Even a Sefer Torah which a Gentile writes, since he is not devoted to idolatry (since Gentiles nowadays are not deemed idolators) is not unfit for use as a certainty but only because of a doubt which requires putting the Torah away. Therefore all the more in this case when the man writes under the guidance of the scribe who stands by his side, there is no doubt at all.

Now in the book *B'nai Yonah,* no. 281, parag. 3, he (Jonah Landsofer of Prague, 1678–1712) writes that a Jewish apostate, although he is in duty bound to put on *tefillin* (and therefore is eligible to write *tefillin*), nevertheless, since he has broken off the yoke of the Torah from himself, he must be now considered as one who does not put on *tefillin* and is therefore ineligible to write them. All the more may he not write a Sefer Torah. However (continues Deutsch) one cannot consider these Sabbath violators as men who have thrown off the yoke of the Torah, since all the sins which they do are committed because they are not accustomed to obey the commandments, and they are by nature and mood not easily taught and guided. The proof that they have not thrown off the Torah completely is the fact that they pay money to earn this *mitzvah* of participating symbolically in the writing of a Torah. Therefore there is no suspicion upon which to invalidate the Sefer Torah.

At all events, in our case, with regard to the writing of the Torah, the fact that they write certain letters in the presence of the scribe does not make this Torah one of the category of "a Torah written by an apostate." And even those authorities who would declare that one who is an apostate because of his desires (not for provocation) is ineligible to write, even such an authority would not declare him ineligible when he writes just a few words in the presence of the scribe. If so, there is no ground for suspicion in this case; and the Sefer Torah is kosher for reading without suspicion or cavil, so it seems clear to me with God's help . . .

. . . and what seems to my humble opinion, I have written in the evening of Wednesday, New Moon of Heshvan, 5661.

51

✡

SLANDERING A SHOHET

Ephraim Zalman Margolioth (born in Brody, 1762; died there, 1828), Galician rabbi, began as a brilliant young student and was in frequent correspondence with Ezekiel Landau, the famous rabbi of Prague. In his native city of Brody, he established a banking house and became wealthy. In 1785 he published an edition of the responsa of Joel Sirkes which earned him great admiration. The following year the rabbis of Brody elected him one of their number. He opened a yeshiva and, being wealthy, maintained it himself. He wrote commentaries on the *Shulhan Arukh* and is best known for his book of responsa, *The House of Ephraim.*

The responsum which we cite deals with a topic which in various forms appears very frequently in the responsa, especially of the last two centuries. It concerns a *shohet,* the official slaughterer of kosher food in the Jewish community. The *shohet* was, of course, an important religious functionary and enjoyed a significant status in the community. Besides having to be technically skilled in his craft, he also was expected to be a learned man, especially as to the laws of slaughtering which constitute a considerable part of Jewish Law. These laws involve complicated instructions concerning the anatomy of the animal slaughtered. The presence, for example, of adhesions on the lungs, which might indicate a diseased animal; or the presence of injuries which might indicate that the animal had been in a dying condition before being slaughtered; or the lack or mutilation of certain vital organs; or the presence of certain foreign bodies, and the like—all of these make the animal unfit for consumption (*trefa*). While, of course, the ultimate decision as to whether a recently slaughtered animal is kosher or *trefa* is made by the rabbi, nevertheless, the question might never be asked of the rabbi if the *shohet* did not first realize that there was a problem to be decided. If he simply passed the meat as kosher, the problem would never come to the rabbi for decision.

Therefore, the *shohet* had to be a learned man, at least in this specific field, and was expected to pass an examination before he received authorization, or a license from the rabbi (*Kabbala*). Also the rabbi could require periodic re-examination. It was not only the knowledge of the *shohet* which was important, but also his character. He was subject to considerable financial temptation, since to declare an animal *trefa* involved considerable loss to the merchants.

Hence, there were frequent disputes in the communities over the character and the knowledge of the *shohet*. It was easy to arouse parts of the community to sudden anger if the charge was made that the *shohet* was giving the community *trefa* food to eat. One of the most bitter controversies of the last century, one that involved scores of rabbis over a wide area, was the dispute over the *shohet* of Berditchev, which was initiated by Solomon Kluger of Brody (see Freehof, *Responsa Literature,* p. 177 ff.). The late Yekuthiel Greenwald wrote an entire book on the disputes with regard to the *shohet* in rabbinic literature (New York, 1945).

In this particular case, therefore, which may be looked upon as typical, or at least of frequent occurrence, a charge was made against the *shohet*. Ephraim Margolioth dismissed the charge as malicious slander without any foundation. Yet the scholar does not merely dismiss the charge outright. He discusses, on the basis of analysis of the talmudic and post-talmudic literature, the nature of such charges, to what extent they need ever be heeded and the status of the religious functionary who is being accused. The responsum is *Yoreh Deah,* no. 1.

TEXT

To the peaceable and faithful of Israel *(II Sam. 2.19), whose* righteousness is like the high mountains *(Psalms 36.7)*, the heads of the myriads of Israel, *the rabbis, leaders and chiefs of the congregation of Jeshurun . . . and those with them, the chosen and the judges of the city.*

Your letter reached me and *you have supported me with dainties* (Song of Songs 2.5). My hands are weak; but your honor, the rabbi, has urged me and strengthened my hands to write these few lines. The decision requires no hesitation, namely, we do not remove this *shohet* from his position and his status. I have already written a long responsum to indicate that even when there is a rumor which does not cease, we may not, on that basis, remove a man from his presumption of being kosher. Similarly, and all the more in this case, when the rumor is merely the voice of a gossiping woman who should be whipped, as is stated in the Talmud (Pes. 113b, where the one who brought the false witness was whipped).

Especially (is this the case) since it is clear that this worthless woman is not concerned with saving people from eating forbidden food (which would be a worthy motive, if she had thought that the *shohet* was negligent in his duties), but her purpose is to malign him. She has carried out her intentions and the city speaks of her. At all events, we are not required to pay any attention to these idle words; for were it not so, what recourse would worthy people ever have when *scoffing men excite the city* (phrase from Prov. 29.8) and bring a malicious report that worthy men have done evil. Indeed, we do not listen to her report. Any rumor that is not confirmed by the court is of no significance. It seems clear that even an especially pious person (the Hebrew phrase is *baal nefesh,* "a person of soul") need not pay attention (to such a rumor).

(Now he feels called upon to discuss some passages in the Talmud which seem to indicate that the rabbis did pay attention to mere rumor. He explains these passages away. The last of these passages is from Moed Katan 18b, in which the Talmud says no one is ever suspected unless there is ground for some suspicion. But the Talmud itself explains that often a man may be suspected because he has enemies. So the Talmud continues: *They envied Moses in the camp* [Psalms 106.16]; it was because of hatred that they did this to him. So where a man has enemies, it is they who send out this rumor about him. He explains that wherever in the Talmud the rabbis seem to pay attention to rumors, they either explain the rumors away or the case refers to some special situation that is not relevant here. So he continues:)

But in the case of this wicked woman and the other woman with her (there seem to have been two slanderers), we can rely upon the presumption that there is no truth in their mouth and we need pay no attention to their voice at all. It seems to me that if a man is nervous (about the meat slaughtered by this *shohet*), and wants to give credence to these women as if they were two witnesses (the legal number of witnesses generally required by the Jewish court), even so he may eat from this *shohet's* slaughtering; because it is an obvious law that if one has committed only one sin, he is still kosher, as are the opinions of Maimonides and the *Shulhan Arukh*.

I have dealt with this matter at length in my (other) responsum and here I will abbreviate. There is no evidence that he is unfit to do slaughtering, all the more since, according to your letter to me, he is a regular student of the Torah and fulfills the commandments, and no whisper of slander has been heard against him in twenty years. Besides, he is adept in *shehita* and has worked in the congregation for thirteen years and no fault has been found in him to justify disgracing and shaming him with harsh words.

(He shows that the identical theme was discussed by Joseph Colon in the 14th–15th century in responsa no. 188, who, he notes, cites the same talmudic references which he has just cited. He continues:)

As for this wicked woman, she should be gagged and let others learn a lesson from her. Are ye not wise and is not wisdom among the aged (cf. Job 12.12)? Gather your strength to remove the stumbling block from the road of the people so that the flock may feed in its pasture in peace (cf. Isa. 5.17).

The words of the unimportant one of the company, the threshold to the scholars (M. Hag. II.7), the young one,

Ephraim Zalman Margolioth of Brody

52

✡

VIOLATING THE SABBATH
TO CONSULT A HASIDIC RABBI

Solomon Kluger (born in Komarow, Poland, 1783; died in
Brody, 1869), was chief rabbinic judge (*dayyan*) and preacher
of Brody. He was rabbi in a number of communities before becoming *dayyan* of Brody, where he remained for over fifty years
(except for a short interval when he left the city). He was a
prolific writer in all fields of rabbinic literature, but perhaps best
known are his commentaries on the *Shulhan Arukh* and his responsa. Kluger was a man of great personal courage and had a
strong sense of his rabbinical responsibility. Perhaps for that
reason he precipitated many disputes, such as the one over
machine-made *matzot* and the *shohet* in Berditchev. (See Freehof, *Responsa Literature,* p. 177 ff., 181 ff.) He also possessed
great independence of mind. It was his decision which made
possible the sending of Jewish bills of divorce (*gittin*) by means
of the post instead of by a hand-messenger. At the time when
Jews started emigrating in vast numbers from eastern Europe,
the possibility of sending a divorce by post was of great importance in preventing many a wife from becoming an *agunah*
(chained to an absent husband and unable to remarry).

This responsum illustrates Solomon Kluger's bold style and
forthrightness of speech. It also reveals the tension which per-

sisted for a long time between the regular rabbis and the Hasidic leaders. A Hasidic rabbi had decided that a Jew could travel on the Sabbath to get a miraculous cure (for his relative) from a Hasidic rabbi living in another town. Kluger denounces this violation of the Sabbath and indicates clearly enough his contempt for such magical cures. The responsum is from *U'Baharta baHayyim*, no. 87.

TEXT

In the year 1836, to the officers and leaders of the community of Schlochov:

My spirit oppresses me (cf. Job 32.18) beyond description, over the violation of the Sabbath which has spread like a burning fire within me over the evil and perverse decision which was made in your community last Sabbath. The teacher directed a certain man to violate the Sabbath, one violation after another: to write a *kvittel* on the Sabbath (i.e., a note, which must be given to a Hasidic rabbi by the person approaching him, describing the help that is needed); and then permitting the Jew to journey more than three miles, which is a violation of the Sabbath limit by biblical law; and on horses owned by Jews; and by taking money outside of the Sabbath limit. All of which, even to carry out their intention, could have been done with much fewer Sabbath violations by sending this (the note) by means of a Gentile. He added sin to iniquity by sending two Jews to two places with *pidyanot* ("redemptions," money-gifts to Hasidic rabbis).

Now, indeed, this decision (to allow this Sabbath violation) is exceedingly perverse from beginning to end. Even though, according to the law, it is obvious that danger to life (e.g., to save a dangerously sick person) sets aside the Sabbath, this (permission) is not allowed except to procure a natural medicine. Even so it has to be a tried, reliable medicine. But (to violate the Sabbath) for miracles and prayers is not permitted in any way at all. Even if the one who prays (for the sick) is like Rabbi Hanina ben Dosa (Ber. 34b; this rabbi was famous for the efficacy of his prayers for the sick), even so the Sabbath could not be violated for him (i.e., to journey to him to ask him to pray for the sick), even as far as doing work prohibited only by rabbinical decree, and much less by doing work prohibited by the Torah itself.

Note in this regard what Rashi says in his commentary to *Taanit* 14a (where there is a discussion whether the *shofar* may be blown on the Sabbath. Rabbi Yosé says that in case a ship is being wrecked, we may blow the *shofar* for help, but not as an adjunct to prayer). Rashi says: "The words 'For help' mean that we may sound the *shofar* to summon people to come and help us; but we may not blow the *shofar* on Sabbath as a prayer; for we are not so confident about the efficacy of our prayers that we would violate the Sabbath by blowing the *shofar* for that purpose." The *Tur* (Jacob ben Asher) quotes this in "Orah Hayyim" 288. Now if in the days of the Talmud and Rabbi Yosé it is said that we are not so confident about our prayers (to violate the Sabbath for them by blowing the *shofar*) what shall we say in comparison, we orphans, the sons of orphans?

> (Kluger enters into a deeper discussion of the commentaries on the *Tur* as to what help is permitted to be sought on the Sabbath. He continues:)

It is clear from our words that by way of nature (i.e., human medicine) even a complete violation of the Sabbath is permitted. But merely to arrange for prayers, even a minor prohibition made by the rabbis is forbidden.

> (He then explains the talmudic phrase, in Shabbat 12a, which says that when visiting the sick on the Sabbath, one should say, "It is the Sabbath so we must not cry out; but help will soon come." He concludes from the phrase that we may not even pray for the sick on the Sabbath, for the spiritual rest of the Sabbath is in itself a source of healing. He continues his responsum as follows:)

The outcome of the matter is: this teacher has violated the Sabbath in many ways. Therefore, if he will retract this decision and confess in public that he made an error, well and good. But if not, let all know that his decisions are perverted and they are like a piece of forbidden food, and people may not rely upon any decision of his. Please tell me who this teacher is and I will not be silent, *nor will I give slumber to mine eyes* until I proclaim his shame before the entire province.

(And he concludes:) With God's help, I will inform all the rabbis and the *tzaddikim* (the Hasidic leaders) of this matter, all of them without exception, so that they may know and answer whether it is right to do this. Also you are permitted to show my letter to every intelligent person (to see) whether these words of mine do not present their own testimony and speak the truth.

These are the words of him who seeks your peace, who speaks the truth in the love of truth, the young one,

Solomon Kluger

53

✡

ENFORCED SYNAGOGUE
ATTENDANCE

Joseph Saul Nathanson (born in Berzan, 1808; died in Lemberg, 1875), Galician rabbi, was the son of Aryeh Lev Nathanson who was rabbi of Berzan. In 1857 he was appointed rabbi of Lemberg, where he remained for eighteen years. He was one of the most creative rabbinic writers of his time and was highly respected as a great legal authority. His approbation of new books was eagerly sought and there are in all likelihood more approbations by him on rabbinic books than by any other rabbi. He wrote commentaries on the *Shulhan Arukh,* but is most famous for his great collection of responsa, *Shoel uMeshiv* (He Asks and He Answers).

The question with which he deals in this responsum is a new and rather modern form of an ancient problem in Jewish (as in all organized) religious life, namely, how to encourage attendance at public worship. From one point of view the task was more difficult in Judaism, not because Jews were less prayerful, but for the opposite reason. The obligation to pray three times a day was deep-rooted in Jewish life, but there was a strong feeling that one did not necessarily need synagogue attendance in order to pray. In the Talmud (particularly in Ber. 8a) there is an illuminating difference of opinion continuing among rabbis of a number of generations, as to whether or not it was indispensable to go to the synagogue in order to pray. One rabbi says that if there is a synagogue in the town and one does not enter into it for worship, he must be looked upon as a bad neighbor. Another rabbi says that although there are twelve synagogues in Tiberias, he prays only in the place where he studies (the scholars considered their study of the Torah to be their primary duty and the place where they studied to be as sacred as the synagogue in which the community worshiped). The law is, also, that workmen engaged in their work could pray on the job, even at the top of a tree.

There were, of course, certain elements in worship which could not be carried out without a congregation of a minimum of ten (*minyan*), such as the reading of the Torah in public, the public *kedushah,* and the like. To overcome this difficulty many of the scholars would gather a *minyan* in their own homes, where they studied, and would conduct, therefore, what might be described as a private-public worship. Essentially the situation was this: Many scholars considered their study their primary duty; the duty to pray three times a day was incumbent upon all; as a personal obligation it could be conducted anywhere, but since certain parts of the prayer required public worship, scholars often gathered a *minyan* of their own. On the other hand, there was concern about maintaining communal worship against these centrifugal motivations. All these mixed moods are reflected in the law as found in the *Shulhan Arukh* 90.9: "A man should strive to pray in the synagogue with the congregation. If he cannot come, let him endeavor to pray at the hour when the congregation is praying." To which Isserles adds: "So with people who live in small settlements where there is no *minyan;* let them pray at the hour when a congregation prays."

The old problem of strengthening the public synagogue worship became a little more difficult in modern times, as Jewish occupations in work and in business became more demanding and less in harmony with the normal schedule of the isolated Jewish community. Now, not only scholars, but also businessmen would tend to pray at home, or perhaps a group of them would have a *minyan* in a house in their own neighborhood. These changing social conditions are reflected in the responsum of Joseph Saul Nathanson.

The former rabbi of a certain town had issued a ban (i.e., a decree) forbidding private groups to worship and insisting that worship take place in the synagogue. The question is asked by the incumbent rabbi of the town, who wants to know whether his predecessor's ban is valid, and whether he can void it. While the question came to Nathanson from a small town, he states that he knows that the situation is similar in large cities too. Of course, as is generally the case in the responsa, social conditions are revealed almost inadvertently. The main discussion is a technical, legal one, namely, may the rabbi issue such a *herem* (decree). The responsum is in vol. III, part A, no. 58, of *Shoel uMeshiv*.

TEXT

Peace to the learned rabbi, Zvi Lippe, rabbi in Grodyczicka:

Question:

Your letter reached me yesterday. Your question deals with the fact that your predecessor once issued a decree on the Sabbath during the "third meal" (the community would gather late Sabbath afternoons for a collation called "the third meal," because the Mishna says [Peah VIII.7] that each person should eat at least three meals on the Sabbath). Joined with him were ten men, who were not the actual leaders of the city but some teachers of children and young people who were not scholars (the present rabbi mentions this fact to throw doubt on the validity of his predecessor's ban). The ban was that no one should pray except in the synagogue or in the public house of study. The purpose of this was that public worship in the synagogue and house of study may not cease. Many of the members of the community were not in favor of this action, but they were overawed by the rabbi and they accepted the decree. Now, since there are men who have not been called up to the Torah more than once every half year because the president dislikes them, therefore (says Nathanson) you (the present rabbi) wish to rescind the *herem.*

(In a small, private-public service, a man can have the honor of being called up to the Torah every Sabbath or every other Sabbath; but in a large congregation, the honor becomes rare.)

Answer:

Now as to what you have said, that the rabbi could not decree for the future, I do not know why he cannot do so. As for your quotation from Ezekiel Landau (I, "Yoreh Deah" 68), he, Landau, "preaches directly by inspiration," (a phrase from the Talmud, Meg. 31b) and I do not know his reason. For if a rabbi sees that he needs to erect a "protective fence" for the Torah and the commandments, just as in our case here, in order that public prayer should not lapse, since this is a small town, why should he not be able to decree a *herem* which will be obligatory upon the coming generations?

(He goes a little deeper into the analysis of the opinions of Ezekiel Landau whom the questioner had quoted, and discusses the limitations on the use of a *herem,* and then continues:)

But (in spite of all limitations on the use of a *herem* in this matter) in our case here, when without the ban the regular service in the study-house or in the synagogue would cease—a situation which we observe even in the large cities, and all the more in the small cities whose inhabitants are few—the ban is all the more valid.

As to your statement that your predecessor's *herem* does not apply on the Sabbath and holidays because certainly there will be a *minyan* on Sabbaths and holidays in the synagogue and in the house of study, this is no good argument. For if people will pray (in their private-public groups on Sabbath and holidays, relying on the fact that there will be a *minyan* without them in the communal synagogue), there will be a diminution of the income of the cantor and the sexton and the like, since the people will donate in the house where they pray. In this way, ultimately, the study-house and the synagogue will fade away. For whence will they get what they need for the study-house? Therefore your desire that they read the Torah in your house, that, too, is not right; for thereby synagogue and study-house worship will lapse, and I myself know this.

> (He means that in Lemberg there were many scholars who gathered *minyanim* in their own homes. While, of course, regular worship went on in these groups, the public synagogues were neglected.)

But, of course, all this applies if the intent of your predecessor was really a worthy one (i.e., "in the name of Heaven") and in order to prevent neglect of services in the synagogue and in the study-house. In that case it was a true "fence" to protect the Torah and it is impossible to annul it. If it were not for selfless intent, it is possible to say that it is not valid. But who can know secret motives? Therefore, please take care not to void the *herem* (of your predecessor), for you have not the power to do this. I am also willing to participate in this matter, namely, that if the entire congregation will tell your predecessor that they all desire that his *herem* be voided (then it can be done) through "opening and regret" (a vow or a promise can be voided by a scholar "opening the way" to the man who has vowed, and thus find a road of which he can say, "I did not mean it to apply in this particular way"). If, also, the members of the community will take upon themselves not to allow the services in the synagogue and the study-house to lapse and if, also, you will cease quarreling on the subject of who is called up to the Torah, then certainly your predecessor will void this *herem*.

May He who maketh peace, grant you peace.

54

✡

SPACE FOR A GRAVE

Hayyim Halberstam (born in Tarnogrod, 1793; died in 1876) represented a remarkable combination of Hasidic leader and talmudic authority. Generally, in those days, the non-Hasidic rabbis were the great Talmud legalists, while the Hasidic leaders exerted their influence through personal piety and mystic ideas, miraculous cures and a jovial sense of brotherhood among their people. But Hayyim Halberstam knew both schools. On his mother's side, he was a descendant of Zvi Ashkenazi (see p. 176 above). He was the pupil and later the son-in-law of Baruch Teomim Fraenkel of Leipnik, Moravia. On the other hand, he studied also under the greatest Hasidic leaders of his time and founded his dynasty in Sanz. The Hasidim of Sanz, led by his descendants, are still a powerful branch of the Hasidic movement.

The most dramatic part of his career concerns the dispute between him, as the head of the Hasidim of Sanz, and the Hasidim of Sadagora. The dispute started because one of the Sadagora dynasty had become a modernist. As the dispute developed, harsh anathemas and bans were issued. The Sadagora Hasidim who had settled in Jerusalem issued so bitter a ban against Hayyim Halberstam that the non-Hasidic rabbis of eastern Europe came to his defense. Usually they would not allow themselves to be drawn into Hasidic affairs.

Halberstam's responsa are studied and quoted, not only by

his followers, but by all who are interested in Jewish Law. The responsum which we cite has considerable social interest. The Jewish communities were always deeply concerned with the management and protection of their cemeteries. Often the questions deal with trees and plants in the cemetery: may the trees be cut down and the wood sold? Generally speaking, the living may not derive material gain from what grows in the cemetery, since the grave and its earth "belong" to the dead. Often there are questions of disinterring the dead. It happened frequently that the nobleman who owned the town confiscated or repossessed part of the cemetery land; or else, in recent years, the development of transportation led the secular authorities to cut a road through the cemetery. During the 19th century, many Austrian municipalities established communal cemeteries and offered the Jewish community a section in this general cemetery: did Jewish Law permit the use of a cemetery which was not entirely separate? Sometimes the authorities (or in older times, the feudal owner) did not permit the Jewish community to buy cemetery land outright: to what extent was it permitted to use land which was merely leased and the tenure terminable at the feudal owner's pleasure?

The specific question dealt within the responsum cited here is one which has been frequently discussed: how much space must be left between graves? Clearly this question was often an urgent one. Cemeteries became crowded and it was difficult to acquire new ground. The Jewish law requires, generally, that there be a space of six handbreadths between graves. Can this requirement be eased and less space be used? May one body be buried in the same grave over another? If so, how much space must be provided between the coffins? There is, for example, an interesting series of questions from the community of Paris (cf. the question addressed to Aryeh Lev of Metz, 18th century, *Sha'agat Aryeh,* n.s., Vilna, 1873, p. 120; and the later question asked of Isaac Shmelkes of Lemberg, *Bet Yitzhak,* "Yoreh Deah," no. 153). The various permitted relaxations of the law are enumerated fully by Abraham Danzig in his *Hokhmat Adam* (in the section "Matzevat Moshe," no. 10).

Incidentally, the responsum cited below reflects an important principle in Jewish legal tradition, namely, the validity of popular custom (*minhag*). Any well-established custom is to be respected, especially if it is an old custom in a community which has had honored rabbinic leaders; for in that case, we may assume that these scholars of past generations had studied the local custom and had approved of it. We therefore accept the custom as valid even when we do not know the specific bases for the approval. Thus the questioner here asks whether it is permitted to bury two bodies in the same grave. Halberstam answers that according to the letter of the law this is not permitted, but that if there is a well-established custom in the community to do so, then the practice cannot be forbidden. The responsum is from *Divrei Hayyim,* II, *"Yoreh Deah,"* no. 136.

TEXT

To my brother, the famous scholar, Avigdor, rabbi of Dikla:

As for your question with regard to the burial of two dead together (i.e., in the same grave), know, dear brother, that it is forbidden to bury two dead without a partition of six handbreadths (of earth) between the graves. Of course, according to Tashbetz (Simon ben Zemah Duran, Algiers, 14–15th century, III, 119), in case one grave is above the other, it is sufficient if there is a separation of three handbreadths; but really (according to the strict law) the second body should be removed. Thus it is decided in *Evel Rabathi* (the post-talmudic booklet on mourning) cited by Nahmanides in his *Law of Man* (a book on rules of mourning) and quoted by Joseph Caro to the *Tur* ("Yoreh Deah" 362).

(Simon ben Zemah Duran explains why only three handbreadths are needed when one coffin is above the other, whereas six are needed when one coffin is alongside the other. When one is above the other, the earth is compressed and the earth-partition is less likely to disintegrate.)

No one disagrees with this decision (i.e., that six handbreadths with coffins side by side, or three with coffins above each other, are required). However, later scholars write that nowadays, since we are in exile, or in times of emergency when it is impossible to find any other place, it is necessary to bury the second body and there is no other way (than with a smaller partition). Thus wrote the Gaon Hai, cited by Joseph Caro to *Tur* 363. But the later scholars are lenient (as to the space requirement) when it is impossible to get another place of burial. This is clear from the words of my grandfather, Zvi Ashkenazi, in his responsum no. 115 (this should be no. 149), and Jacob Reischer of Metz, 18th century, *Shebut Yaacob,* section III (this should be section II, no. 95). However, since the book is not readily available, I will give you a transcript of his words. Thus says the *Shebut Yaacob* in II, no. 95 (here the reference is correctly given): "With regard to the distance between the bodies, although the clear law is given in 'Yoreh Deah' 362 that the space between one and the other should be six handbreadths, nevertheless, 'go forth and see what the people say' (a phrase from the Talmud, Ber. 45a, introducing a popular custom). In all the scattered dwelling-places of Israel they bury the dead one alongside the other and one over the other. Now, although this is not according to the law, it seems to me that this custom (of close burial) has spread in our exile because we are not given room. What arduous efforts do we need to expend in all places to get the little space that we have! So it is sufficient if we keep to the limited space. After all, these laws were meant to apply only when we had plenty of space. This, too, was the opinion of the *Turei Zahav"* (David haLevi, 16–17th century, to *Shulhan Arukh,* "Yoreh Deah" 364).

He quotes Solomon Luria, who said, "As for the fact that our modern custom no longer holds with regard to *met mitzvah* (a body found dead in the field, which according to the old law had to be buried where the body was found), it is because the land is not ours and we do not have permission to bury everywhere (where a corpse might be found). So it is, continues Jacob Reischer, in this case. Since, however, your settlement is a new one and you still have space, you are still able to bury according to the legal requirements of space between graves."

(Then Halberstam continues as follows:)

All (the laws of space between graves) are for the purpose of avoiding shame to the dead (if they are crowded), as is clear in the citation from Avel Rabathi cited above. Thus in the case that you ask about, according to the letter of the law, we should disinter the second body which is buried too close, either beside the other grave or above it. But, if it seems to be the custom to bury so closely in your community, then we have no right to disagree with the famous scholars of your community of the past. For certainly this custom of yours (of close burial) was carried out according to the opinion of these great scholars. If, therefore, it is known to you that this has been the custom in the past, then it is impossible to change the matter (i.e., to disinter the second body) because of the "fear of judgment" (a phrase used with regard to unnecessarily disturbing a body), since the bodies have already been buried correctly (according to the custom endorsed by past scholars). But hereafter, you should seek a place to bury (with proper space).

Signed in the month of Ab, 1861.

55

✡

SOLDIER KOHEN—AND THE JEWISH DEAD

Menahem-Mendel of Lubovitch (born in Liozne, White Russia, 1789; died in Lubovitch, 1866) was the third in the great HaBaD dynasty of Hasidim founded by Shneor-Zalman of Ladi. This Lithuanian, or White Russian, branch of the Hasidic movement was intellectual from the very start. The founder of it was a great talmudist and his version of the *Shulhan Arukh* is cited by scholars of all schools. Menahem-Mendel was therefore in the true tradition of his particular branch of Hasidism when he became a legal authority. His six-volume collection of responsa, *Zemah Zedek,* is widely used.

The responsum which we cite deals with a soldier, who is also a kohen, who is compelled to come into contact with the dead. According to the biblical law, the priest may not come in contact with the dead except when this duty is incumbent upon him in connection with the burial of his close relatives. Otherwise, priests do not enter cemeteries or funeral parlors, or the like. The question asked of Menahem-Mendel is an outgrowth of the fact that there was compulsory military service in czarist Russia and therefore kohanim had to serve in the army. A similar question arose a few years ago in the United States during the selective service period preceding World War II; i.e., may a kohen under compulsory service come into contact with the dead when this is part of his military duty? The responsum cited is "Yoreh Deah" 238.

TEXT

Question:

A Jew, a kohen, a soldier, serves in the military hospital. Is he permitted to defile himself to bury a dead Jew? Is such a Jew to be considered a *met mitzvah?* (If a body is found in the road, it is mandatory, a *mitzvah,* upon everyone, even upon a priest who finds him, to bury him. But it is possible to question whether this dead soldier is a *met mitzvah* and hence whether the priest is in duty bound to bury him). If he does not concern himself with the burial, the Jew will still be buried, but by Gentile soldiers, who likewise are on service in the hospital.

Answer:

The Mishna (Naz. VII.1) says: "Neither a high priest nor a nazirite may defile himself with the burial even of his relatives (an ordinary priest may conduct the burial of his seven categories of relative), but they may defile themselves for a *met mitzvah."* Now the Jerusalem Talmud to this chapter says: "What would be described as a case of *met mitzvah?* All such cases where, if one should cry out for others to come and bury this dead, and no inhabitants of the city come (then it is a *met mitzvah* and it is one's duty to bury him). But if members of the city do come, then he (the priest) must withdraw from the task. How many must come (for him to be free from the task)? As many as for a full funeral cortège . . ."

> (He then proceeds to elaborate on the law as given in the Jerusalem Talmud as to when the priest may and may not avoid burying the body.)

Therefore, all the more in our case, where there is no other Israelite available, though there are Gentiles, this priest must defile himself. Furthermore, because he (the priest) is actually needed, since (otherwise) the body will not be buried as soon (as Jewish Law requires) if he withdraws from the task. Perhaps, too, they will not bury him in a grave as deep as Jews bury their dead.

(Now he concedes that it is possible to argue that it is not really a case of *met mitzvah*. He puts this supposititious argument as follows:)

From this point of view we might, indeed, say that even though there are no other Jews but this priest, nevertheless, if he does not engage in the task, the other, non-Jewish, soldiers are actually commanded to bury him. It is possible on that basis perhaps to say that this is not a *met mitzvah* and therefore the burial is not incumbent upon the priest especially. Nor can one particularly object to the fact that these are non-Jews who would bury him, for we are, in fact, told in the Talmud (Betza 6a) that if a man dies on the first day of a holiday, Gentiles may bury him.

(This possibility that the duty may, after all, not be deemed incumbent upon the priest, he dismisses by saying the following:)

But in our case, even by military law, the burial is incumbent upon him as upon other soldiers. Perhaps even all the more is it his military duty since he is a Jew. Hence the situation is like that described in the Palestinian Talmud, that he should not withdraw from his duty.

(He now proceeds to quote a comment of Rashi to the effect that the defiling of priests is not even relevant in such a case.)

For thus wrote Rashi, to Berakhot 20a, that the law concerning uncleanness of priests is void in the case of a nazirite and a kohen who must defile themselves for a *met mitzvah*. This is due to the honor which must be paid to human beings (i.e., the respect due to all). Therefore, we too say that because of the respect due to all human beings, the commandment of avoiding uncleanness does not even apply to a *met mitzvah*.

(And he concludes:) Therefore, we should perhaps be lenient in this matter, especially because of Rashi's statement that uncleanness of priests is permitted for a *met mitzvah*.

(He ends with the pious wish:)

May God destroy death forever (Isa. 25.8).

56

✡

UNAUTHORIZED TORAH READING

Naftali-Zvi Yehudah Berlin (N'tziv: born in Mir, 1817; died in Warsaw, 1893) was head of the famous yeshiva of Volozhin founded by Hayyim of Volozhin, the pupil of Elijah of Vilna. This most famous of all Russian yeshivas experienced many difficulties during the administration of Naftali Berlin. There was an internal revolt advocating another style of Talmud teaching from the one which he pursued. There was a struggle with the Maskilim, the modernists, who wanted the yeshiva to become like a modern Western Jewish seminary. In 1879, the yeshiva was closed by order of the government. Naftali Berlin was able to secure its reopening in 1881. He was perhaps the best known yeshiva head of the century and many questions came to him for his solution. Besides his book of responsa, *Meshiv Davar,* he is famous for his commentary on the *She'eltot* of the Gaon Ahai.

Since, in order to maintain the yeshiva, he developed a widespread system of solicitation by emissaries, especially in the United States, he and his yeshiva were especially honored in America. As a result, there are many responsa in his collection which answered inquiries by American rabbis.

The responsum which we will cite was addressed to a rabbi in Cincinnati. It touches a well known problem in Jewish Law: to what extent may one add to the ritual traditionally observed? May additional services be instituted? The question is debated

vehemently nowadays. Orthodox circles are still in disagreement
as to whether the celebration of Independence Day of Israel,
for example, may be accompanied by the reading of the *Hallel*
Psalms. Would not such a reading constitute an unauthorized addition to the traditional list of occasions when the *Hallel* may be
recited?

The question asked here is not quite of such wide import, but
it involves all the principles which are cited nowadays in the
discussion of the Independence Day services. The specific question was this: A congregation in Cincinnati built a new Ark for
its synagogue. The dedicatory celebration took place on a Sunday. One of the leaders of the congregation wanted the Torah
read and himself called up for this privilege. Is this permissible?
The rabbi, whose name is not given, sent the question from Cincinnati to Volozhin, and the following is Naftali Z. Y. Berlin's
answer. It is in vol. I, no. 16.

TEXT

To the honored rabbi in the city of Cincinnati in America:

Question:

Your honor asks about the following matter that happened in
a certain congregation in your city. The congregation had the
privilege of dedicating a new Ark. In the celebration, they in the
joy of their hearts marched around with the scrolls of the Law.
One of the men desired to read from the Torah, in public reading, on that day which was Sunday. You, your honor, forbade it
and explained your reason for the prohibition, namely, that if
one reads the Torah in public at a time not fixed by our sages,
such a one is violating the prohibition against "adding" (to the
commandments of God). This (you said) is according to the
opinion of Mordecai (ben Hillel) in his notes to the first chapter
of Megillah, with regard to reading the Megillah on the 15th day
(of Adar in addition to the 13th or 14th). If the reader (says
Mordecai) intends this to be a public reading it is a violation
(of the prohibition against adding to God's commandments).

Answer:

If your reason is based only upon the sin of "adding," it is no valid argument. You know well that the sin of "adding" does not apply to the reading of the Torah. This we know from the Talmud (Er. 96a). Furthermore, with regard to the talmudic statement that one who sleeps (in the *sukkah*) on the eighth day is to be punished (because the commandment is to dwell in the *sukkah* for *seven* days, and this man would be adding one day), Rashi says that we (in Europe) nevertheless do dwell in the *sukkah* on the eighth day because of the doubt (as to the actual date; the day might actually be the seventh day). But since it is not actually the time and since we do not intend it to be (the formal observance), this is not really an "addition" (on our part). Therefore we are permitted to do so; for should it actually be the eighth day (by the true calendar), then (understand that) we do not intend this to be the actual *mitzvah,* of dwelling in the *sukkah*. Hence, this cannot be considered an unauthorized addition (when we stay in the *sukkah* on the eighth day). Thus far the words of Rashi. (Berlin continues:)

For this reason the prohibition against adding is not involved. But even if so, we still have the difficulty with regard to the second day of holidays outside of Palestine. We read the Torah (on the second day) and pronounce a blessing over it. In that case, we cannot apply the statement of Rashi that we do not mean this to be a fulfilment of the commandment (should it actually be a non-holiday). After all, we do recite a blessing on that day (and the law prohibits a blessing to be recited in vain. How, then, can we recite a blessing over the Torah on the second day of holidays which may in truth not be a holiday at all according to the correct calendar?).

> (Then Berlin goes more deeply into the problem of our reading the Torah publicly and reciting a blessing on a day which the Bible does not authorize, since the Bible says that there are seven days of Passover and one day of Shavuot, etc. He continues as follows:)

Yet, in truth, Solomon ben Adret in his notes to the Talmud (R. H., p. 16) says that the Torah reading on the second day

of holidays presents no difficulty at all, because it is an observance which was decreed by our ancient sages.

> (Berlin now discusses certain differences in their opinions
> between Rashi and Solomon ben Adret. He concludes as
> follows:)

Let us return to our subject, namely, that in the mere reading
of the Torah (at that Sunday meeting in Cincinnati) there is no
violation of the commandment "not to add." But it is clear that
to read the Torah and pronounce the blessing on a day that the
rabbis did not ordain for the reading of the Torah, would be
reciting a blessing in vain (which is a sin). So it is clear, however, that to read the Torah *without a blessing* does not involve
any prohibition and it is the same as a person merely reading
the Torah.

You are right in calling attention to the fact that there is, after
all, some prohibition (to read it in public even without a blessing) on a day in which there is no required reading at all. (I.e., on
a day when there is a required reading, it might not be harmful
to read more in the Torah than is required; but it is wrong to
take out the Torah on a day when no reading at all is required.)
For (continues Berlin) to take out and read the Torah on a day
when no Torah reading is ordained must certainly be prohibited.
For how shall we deal with this reading? If we read without a
blessing at all, then we must be concerned about the opinion of
the Palestinian Talmud that every public reading of the Torah
requires a blessing. On the other hand, to read the Torah with a
blessing on a day in which the rabbis have not ordained any reading, then the blessing has been recited in vain (which is a sin).
This prohibition would apply also to taking out and reading the
Torah, even on a day for which it was ordained, but doing so
not at the proper time of day, as, for example, reading it after
the service is over or in the evening.

In truth, I do not know for what reason that man was so eager
to do this deed. It is an action whose sources are unknown. (I.e.,
sometimes a local custom must receive consideration if it has a
source which can be found in a decision of some worthy scholar.
But if it has no such origin, then it has no value.) If this man is

not a mere "reed-cutter" (a talmudic phrase from Shab. 95a meaning a mere ignoramus), then it would be right for him to explain from what source he got the idea. If he has no proper source for it, then the whole notion is only folly and pride, an act of grandeur to impress the mob. In general, for the present I know of no source for such a suggestion. Therefore, your honor was right in preventing this. Pay no attention to anyone who is grieved at this decision. Such a person's *disgrace will return to his own bosom,* and *it is an honor to a man to cease from strife* (Prov. 20.3).

May God make us worthy of the blessing, *All Thy children will be taught by the Lord and Thy children will have great peace* (Isa. 54.3).

These are the words of him who is heavily burdened,

Naftali-Zvi Yehudah Berlin

57

✡

RELIANCE ON OFFICIAL
REPORT OF DEATH

Isaac Elkanan Spektor (born 1817; died in Kovna, 1896) was the foremost Lithuanian rabbi of his time. In his early years he was poverty-stricken; but he had no lack of teachers, because he was a child-genius (*ilui*). Married at the age of thirteen, he held a series of small positions until finally, in 1864, he was elected rabbi of the great community of Kovna. Here he became prominent. He visited St. Petersburg a number of times in behalf of problems that concerned all of Russian Jewry. He was interested in the problems of world Jewry.

His great fame rests upon his responsa, or perhaps, too, the great range of his responsa was the result of his world fame. In his day, the great stream of Russian Jewry immigrated into the western lands, particularly the United States. This immigration, in which generally the husband alone traveled overseas, often resulted in estrangement and the break-up of families; husbands sometimes disappeared into the new world and never were heard from again. The problem of the *agunah* (the chained woman, who could not remarry because she had not received a proper bill of divorcement from her husband) became greatly aggravated. Isaac Elkanan Spektor performed a great service in this regard. Though strictly traditional in attitude, he managed by brilliant reasoning to find relaxations of the laws of evidence and, in fact, many of his decisions relaxing the laws of evidence (of a husband's reported death) became a permanent part of Jewish legal tradition. In his volume of responsa, *Be'er Yitzhak* (The Well of Isaac), no. 5, there is a long responsum in which, with meticulous attention to every detail of the literature, he proves that a government declaration of a man's death is acceptable in the Jewish court of law. Hitherto, the testimony of a Gentile was accepted in the case of an *agunah*, provided that the Gentile testified "in innocence." Such simple "innocence" of testimony could hardly be ascribed to an official report of a government. A government report was a conscious statement, aware of its consequences as to a woman's right to remarry. Yet, Spektor proved that, in spite of the absence of the old requirement of simple "innocence," the government report is to be accepted. This, of course, greatly eased the situation in wartime, because often it would be hard, otherwise, to find adequate and acceptable testimony of a man's death, and his wife would remain permanently an *agunah*.

The specific case in this responsum was not precisely one in which a woman's husband had disappeared. The woman's husband had died. That was established. But he had died childless. The woman, therefore, could not remarry until she went through the ceremony of *halitzah* (release by the deceased husband's brother). But she could not obtain this release because the husband's brother was away at war. Now the government, in response to an inquiry, reported that he had been killed in action. It was in this case that Spektor proved the acceptability in a Jewish court of the government report.

In the responsum which we now cite, the case is one in which the woman's husband was himself a soldier and the government reported him dead. Here Spektor refers to his previous long responsum and takes its conclusion to be an established principle, namely, that government reports are to be accepted in Jewish Law. The responsum cited is from *Ain Yitzhak* (The Fountain of Isaac), "Eben haEzer," no. 19.

TEXT

Question:

I was asked by a certain eminent rabbi with regard to an *agunah,* as follows: One witness testified that a Jewish soldier had told him that his comrade-soldier was slain in battle while he stood by him on the battleline. Also there came a report from the army to inform his wife that her husband had been killed in battle. Your honor has debated the matter and come to the conclusion that she is permitted to be remarried. Now you ask me to express my opinion on this case.

Answer:

I shall answer you briefly, namely, that I, too, agree to be lenient in this matter. This is in accordance with a conclusion that I came to in my book *Be'er Yitzhak,* "Eben haEzer," no. 5, that one can rely upon the official testimony of the courts more than upon the words of one witness. For we see that their (the official) testimony is more worthy than that of one witness, as I have written and proved in my book. Certainly, when we have two witnesses to testify that he was killed in war, we hold that we should be lenient, as is explained in the *Shulhan Arukh,* "Eben haEzer" 17.50. (See note of Isserles.) Therefore, if one witness transmits the testimony of two witnesses, this is the same as if the two witnesses were in our presence. In that case we are not concerned with the possibility of the testimony being based upon mere guesswork.

(The Talmud, Yeb. 114b, says that if a woman comes and reports that there was a war in the land in which she and her husband were traveling, and that her husband was killed in war, we do not accept her testimony because we suspect that, though her husband disappeared, she merely guesses, on the basis of probability, that since there was a war going on, her husband must have been killed in the war. Spektor here says that this testimony in the case that he is discussing is not merely testimony based upon guesswork or probability.)

In the case of an *agunah,* one witness is believed whenever there is no reason for concern that the testimony is a mere estimate or guess. Therefore, according to this witness' testimony that he heard of the husband's death through two witnesses, he is believed, since the testimony of two witnesses is not subject to the suspicion that it might be a mere assumption. Therefore the testimony of this one witness is sufficient, and this is the pivot of the opinion of the *Zemah Zedek* (Menahem-Mendel of Lubovitch, "Eben haEzer," no. 88).

This, then, is the situation in our case here. There is before us testimony of the officers that the husband was killed in the war. They would not record that he was killed except after careful investigation of the matter; for if they did not look into the matter carefully, then it might turn out that he was not killed after all, but had been captured by the enemy facing them. Afterwards, when there is peace and each of the armies returns their captives, he would be found to be alive. Thus the officers of the army would prove to be falsifiers if they had recorded that he had been killed. This would be a shame and a disgrace for them. Therefore it seems obvious that they had investigated the matter very carefully. So this is exactly the same situation as when the head of the court is together with his scribe, as in the Talmud (Git. 19b) and the *Shulhan Arukh* ("Hoshen Mishpat," no. 45.2, note of Isserles), that we rely upon the scribe, since he has a true verification (i.e., that the head of the court can verify the scribe's words). So it is here, that those soldiers who are appointed to report the casualties in battle have verification so that the higher officers appointed over the matter are to be trusted.

(He continues with this argument and ends the paragraph as follows:)

It appears from your letter that the report of the army officers was not based upon the testimony of the same two soldiers whose testimony was reported to you by this one witness. The government has special officers appointed for this purpose (to record casualties). Therefore we have a firm foundation to free her, with the help of God, from the chains of being an *agunah.*

58

✡

RELYING ON GENTILE CHEMISTS

Shalom Mordecai Schwadron (Maharsham: born in 1835) was the leading Galician authority of the past century, and may be considered the chief rabbinic authority of the entire Jewish world after Isaac Elkanan Spektor of Kovna. Isaac Herzog, the late chief rabbi of Israel, said of him: ". . . the true eminence, accepted as the outstanding decisor in all the scattered dwelling-places of Israel." His responsa, which have appeared so far in six volumes, were sent to inquirers all over the Jewish world.

The responsum we cite deals with a problem which is of increasing concern in Jewish Law, namely, to what extent the opinion of a Gentile scientist is to be accepted as testimony in deciding religious matters. For example, the question of whether the use of a microphone or loudspeaker is permissible on the Sabbath is based upon the prohibition against kindling or increasing fire on the Sabbath. A scientist may answer that talking through the loudspeaker does not increase the electric spark. His answer might well be decisive in determining the permissibility of using the microphone, provided that the testimony of a Gentile expert is acceptable in deciding a Jewish religious question.

Schwadron here takes up one of the earliest of such modern inquiries. It concerns the question of canned oil prepared in America. The Gentile chemist employed by the factory says that the oil is composed of pure vegetable (cottonseed) oil. There was some concern, however, that perhaps oil from an unclean or an improperly slaughtered clean animal could be mixed in with the oil. The question then is: can the testimony of a Gentile scientist be conclusive in determining questions of kosher and *trefa?* The responsum cited is from vol. III, no. 215.

TEXT

To the eminent rabbi, Jacob Teomim, rabbi of Tarnigrod . . . :

Question:

This is with regard to your question concerning the oils which come from America. According to what a rabbi wrote to you from New York, most such oils are made from incorrectly-slaughtered or non-kosher animals. But there is one factory which makes it from cottonseed oil ("the wool of a vine"). Yet this oil is for the present prepared without rabbinical supervision. We may, therefore, be concerned with the danger of adulteration, and the like. Your honor is in doubt whether we can rely on a (Gentile) chemist to test the oil. You referred to the responsa *Shoel uMeshiv,* III, A, 377 (by Joseph Saul Nathanson), in which he expresses confidence in such a chemical test, but only when combined with other reasons and also if the oil is used in the proportion of one in sixty or less. But in our case there is concern about all the oil—whether it is from non-kosher animals. Therefore, one cannot rely upon the abovementioned responsum. Thus far is your question.

Answer:

(Schwadron begins his responsum by discussing all the varieties of reliance upon Gentile merchants, cooks, or experts. He discusses the principle that a man will not allow his professional reputation to be hurt by giving a wrong opinion, or that a merchant would lose his customers if he sold the wrong kind of goods. When are such people to be trusted and when not? He concludes from the discussion that it is possible to be lenient in this particular case. But then he turns to indicate that the possibility of leniency must here be set aside. He continues in this vein, as follows:)

But we can object in this case (to accepting this oil). The situation would be different if anyone could taste the food and judge its contents; or if the Gentile cook were an expert (whose trained palate could judge) and if it were as easy to expose the cook's deception if he were falsifying. Under such circumstances, such an expert could well be trusted. But, in our case, no average person can detect whether the oil (is what is claimed for it) except the chemist. Now, if we wish to check this chemist's opinion by consulting another chemist, if there is such a person in the city, we would have to go to great expense in the matter. Besides, the original chemist could deny this one's testimony, and at best we would have one witness testifying against another. Who could know which one of them is telling the truth? We could not tell which one was false. Therefore, under these circumstances, when we cannot check one opinion against another, the original chemist, all would agree, is not to be trusted. For thus Isaac bar Sheshet proved at length in his responsum no. 154, when he explains why, in testimony with regard to a woman (being freed for remarriage), one witness is not sufficient (except by permission of rabbinical law rather than biblical law); for this is not a matter whose truth would ultimately be revealed (how could we ever know what was the truth). Therefore one witness ought not to be sufficient.

(He continues with an analysis of why one witness in most cases is not to be trusted, since his testimony cannot be tested. He concludes as follows:)

This is precisely our case. Therefore it seems that it is impossible to rely upon this (namely, the statement of the manufacturer's chemist) unless we tell the expert that we intend to inquire of two other chemists equally expert. If we did that, it would be what the Law calls a situation whose truth will eventually come out into the open. In that case, the expert would not harm his professional reputation and he would himself, then, check his own opinion by another expert (to be sure that his opinions will not be disproved by our inquiries).

Now this I will tell you: Today I consulted the apothecary of this city. He said to me that indeed there are to be found chemical experts in many places who know how to test whether the oil is made entirely of animal fat or entirely of vegetable oil. But not every chemist could give trustworthy testimony as to whether or not there is an *admixture* of oils, unless he is a specialist in food studies. Such specialists are not found in Galicia, not even in Lemberg, except perhaps in Vienna and the like. Therefore, your honor knows well what he has to do under the circumstances.

59

✡

CONVERTING FOR MARRIAGE

David Hoffmann (born in Verbo, Hungary, 1843; died in Berlin, 1921) was the rector of the Orthodox rabbinical seminary in Berlin. Among his works were an introduction to the *halakhic midrashim,* a book in defense of the *Shulhan Arukh* against antisemitic charges, and his volume of responsa, *Melammed l'Ho'il* ("He Teacheth [thee] for [thy] Benefit," a reference to the verse in Isa. 48.17). These responsa have been widely used. They are, of course, strict in their conclusions, yet reveal a keener awareness than, perhaps, an East-European rabbi might have of the problems and the pressures of modern life.

The responsum which we cite is an evidence of the increased contact of Jews with non-Jews and, especially in western Europe, resultant intermarriage. According to the strict inter-pretation of the law, it is not proper to convert any Gentile to Judaism if it is known beforehand that this Gentile means to be converted in order to marry a Jew. In other words, conversion should be purely out of religious convictions. Yet in actual human experience, it is rare that a Gentile chooses Judaism without other motivation. Therefore, the problem arises whether to admit to Judaism those of whom it is definitely known that their con-version is for the purpose of marrying a Jew. David Hoffmann realized that such conversions must be made. He was able to build his case more strongly because the Christian man involved is already married to the Jewess by civil law. In his discussion, carried out in his usual clear, terse fashion, he presents the essential attitude of Jewish legal tradition toward converts. The responsum is "Yoreh Deah," no. 83.

TEXT

It is made clear in the *Shulhan Arukh,* "Yoreh Deah," no. 268.12, that we do not receive any proselyte who comes to be converted because he desires a certain Jewish woman. However, the *tosafot* in Yebamot 24b already raises an objection against this point of view (which is, of course, older than the *Shulhan Arukh*). The objection is based upon the fact reported in the Talmud, Shabbat 31a, that a Gentile came to Hillel to be converted, and said, "I want to become a high priest" (therefore the conversion was not for pure spiritual motives); nevertheless, Hillel did convert him. So in Menahot 44a we are told that a woman came to Rabbi Hiyyah and said that she wanted to be converted in order to marry a young scholar. (Here, again, where the motive was not purely spiritual, Rabbi Hiyyah converted her.) The *tosafot* answers its own objection by saying that they, Hillel and Rabbi Hiyyah, were confident that these candidates would ultimately become sincerely selfless in their motivations. So Joseph Caro, *Bet Joseph,* cited by the Shakh (Sabbatai Cohen) at the end of section 23, says that from this statement (of the *tosafot* that Hillel and Hiyyah foresaw a potential noble intent in these candidates) we can derive the principle that (whether to convert such candidates or not) depends upon the judgment of the court.

Thus when it is clear to the eyes of the court that the candidate really has a spiritual motive (literally, is converting "for the sake of Heaven") then, even though he has in mind (marrying) a certain Jewess, it is permitted to accept him as a proselyte.

Now, consider, in this case before us that he has already married the Jewish woman and she has already given herself to him and is pregnant by him. So it is clear that she is willing to be married to him even if he does not convert. That being the case, there is some justification in our holding the point of view that he is converting for a spiritual motive (since the girl is married to him in any case, whether he converts or not).

Furthermore, if we do not accept him, she will be married to him in sin, because (see the responsa of Moses Schick, "Eben haEzer" 37) it is forbidden by the Torah for a Jewess to be married to a Gentile. If so, it is better that we accept him as a proselyte than that she should be married in sin. Now, you might raise the objection that we never may say to a man, "Sin thou, in order that someone else may gain merit." (This phrase comes from the Tosefta, Hal. I.9, and he explains at once its application here.) The objection is: How can we ask the court (i.e., of rabbis) to commit the sin of accepting a proselyte who is not converting for a pure purpose, in order to deliver this woman from the great evil that all her life she will live in sin; has she not committed the first sin herself?

Against this objection one can say, first of all, that although she began with a sin that she gave herself to a non-Jew, it finally becomes a situation in which she is helpless, since she is now pregnant and cannot endure her shame unless she be married to him (by Jewish Law) and she is afraid that no other man will want to marry her and she will have to remain forlorn all her life. . . . Furthermore, if she remains married to this man (who remains a Gentile), then her children, which by Jewish Law are full Jews (since in mixed marriages the children follow the status of the mother), will follow their father into Gentile life and will thus be sinners. And what sin have these innocent sheep committed (that we should permit them to be weaned away from Judaism)? Since this is the case, it is better that the court (itself) should commit the minor sin of accepting this proselyte, so as to accustom him to Jewish life in order that there may be worthy Jewish children from this couple. But, at all events, the court must warn the Gentile to be very careful to fulfill Jewish religious Law, especially with regard to the Sabbath and forbidden food. And it would be well to receive an affirmation from him in lieu of a formal oath.

60

✡

CONCENTRATION CAMPS AND REMARRIAGE

Isaac Jacob Weiss was rabbi in Grosswardein, Rumania, and is now rabbi in Manchester, England. He had general and personal experience with the Nazi concentration camps, and has devoted much of his energy to solving the religious problem of the marital status of husbands and wives whose spouses have disappeared.

The problem of the *agun* and *agunah* (the man or woman in whose behalf no acceptable evidence can be adduced as to the death of their spouses and who, therefore, cannot remarry according to Jewish Law) constitutes, as is well known, one of the thorniest problems in Jewish legal tradition. Even in talmudic times, the laws of testimony were relaxed in their behalf. But even so, the problem was only mitigated, but not solved. Isaac Elkanan Spektor (p. 288, above) was the modern rabbi who made most progress towards solution of this problem during the years of mass immigration from eastern Europe, which separated families and often left wives with husbands who were untraceable, yet whose death could not be proved.

The massiveness of the problem which confronted Isaac Elkanan Spektor is reduced almost to tiny proportions in contrast with the problem confronting Jewish Law today. Millions of Jewish men and women have disappeared, leaving no trace. On the basis of what evidence, then, other than mere presumption of death, which is insufficient in the Law, can thousands of fugitives who survived be permitted remarriage within Jewish Law? It is to this problem that Rabbi Isaac J. Weiss devoted himself. In volume one of his work, *Minhat Yitzhak*, the first five responsa analyze the law in order to find such permission for the survivors of the concentration camps. He arrives at his solution by a subtle analysis of all the relevant sources; and certain groups of rabbis have agreed with his conclusions.

From the point of view of general Jewish history, there is an additional significance to these five responsa. In order to prove his case, he describes vividly the circumstances surrounding the lives of those who were taken to the camps. His chief legal purpose is to show the high degree of improbability that any one particular person survived. But in citing these facts, he adds to the Jewish legal literature one more eyewitness account of an historic event. Such eyewitness accounts come into the legal literature only by way of illustration to a legal point and are, therefore, all the more trustworthy. So Jair Hayyim Bachrach, in the 17th century, in answer to a legal question (see p.171, above) as to whether the pious practices of the earlier generation are incumbent upon the next generation, gives an eyewitness account of the destruction of Worms by the French armies. Therefore, in giving the excerpts from Weiss' responsa, we will mention enough of the legal matter for the problem to be clear, but cite primarily the historic description of the situation in the concentration camps.

TEXT

(The first responsum was a legal essay, addressed to a group of leading rabbis immediately after World War II, on the question of the presumption of death of those taken to concentration camps. He begins as follows:)

This is with regard to those thousands of women who are *agunot*, referring specifically to the remnant which escaped from the death camps, Auschwitz, etc., which were founded for the purpose of destroying our people, young, old, children and women. The procedure was this: When, after great worry and grief, family groups came to those places (Auschwitz, etc.), they (the Nazis) separated them from each other, one going to the right for a temporary continuation of life and the other group going to the left to immediate death, on the road that led to the crematorium, (of which group) we are told not one soul escaped. As for those who were left for temporary survival, these too were afterwards condemned to die by horrible deaths. Thus died, for the sanctification of God's Name, about 6,000,000 Jews. There were left approximately 300,000 in all the lands of Europe into which the evil government had spread; may its name be blotted out.

> (Jacob Weiss begins the legal discussion with the passage at the end of tractate Yebamot which deals with the question of the disappearance of a husband, either through his drowning in unlimited waters, where it could not be known whether he survived or not, or else through his being in a city under siege in which it could not be proved whether he escaped or not. He begins by quoting Mordecai—Mordecai ben Hillel, pupil of Meir of Rothenburg—whose great legal work, the *Mordecai,* is now published as an appendix to the Code of Isaac Alfasi.)

Now in my humble opinion the decision in this matter depends upon a premise with regard to people going down in unlimited waters and whose memory is lost. In the *Mordecai,* at the end of tractate Yebamot, there appears the following: "In the answer of Rabbi Eliezer of Verdun there is a careful analysis of the statement of the rabbis (the Talmud) that if a man goes down in unlimited waters, his wife is prohibited (from remarriage). Now it does not say that she is prohibited *forever.* Therefore, since 'forever' is not said in the rabbinical statement, it seems reasonable to assume that our rabbis put it up to the sages of every generation to study and come to conclusions with regard to the circumstances of their own generation. So he makes a strong effort to find grounds for permission (for remarriage) for a woman who was an *agunah* for four years and there are **many** presumptions indicating that her husband was really drowned, for the articles which he took with him onto the ship were found on the shore, etc."

(Jacob Weiss then takes up the various objections which were raised to the statement of this French rabbi quoted by the *Mordecai,* namely, that the rabbis of each generation are given a fair amount of latitude to decide, each in his respective generation, when to permit a woman to remarry if her husband disappeared without a trace. He weighs all these objections. He moves, then, into the analogous problem discussed in the Talmud of people who are in a besieged city. This involves the question of probability of survival. What degree of probability must there be for us to declare the woman free to remarry? After discussing these matters, Jacob Weiss describes in more detail the procedure in the concentration camps for the purpose of indicating how high is the probability that none who went there survived. This is from the second responsum:)

According to what is known to us, the order of the killing was conducted as follows: first they selected a large proportion for death; the few that were left they divided into camps, and from those camps they constantly chose people to be killed. In the camp itself, people were killed in various ways. Of the few that were left, they led them so far on foot, making them run, that many of them died on the road. Very few were those who remained to move on from one exile to another; and every time they were mixed up with other men and many of those died. So a minimum of a minimum were left.

(All this is for the purpose of showing that there is an overwhelming presumption that the survivors are truly widowed and are free. He ends the responsum saying that before the decision to free these people to remarry can be carried out:)

. . . we need in this the agreement of the great rabbis of the generation. (Then comes the following footnote:) As is known, the great rabbis of the generation have already agreed to permit (remarriage). Nevertheless, they wrote that every individual *agunah* (whose case is presented) must present as testimony a record of all the details of the life of the couple in the years of peace, and the circumstances under which the husband was sent to Auschwitz, etc.

(In other words, the rabbis agreed to deal with this matter leniently, but not with a blanket agreement. Each case must be weighed individually, but will be decided liberally.)

61

✡

JEWS IN SAHARA CARAVANS

Joseph Messas, rabbi in Tlemcen, Algiers, published in 1933 a volume of his responsa called *Mayim Hayyim*. His responsa are answers to questions mostly from west North African Jewry, but often from Arabic Jews in southwest Europe, as, for example, Marseilles or Gibraltar. The responsum which we cite is of special interest, partly because of the subject itself and partly because of the picture which it gives incidentally (as is the way with responsa) of some aspects of the social and economic life of the Jews of North Africa.

The problem concerns the question of reading, in the public Sabbath service, not from the regular parchment Torah scroll, but from a printed Bible. If such reading is permissible, then the blessing over the Torah may properly be recited by each of the seven men called up to the reading. But if such reading from a printed Bible is not permissible, then the blessing would be a *berakha l'vatala,* a vain blessing, the reciting of which is a violation of rabbinic law. Incidentally, in the discussion of this question, he cites a manuscript responsum from the earlier rabbis of Marakesh, Morocco, which tells of a similar question asked by the Jews who would spend several weeks with a desert caravan. This reveals the fact that the Jews participated in the great trans-Sahara caravan trade between Arabic North Africa and Negro Africa, usually going from Marakesh to Timbuktu. The responsum is no. 79.

TEXT

In answer to a young scholar who prefers to remain anonymous:

Question:

Your question, my friend, concerns an occurrence among certain Jewish men who live at the seashore. There was found among them a teacher who was appointed by them to be the *hazzan*. In the morning prayer (on Sabbath) he called up seven men (to the Scriptural) reading from a printed Bible, each one reciting the blessing before and after the portion. He took the prophetical portion for himself, and blessed before and after it. Did he do right or not?

Answer:

This matter was a subject of disagreement among the earlier scholars. Maimonides, of blessed memory, in his responsum no. 19, answered his pupil, Rabbi Ephraim, that where there is no Sefer Torah, the people may read in a *Humash* (the Five Books of Moses in book form) in public; they may even recite the portion by heart, and pronounce the blessings before and after each portion; for the blessings were not ordained specifically for the scroll of the Torah but for the *reading* of the Torah. Six of the great scholars of Narbonne agreed with Maimonides in this and he and they gave various proofs for their decision. But Solomon ben Adret in his responsum, which our teacher, *The House of Joseph* (Joseph Caro), cites in *Tur,* "Orah Hayyim," no. 143, expresses astonishment at their opinion. He refutes all their proofs and writes that Maimonides, of blessed memory, wrote this opinion in his youth, but had changed his mind and prohibited such reading (from a book) in his *Yad* ("The Laws of Sefer Torah," X.1). Also, Rabbenu Tam and the *Mordecai,* etc., and many of the earlier and later decisors agree to prohibit blessings over the book (i.e., not the scroll) in public reading, as our teacher Joseph Caro mentions there. He (Caro) quotes the Raviah (the Rhineland scholar, Eliezer ben Joel haLevi) whose opinion he found in a manuscript that, if one reads from the *Humash* and recites the Torah blessing, the sages do not think well of him, and his blessings are "vain" blessings. Thus, too, do the *Tur* and Caro himself decide, and this is the opinion of all the later scholars. See also the opinion of Hayyim Heskiah deSilva, in paragraph 143, who also refutes the opinions of Maimonides.

(Messas continues, as follows:)

There is in my hand a copy of a manuscript responsum from the old rabbis of Marakesh, of blessed memory. They were asked concerning a caravan that journeys in the desert, in which there are ten Jews and more. Are they in duty bound to read on the Sabbath and Monday and Thursday from a printed Bible and recite the blessing over it? They answered that to recite the blessings (over a printed book) is certainly, absolutely, forbidden. He who does recite such a blessing incurs a public sin and he deserves serious punishment. But even without a blessing, it is forbidden to read (as a public reading) with a *minyan* of ten from a printed *Humash*. The decisors only permitted such reading when there was no Sefer Torah and in order that the reading of the Torah should not be forgotten. But this applies only when they rest for many Sabbaths on their journey, or are in villages which have no scroll, as is cited in the responsum of Solomon ben Adret quoted by the *Bet Joseph* (Caro to the *Tur*). However, if they spend only one or two Sabbaths (in the desert) then they should not read at all, for the reading was ordained only from the scroll. But, they are obliged to read (privately) twice from the Hebrew and once from the Aramaic after the services are over, in order that they should not neglect the weekly portion. Thus far are their words (of the rabbis of Marakesh).

(Messas, of course, agrees with the rabbis of Marakesh and ends with an indignant letter addressed to the man who acted as cantor and conducted the reading from the printed book.)

62

✡

ARTIFICIAL INSEMINATION

Aaron Walkin (born in 1863; died during World War II, in Europe) was the rabbi of Pinsk-Karlin. His responsa, *Zekan Aharon,* in two parts, are widely used in modern times. The responsum which we cite deals with the question of artificial insemination, a problem which is being widely discussed nowadays by every great religious tradition and by the courts. The chief question is whether such a child is to be deemed the legitimate child of the parents.

Aaron Walkin, of course, deals with the easier form of the question, namely, when the donor of the seed is not a stranger, but the husband himself. The questions involved are whether a child thus born without the normal sexual relationship is to be deemed the man's child, in the sense that the Law requires him to fulfill the duty of "increase and multiply" (which requires at least one son and one daughter); also whether the very taking of the seed from the man by the physician is not a violation of Jewish Law.

It seems strange that with regard to so recently invented a procedure as artificial insemination, it is possible to have responsa built in the usual fashion upon the foundation of older precedents in the Law. How could there be any precedents for this new procedure? The precedent comes from the fact that the Talmud and, indeed, the medieval physicians, Jewish and Moslem, believed that a woman could be impregnated by male seed that happened to be present in a bath. Since the seed entered her not in the normal way of sexual relationship, this belief in the possibility of such impregnation serves as a precedent for all new responsa on this subject. The responsum is from vol. II, "Eben haEzer" 97.

TEXT

Question:

This relates to your question about a couple who were not blessed with children. The physician advised the taking of seed from the husband which the doctor would then inject into the woman's womb. In this way she would become pregnant. Is it permitted to do so? You (the questioner) cite the rabbi of Berzan (Shalom Mordecai Schwadron) in his responsa, vol. III. He was asked about this matter and decided that it would be permitted, provided two other rabbis agreed to his decision. Since this book is not in my possession, I do not know his arguments and his reasons. Therefore I will write only what God teaches me after I have studied the matter.

Answer:

You did not explain what was the basis for your doubts. As for myself, I find three doubts: one, as to whether it is permitted to take the seed from the man on the assurance of the doctor that the wife will thereby be surely impregnated; secondly, whether the insertion of the tube into the womb may not produce blood; and third, whether by means of such an artificial impregnation the child who would be born should be considered his child, so he may be deemed to have fulfilled thereby the commandment, "increase and multiply." Perhaps it should be argued that the child would not be considered completely his son, to be part of his family, unless the child is born from normal sexual relationships.

(He takes up these various doubts and deals with them:)

As for the doubt about whether it is permitted to follow this procedure because of the prohibition against "bringing forth seed in vain," if we follow the earlier sages, it seems that the Talmud and the decisors agree that doctors are to be trusted even in cases where prohibitions (of the religious law) are involved. If, then, the doctors' words are correct, that by this procedure it will be easier for her to become pregnant, since this is the physical nature of this woman, then this procedure (of taking the seed) is not "in vain" at all. On the contrary, it is for the purpose of achieving pregnancy more easily. The rabbis forbade bringing forth seed in order to destroy it, but here there is no destruction; it is placed into the womb of the wife in order that she shall be impregnated. Then, clearly, there is nothing wrong with this procedure.

(He then discusses various opinions on related questions and concludes as follows:)

The summary of my words is that I do not see in this procedure any sound basis for prohibition . . . and since you tell me that Rabbi Shalom Mordecai Schwadron agrees to permit this, but only makes the condition that two other rabbis agree with him, behold, I carry (the burden of decision) with him, and I count myself with him among those who permit it. May God agree with us that there may be given enduring seed to all men of Israel, in order that they may not need these devices, and in this blessing are included those who follow our decision.

This is the wish of him who blesses you,

Aaron Walkin

63

✡

HYDROPONICS

Ben-Zion Uziel (born in Jerusalem, 1880; died in 1954) was the chief Sephardi rabbi of Palestine. His responsa are models of clarity. His literary style combines the old rabbinic legal style with modern Hebrew usage. The construction of each of his responsa is systematic. He usually begins with the tabulation *seriatim* of the legal principles involved, or the subdivisions of the problem. He was always concerned with modern social attitudes and scientific discoveries in relation to their bearing upon traditional Jewish life. His collection of responsa, *Mishpetei Uziel* (The Judgments of Uziel), have appeared in five volumes.

The problem which he deals with in the responsum which we cite concerns the possible relevance of a modern agricultural invention upon one of the Jewish agricultural laws. The biblical law forbids any field or vineyard work in the sabbatical year. This law, of course, applies only to agriculture in Palestine. As the Jewish settlements developed in Palestine in recent years and the inhabitants grew to depend upon their own agriculture, the law requiring cessation of all agricultural work every seven years would have been a great burden upon the economy. It would have burdened the whole country, but most especially those colonies which observed the sabbatical year. Ben-Zion Uziel had heard that the American armed forces on the isolated sterile islands in the Pacific had managed to grow fresh vegetables in tanks by the new process known as hydroponics.

The question immediately presented itself to him with regard to the possible effect of this new process on the laws of the sabbatical year. Suppose the Orthodox colonies in Israel, during the sabbatical year, were to raise their crops in tanks, by hydroponics. Would this be permissible?

On the presumption that the Talmud is the foundation of all Jewish Law, no full-dress responsum can do other than begin with the Talmud in finding either a precedent or an applicable principle. How could a precedent be found for this innovation? But Ben-Zion Uziel finds such a precedent in the Talmud, just as those responsa on artificial insemination, also a new invention, found talmudic precedent (see p. 309).

The responsum cited is in the second sequence of *Mishpetei Uziel,* "Yoreh Deah," no. 103. It is addressed to Rabbi A. M. Hirshberg in Chicago, who encloses the following question, which came to him from Tel Aviv.

TEXT

Question:

I was asked (says Rabbi Hirshberg) by my friend Benjamin Mintz of Tel Aviv with regard to hydroponics, by which one can sow without soil. Can one sow there (in those tanks) in the sabbatical year (without violation of the biblical law)? The year 1951 will be a sabbatical year and the *kibbutzim* (agricultural settlements) of the Poale Agudat Yisrael (Orthodox Workers Party) do not plow or sow in the sabbatical year. They are careful to follow all the (strict) opinions which do not rely upon such alleviations as selling the land to a Gentile, etc., as was done beginning with the year 1942. Now this is a matter of great necessity, as can be understood, for the colonies of this group. Besides, if this can really be permitted, then perhaps other colonies (not so Orthodox) will also do the same in the sabbatical year. Therefore, he wants to know whether there is any permission to be found for this procedure.

(Rabbi Hirshberg's letter to Ben-Zion Uziel continues as follows:)

The procedure known as hydroponics is a new American invention. They take large tanks, and it makes no difference whether they are stone or metal or wood; they put water and chemicals and fertilizer into these tanks; and they sow in these, just as they would sow in the earth. I have heard in Washington, from the Department of Agriculture, that American soldiers who were in the South Pacific during the last war made use of hydroponics and raised all vegetables that were not hitherto found there.

Answer:

At first glance (said Ben-Zion Uziel) it would seem that we may permit this right off. For, behold, all the commandments of the sabbatical year depend upon the earth itself, as it is written, *The earth shall rest as a Sabbath to the Lord; you shall not sow your fields nor prune your vineyards* (Lev. 25.4). Then the commandment is for the earth to rest; and in hydroponics there is no working of the earth and (the tanks cannot be) called "your field and your vineyard."

But after a little meditation, it appears that this is not so, i.e., we cannot permit hydroponics. We learn in the Mishna (Hal. II.2) that if earth from outside of Palestine is brought by a ship to Palestine, this earth comes under the laws of tithes and sabbatical year. Said Rabbi Judah (there in the Mishna): "When does this apply? When the ship touches (the shore)." Maimonides explains this as follows: "When foreign earth comes to Palestine in a ship and they sow in that earth on the ship, the crop comes under all the Palestinian agricultural laws, that is, provided the ship touches (the Palestinian) earth." In his book of laws ("Laws of Heave-Offering," I.3), Maimonides says: "Earth from outside of Palestine that comes to the Land and touches the earth, he who sows in it must give heave-offering, tithes, and follow the sabbatical year as if he were sowing in Palestine." Now (continues Uziel) any ship is either of wood or of metal and is not pierced at all (a pierced flower-pot is deemed part of the earth, being in contact with it, but a non-pierced flower-pot is a separate entity in certain legal situations). Nevertheless, he who sows in it, even though the earth is from outside of Palestine, must follow the laws of heave-offering and sabbatical year. Therefore we can conclude from this that with regard to the case (of hydroponics) which does not have any soil at all from outside of the Land and the water in which they sow is found in vessels (i.e., it is Palestinian water) that surely it does not free the one who sows in it from the laws of the sabbatical year, neither with regard to sowing or reaping, since (their contents) are indeed from Palestine and the biblical words, *thy field and thy vineyard* certainly apply to them.

> (He goes into various opinions of the older scholars on the type of vessel involved, earthenware or wood, and also whether the ship that is not right up against the pier is nevertheless in contact with Palestine by means of the intervening water. He concludes that the intervening space of water, instead of separating the ship from the Land, really unites it with the Land. So he concludes:)

For the decision on the law, it seems to me that all the prohibitions of the sabbatical year remain in full force with regard to the new invention of sowing in tanks of water, which is called "hydroponics," whether they (the containers) are made of earthenware or wood or metal, and even if they are not pierced.

What appears to my humble opinion I have written.